This Happened in America

Harold Rugg and the
Censure of Social Studies

a volume in

Studies in the History of Education

Series Editor:
Karen L. Riley
Auburn University–Montgomery

Studies in the History of Education

Karen L. Riley, Series Editor

Language of the Land: Policy, Politics, Identity (2007)
edited by Katherine Schuster and David Witkosky

Educational Research, the National Agenda,
and Educational Reform: A History (2007)
by Erwin V. Johanningmeier and Theresa R. Richardson

Social Reconstruction: People, Politic, Perspectives (2006)
edited by Karen L. Riley

This Happened in America

Harold Rugg and the
Censure of Social Studies

by

Ronald W. Evans
San Diego State University

Information Age Publishing, Inc.
Charlotte, North Carolina • www.infoagepub.com

Library of Congress Cataloging-in-Publication Data

Evans, Ronald W.
  This happened in America : Harold Rugg and the censure of social studies / by Ronald W.
Evans.
     p. cm. — (Studies in the history of education)
  Includes bibliographical references.
  ISBN-13: 978-1-59311-765-8 (pbk.)
  ISBN-13: 978-1-59311-766-5 (hardcover) 1. Rugg, Harold Ordway, 1886-1960.
2. Educators—United States—Biography. 3. Social sciences—Study and teaching—United
States—History—20th century. 4. Social sciences—Textbooks—Censorship—United States.
I. Title.
  LB885.R732E93 2007
  370.92--dc22
  [B]

                                                                                      2007020557

ISBN 13: 978-1-59311-765-8 (pbk.)
          978-1-59311-766-5 (hardcover)
ISBN 10: 1-59311-765-5 (pbk.)
          1-59311-766-3 (hardcover)

Portions of the introduction and conclusion are adapted and reprinted by permission of the publisher. From Ronald W. Evans, Social studies vs. the United States of America: Harold Rugg
and teaching for social justice, in K. L. Riley (Ed.), *Social Reconstruction: People, Politics,
Perspectives,* pp. 45-68, Greenwich, CT: Information Age Publishing, © 2006. And from
Ronald W. Evans, Harold Rugg: Apostle of the modern social studies curriculum, in Totten, S.
& Pedersen, J. (Eds.), *Addressing social issues in the classroom and beyond: The pedagogical
efforts of pioneers in the field,* Greenwich, CT: Information Age Publishing, © 2007. All rights
reserved.

Limited portions of chapters five and six are adapted and reprinted by permission of the pub-
lisher. From Ronald W. Evans, *The Social Studies Wars: What Should We Teach the Children?,*
New York: Teachers College Press, © 2004 by Teachers College, Columbia University.
All rights reserved.

To Harold Rugg

CONTENTS

PREFACE AND ACKNOWLEDGMENTS

As I send this book to press, I would like to take a moment to acknowledge the many people who contributed to the process of researching, preparing, and writing the manuscript. I first heard of Harold Rugg from my late mentor Richard E. Gross. As I sat in on and assisted with social studies methods classes, and participated in seminar discussions during my years in graduate school, he shared many stories about Rugg that were my original inspiration.

I would like to thank all the archivists who provided access to manuscript collections, photographs, and other materials. Unfortunately, there is no large collection of Rugg papers. Nonetheless, materials on Rugg and his critics are available at a number of repositories. Archival materials were obtained during visits to the following collections: Progressive Education Association Archives, B. Othaniel Smith papers, and Archibald Anderson papers, University of Illinois at Urbana-Champaign; John Dewey papers and George S. Counts papers, Special Collections, Morris Library, and John Dewey Center, Southern Illinois University, Carbondale; William F. Russell papers, Harold and Earl Rugg Textbook Collection, and the Archives of the National Council for the Social Studies, Gottesman Libraries, Teachers College, Columbia University; Nicholas Murray Butler papers, George Sokolsky papers, Butler Library, Columbia University; William F. Russell papers, Columbiana Collection, Low

This Happened in Ameica: Harold Rugg and the Censure of Social Studies
pp. ix–xii
Copyright © 2007 by Information Age Publishing

Library, Columbia University; Oral History Collection, Butler Library, Columbia University; Franz Boas papers, Library of the American Philosophical Association, Philadelphia; Manuscript Collection of the National Association of Manufacturers, Hagley Museum and Library, Wilmington, Delaware; Myers G. Lowman papers, Sidney Hook papers, Paul R. Hanna Collection, National Republic Records, George E. Sokolsky papers, R. Freeman Butts papers, and American Legion papers, Hoover Institution and Archive, Stanford, California; and, the Amos A. Fries papers and Merwin K. Hart papers, Special Collections, University of Oregon.

In addition, valuable materials were procured from Rauner Special Collections, Dartmouth College Library; The Earl and Harold Rugg manuscript collection, University of Northern Colorado; the archives of the Federal Bureau of Investigation; and, the Rockefeller Archive Center, Sleepy Hollow, New York. Also, a collection of audiotapes from Rugg's later years was acquired from George Allen Kay who wrote one of the earliest dissertations on Harold Rugg.

Valuable insights, details of Rugg's personal life, photographs and other materials were obtained from several Rugg family members and friends including his step daughter, Katharine Alling; nephews John E. Rugg and Brian E. Rugg; and from current and former Woodstock residents Alf Evers, Ned Chase, Eileen Cramer, and Bruce Bodner during and after a visit to Woodstock. I owe them a special thank you for the help they supplied by sharing photographs and other materials and information, and for the time they spent sharing their memories.

I would like to acknowledge David Ment, former archivist at Milbank Memorial Library, who provided extensive assistance in searching the Teachers College collections. In addition, I owe a special thank you to Margaret Smith-Crocco who helped me procure materials from the Teachers College manuscript collections during a period when the archive was closed for renovation.

I would like to acknowledge previous scholars who have done a great deal of substantive and path-breaking work on Rugg, including Elmer Winters, George Kay, Peter Carbone, Murry Nelson, and Jonathan Zimmerman. The reader will note that I have treated several dissertations as primary source materials in the referencing of sources when the document cited is no longer available. This is especially true for Orville Jones' dissertation on the American Legion's activities in textbook criticism (1957). Most of the letters cited by Jones are lost, and are no longer available at the National Library of the American Legion. Though treating these documents as primary sources does not conform to the specific guidelines of American Psychological Association style, it provides the reader and future Rugg scholars with more detailed information in a more elegant form. The reader will note that the full source is provided for each item in the reference list, rather than in parentheses in the text. I would also like to thank my friends and colleagues at San Diego State University who supported this work with several small grants to fund archival visits, and a generous sabbatical leave during which I did most of the writing

I would like to thank my editor, Karen L. Riley, and publisher, George Johnson at Information Age Publishing who have made publication of this work possible. I would also like to thank my children, Katie, Mira, and Kai who have helped me keep a sense of balance, even though this was at times a nearly all-consuming obsession. Finally, I would like to thank my wife Mika for her support of my work and her patient endurance with this preoccupation. Though many others contributed to the completion of this work, I assume full responsibility for the accounts, interpretations, and conclusions presented.

INTRODUCTION

Harold Rugg, Education, and Social Justice

Sometimes, I lie awake at night, thinking of Harold Rugg, about his vision for American democracy, and his vision for social studies education. I think about what happened to him, to his progressive vision, and of the possibilities and potential his vision raised. There is, it seems, so little left of the progressive vision in schools with the current trend toward the reification of the disciplines of history, geography, and civics as the core of social studies and the machine like standardization wrought by testing mania. Rugg's story informs us that social studies as a broad and integrated field of study has potential for the development of thoughtful and caring citizens. His work threw critical light on our collective responsibility for social justice and reminds us of our unrealized potential to create a truly democratic "civilization of abundance, toleration, and beauty," and to live out the meaning of our creed. The Rugg story also suggests that it is possible to influence the course of events. Rugg had a real impact. His work in educating citizens brought an integrated and issues-centered approach to social studies, as embodied in his textbooks, to a large segment of American school children during the 1930s and influenced a generation of Americans. His boldly stated social ideas inspired the admiration of forward-looking citizens across the nation and around the world.

This Happened in Ameica: Harold Rugg and the Censure of Social Studies
pp. xiii–xix

Who was Harold Rugg and why should we care about his story? Rugg was one of a small group of leaders of the progressive education movement centered at Teachers College, Columbia University, and among the social frontier group that emerged in the 1930s to argue that schools should play a stronger role in helping to reconstruct or improve the society. He was the author of an innovative and best selling series of social studies textbooks which came under attack from patriotic and business groups in the prelude to U.S. involvement in World War II. The story of his rise and fall encapsulates a significant and central story in the history of American education, and, when combined with subsequent events, reveals a great deal about the direction of schooling in American life, the road not taken, and the possibilities for the future.

Rugg's career "virtually represents in miniature the panorama of educational ideologies that characterized twentieth century curriculum reform in America: scientific curriculum making, child-centered education, and most notably, social reconstructionism" (Kliebard & Wegner, 1987, p. 269). It is in this sense that Rugg's story is biography writ large. His life and story embody many of the challenges of life in a modern or postmodern society marked by concentration of wealth and power, disparity in income and standard of living, and issues of social conflict and difference. Moreover, Rugg's thoughts, and the ideas of his detractors, encapsulate elements of the entire spectrum of ideologies that influenced the making of the social studies curriculum, a projection of broad social issues on the smaller screen of school curricula. Among those competing ideologies are education for social efficiency in the form of scientific curriculum making, social studies as social science inquiry, social studies as traditional history and civics, social studies as an issues-oriented and integrated field of study, and social studies as education for social reconstructionism. As I have argued elsewhere, the battles among the competing versions of social studies represent the larger ideological struggles for hegemony and social direction in the modern era (Evans, 2004). Proposals for change in the field of social studies often serve as a lightning rod for commentary and criticism regarding the nature of the field, the purposes of schooling, and competing visions of the worthy society. At the level of ideals, visions, and values, at certain times in the past social studies movements have challenged either American institutions or a segment of American's beliefs about the good way of life. These challenges have often provoked severe criticism from various groups interested in preserving their particular version of "the American way."

Perhaps most notably, Rugg created an avant-garde social studies program, a prototype for a unified, interdisciplinary curriculum focused on issues and problems and aimed at education for social justice. He was the American father of democratic education, and of teaching for social justice, in social studies. Moreover, in educational thought and practice, rationale is important. Rugg's work was built on a thoughtful rationale that combined student interest with social worth, a powerful combination that still has appeal.

At the peak of their popularity, the Rugg textbooks were censured by a media storm fed by conservative patriotic and business groups who, in an un-American fashion, did not want school children, or their parents for that matter, raising questions about the basic structures of American life and the capitalist economic system. Rugg's story reminds us that education is always political, and can never be neutral. It also tells us what can happen to a good idea, and to precious freedoms, in a society in which the media, public sentiment, and school policy are subject to manipulation, to the manufactured crises that seem to beset our schools again and again, and which have an inordinate influence on how we educate citizens (Berliner & Biddle, 1995). The attack on Rugg, on his ideas and school materials, was perhaps the first major battle of what I have previously termed the war on social studies. Since that time, the field has served as a frequent flashpoint in the culture wars over schooling (Evans, 2004; Gaddy, Hall, & Marzano, 1996). Rugg became, for a time, the leading warrior for progressive social studies, and its most formidable advocate and defender. Though Rugg would lose the battle over his textbooks, he fought gallantly for his ideas and for a progressive vision. His was a battle many educators of progressive mind are still fighting, and, unfortunately, often still losing.

Rugg's story also illustrates the point that being a social critic, whether a progressive reformer (Rugg was), socialist (Rugg's critics thought he was), or communist (some critics called him this), and having a dissenting position from the mainstream can lead to problems. That being a non-conformist or Bohemian, as Rugg was, can be dangerous, especially so in education. The culture assumes and seems to support a mythical and "apolitical" view of education as socialization—suggesting that it's okay to have some discussions of central issues in American life within a framework of balance and teacher neutrality. However, to openly declare allegiance to ideas that challenge capitalism and its most basic assumptions can, and has—on many occasions—led to serious repercussions. Rugg's work and fearless advocacy of certain ideas made it clear that he placed higher value on human rights than on private property, that he wanted students to wrestle with the issues raised by the dilemmas of capitalism, and that he wanted schools to teach about the social world, past and present, as if people mattered.

The timing of Rugg's life and the context in which he developed may help us understand his orientation. The problems of capitalist industrial society had begun to emerge most acutely by the 1890s as Rugg was grow-

ing up in a small industrial city in Massachusetts. He was exposed to the
central dilemmas of the time during his youth, by directly observing the
consequences of wealth, power and poverty which were brought to light
during the takeoff phase of the industrial revolution. These were formative years for Rugg, as we shall see, and they lay the groundwork for both
his emerging social philosophy and his vision for social studies reform.
Moreover, his adult life spanned some of the most crucial years in the
development of the American nation. From the turn of the twentieth century until his death, he was influenced by a maelstrom of cataclysmic
events including the industrial revolution, the progressive era, World War
I, the great depression, the Second World War, and the cold war.

Equally important to a full understanding of Rugg's journey is an
understanding of Rugg's persona. He was profoundly influenced by the
circumstances of his surroundings. As a youth, he was a victim of "not
enough," of not having the resources of a level playing field. This fact
gave Rugg a deep feeling of inferiority for which he compensated with a
drive to succeed far beyond his humble origins. In part, that feeling of
inferiority also created in Rugg a huge ego, an attitude of arrogance, and
a boldness which would, at times, come to haunt him. He was a serious
thinker, a brilliant and hard working writer, and an enthralling lecturer
whose verbal acumen, in both writing and speaking, would help him build
a powerful reputation. His bold style in putting forth his beliefs was a key
part of his success, and contributed to his eventual downfall. Despite the
many fine attributes that went into Rugg's persona, he was undermined
by what some might see as his flaws. He was, by his own admission, a person who seemed to be, "always in a hurry," to write his next book, make
his next speech, or to meet his next challenge. Though he was polite to a
fault, his personal life was, at times, turbulent, dominated by a shadow
side. Consequently, he was sometimes the subject of rumor and innuendo.
Moreover, he was, frequently challenged: some viewed has scholarship as
shallow; more than one of his critics questioned his veracity; at least a few
of his colleagues doubted his morality, at least in private. All of these qualities coalesced in the persona of an educator who challenged the received
wisdom of his culture, and who, in turn, suffered the consequences of
being constantly confronted by one controversy or another. That is not to
imply that he didn't enjoy it, at least to a point.

As a scholar focused on citizenship education, Rugg arrived at a set of
beliefs and chose a course of action that, at a crucial time in our nation's
history, raised the suspicions of many Americans. His textbooks were
never as forthright as his speeches and other writings. Yet, inevitably it
seems, school materials take on a hue or tint, and lean toward socializing
or counter-socializing. When counter-socialization is emphasized, raising
questions about the contradictions in American culture, exposing the

hypocrisy apparent in a "land of opportunity" in which opportunities are not presented equitably, it can raise the suspicions and even the ire of conservative activists.

Rugg's life and work, and the controversy over his textbooks, have great resonance today, in the twenty-first century. The Rugg story raises serious questions about the rationale and purposes of schooling for citizenship: What kind of citizens and citizen education do we want? How far can and should schools go in providing opportunities for social criticism? What kinds of activities and materials are appropriate in support of education for social justice? What are its limits, if any? And, behind all of these questions, Whose version of the American way should schools support?

While Rugg's broader social philosophy is important and lay behind much of his work in the social studies field, I believe that Rugg's ideas on questions related to the purposes and meaning of social studies instruction remain especially relevant. Revisiting Rugg's ideas may cause us to reflect on several important questions, centered on, "Whither social studies?," and "Whither the United States of America?" His work and legacy are also especially helpful for teachers as they attempt to craft interesting approaches to teaching and as they ponder issues of teacher belief, balance of treatment, and the thorny issue of "neutrality," sometimes framed as a discussion of teacher "impartiality," as if either were really possible.

In thinking over the issues raised by the Rugg story that have continuing relevance, the following thoughts and questions emerge which might serve as a schema for readers, as we reflect on Rugg as a case study relevant to key issues in the social studies field:

Definition of social studies: How should we define social studies? What is the nature of the field? What are our central aims or purposes? What rationales are most powerful? In the case of Rugg's work, as a significant social studies theorist and as an advocate of social reconstructionism, what were his main contributions to teaching social studies and to teaching for social justice?

Curriculum scope and sequence: What kind of vision should serve as a guide to organizing the social studies curriculum? Should social studies be thought of as a unified field or as a federation of discrete but interrelated disciplines? What should be the role of history and the social science disciplines? Should they serve as a rich and important source for social studies content and processes or as the definitive framework for the curriculum? What role should broad social issues of past and present play in the curriculum? What is at the heart of social studies: disciplines, issues, or some combination? (Rugg had a clear position on this question, favoring a unified field. In his view the disciplines were an important source of knowledge, but provided an inadequate framework for educating citizens.)

xviii   R. W. EVANS

Pedagogy: What is the relationship between content and pedagogy? How might content and pedagogy be creatively combined to create problem-centered or problem-posing forms of social studies education? How might we raise the general level of classroom practice so that more students experience dialogical, reflective, and problem-posing forms of education? (Rugg offered innovative thoughts on these questions.)

How might we more effectively address the failure of many teachers to go beyond the most pedantic type of textbook driven curricula? What are the limits or obstacles to reform in social studies? (Rugg framed this as "the problem with the old system," but gave little explicit attention to obstacles. However, it is clear that by the 1930s, Rugg was keenly aware that most teachers were simply teaching out of his books, rather than really challenging students to think for themselves.)

Textbooks and materials: How might we effectively address the problems with social studies textbooks and materials that students find uninteresting and that many scholars have described as filled with distortions, omissions, and "lies"? (This was probably Rugg's greatest contribution, creating an innovative and bestselling textbook series, along with supporting materials.)

Indoctrination/social criticism: How might we develop a reasonable, fair and balanced approach to teaching topics that may prove controversial and yet still remain true to our democratic values and commitment to social justice? What role should social criticism play in the classroom? What role should social criticism play in textual materials? (This was the dilemma that proved Rugg's undoing.)

Censorship: What are the limits on freedom to teach and freedom to learn in a democratic society? What role have interest groups critical of social studies and of theorists such as Rugg played in the evolution of the social studies curriculum? (Rugg underestimated the power and influence of interest groups such as the American Legion and the National Association of Manufacturers. Since the 1940s, and especially in recent years, interest groups have strongly and repeatedly influenced the direction of social studies reform.)

I believe that we can learn a great deal on each of these topics by studying the Rugg story in some depth. Harold Rugg was one of the originators of education for social justice, a seminal figure in the movement for social reconstructionism in education during the 1930s. Education for social justice has had many advocates over the years and seems a permanent interest group in the panoply of educational thought. The literature on education for social justice has mushroomed since the 1970s, an offshoot of critiques of society, and of schooling, developed in many quarters (Ayers, Hunt, & Quinn, 1998). Unlike many recent educational reformers and advocates for social justice, Rugg's work achieved a strong presence in schools. Ultimately, the Rugg story, his life and work, challenges us to make a difference in schools.

REFERENCES

Ayers, W., Hunt, J. A., & Quinn, T. (Eds.). (1998). *Teaching for social justice: A democracy and education reader.* New York: The New Press, Teachers College Press.

Berliner, D., & Biddle, B. J. (1995). *The manufactured crisis: Myths, fraud, and the attack on America's public schools.* Reading, MA: Addison-Wesley.

Evans, R. W. (2004). *The social studies wars: What should we teach the children?* New York: Teachers College Press.

Gaddy, B. B., Hall, W. T., & Marzano, R. J. (1996). *School wars: Resolving our conflicts over religion and values.* San Francisco: Jossey-Bass.

Kleibard, H. M., & Wegner, G. (1987). Harold Rugg and the reconstruction of the social studies curriculum: The treatment of the "great war" in his textbook series. In T. S. Popkewitz (Ed.), *The formation of the school subjects: The struggle for creating an American institution* (pp. 268-287). New York: Falmer.

CHAPTER 1

ANSWERING THE CALL

The great transition, from the late nineteenth to the early twentieth century, was the best of times, and it was the worst of times. It was a time of growth and opportunity, it was a time of poverty and oppression. For some, it was a time of fabulous riches and development of empire, while for others it was a time of domination and exploitation. It was a time of accumulation of great wealth, and it was a time marked by extreme poverty and deprivation. It was above all a time of contrasts and a time of questions, in which the choices and the direction of the American nation and the world lay clearly open, at least for a while. It was a time during which a range of issues related to wealth and poverty, power and empire were discussed, debated, and contested like never before.

It was into this time of contrasts that Harold Rugg was born, a boy from a mill town who would become one of the most influential educators of the twentieth century. How does it happen that a child from humble origins becomes a famous and influential thinker, a public personality? How does it happen, that one child in similar circumstances conforms to social norms, and another child rebels? The origin and development of Harold Rugg's life and career makes for an interesting story. It is a story marked by hard work and initiative, a Puritan work ethic, good fortune, strength of personality, the motive of new interest, a persistent feeling of inferiority, fear of failure and impoverishment, the grand vision of creating a new day, and a certain boldness of character. Harold Rugg developed from the child of an undistinguished skilled artisan into one of the leading and

This Happened in Ameica: Harold Rugg and the Censure of Social Studies
pp. 1–23
1

most controversial educational thinkers of his time. He was, in many ways, a visionary who captured the essence of the Deweyan turn in educational thought and applied it to the reconstruction of social studies education, through which, Rugg hoped, he would help engineer a new society.

In this chapter we shall trace Rugg's origins in a conservative New England industrial town, his matriculation at Dartmouth, his gradual growth into academia, his ideological transition from New England Yankee conservatism to a liberal social criticism, and his eventual arrival as a leading scholar in the field of social studies education. As we trace Rugg's journey, we will be mindful of his developing persona, shaped in part by a strong Puritan work ethic and desire for material success. Rugg was a complex and interesting character, strongly influenced by the cauldron of his times. In the period from 1890 to 1920, not only did Rugg grow to adulthood and begin his career, the nation was in a period of transition from an agrarian, rural, and largely pastoral landscape, to one that was increasingly urban and industrial and beset with a multitude of associated problems. American economic, social and cultural expansion from the late nineteenth century into the early decades of the twentieth century created many opportunities and raised poignant issues and questions which confronted all citizens: the role of government in regulating business and providing for the general welfare, the role of capital and labor in American life, the changing face of the American people brought by new immigration, the emerging role of the United States in world affairs and the question of empire. In each case, the issues inspired conflicting and divisive viewpoints representing a range of possibilities, from laissez faire individualism on one end of the spectrum to totalitarian state socialism at the other end, with a thousand variations in between. Though Rugg had some awareness of these issues as he grew to adulthood, his true awakening to the transformation that was occurring in American society and the world, and the call to do something about it, came during a particular period of his life, and it came as something of a shock. Rugg grew from modest and inauspicious beginnings to become one of the most famous and infamous educators of his time. As we trace the pattern of his early years, we shall bear in mind the question, How did it happen, how did he come to be who he was?

The Family. Harold O. Rugg, the leading progressive social studies educator of the twentieth century, was born Harold Ordway Rugg, in Fitchburg, Massachusetts on January 17, 1886, the son of Edward Francis and Merion Abbie (Davidson) Rugg. Rugg later described himself as a ninth generation New Englander. His earliest American forebear was John Rugg, most probably a Puritan from northern England, who arrived in Lancaster, Massachusetts, as a young man in 1654, aligning himself with, then marrying into the prominent Prescott family, the first White settlers in Worcester County (B. E. Rugg, 2005). Thus began the story of the Rugg family in New England.

According to a family story, passed down through the generations, and related by Harold and his brother Earle, the Rugg family was at least partially responsible for setting off the American Revolution. Asa Rugg, 22 years old, was living in Lexington at the time, and serving as a minuteman in the Continental Militia. Apparently, Asa was something of a ne'er-do-well and a drinker. On the morning of April 19, 1775, he was sleeping off a drunken spree in a Lexington tavern when he awoke to the sound and sight of British redcoats on Lexington Green. As we know, the question of who fired the first shot between redcoats and colonists has always been subject to dispute. According to the Rugg brothers, that first shot was fired by Asa, from the window of the tavern. As a punch line, Harold would add, "If it hadn't been for Asa, we'd all be speaking French" (B. E. Rugg, 2005).

The Rugg family lived in Lancaster and in Worcester County for many generations. Harold Rugg's father, Edward Francis Rugg, was born in Lancaster, Massachusetts on October 15, 1854, and lived in Worcester County his entire life. His mother, Merion Abbie Davidson, was born on May 12, 1862, in Sterling, a small town near Lancaster. They met in the early 1880s and were married on May 22, 1883 in Sterling. Shortly after that, they settled in the town of Fitchburg.

Fitchburg, Massachusetts, at the time of Rugg's birth, was in most ways typical of the northeastern industrial towns of the 1880s. Fitchburg was organized as a town in north central Massachusetts in 1764, and incorporated as a city in 1812. In 1880 it had a population of slightly more than 12,000 persons. During that decade it nearly doubled in population, mirroring the urban population growth in the nation, driven by the takeoff phase of the industrial revolution. By 1890 the city had a population of 22,037. Fitchburg incorporated relatively large numbers of new immigrants into its industries and textile mills and provided Rugg with first-hand experience with the social meanness of an emerging industrial civilization. Fitchburg society was composed of several distinct social classes with mill workers and laborers at the bottom, shopkeepers and skilled workers in the middle, and with a very small elite made up mostly of mill and factory owners and their families. Though the 1890s have been referred to as "Fitchburg's finest hour" that description was undoubtedly most appropriate for the owners of factories and stores and was less applicable to the working classes (Fitchburg Historical Society, 1972; Nelson, 1975; Winters, 1968).

Rugg's father, a thin man with large hands, was employed as a carpenter and cabinetmaker. As a skilled craftsman, Edward Rugg could have earned steady wages throughout his adult life. However, his independence probably cost him, and his family, difficulties and displacement resulting from job losses. The elder Rugg struggled with a "rigid economic order" and suffered due to "refusal to join the carpenters' union and criticism of his employer or of his politics" (H. O. Rugg, 1941, p. 174). Later describing himself as the product of a "lower middle-class" family, Rugg's youth was scarred by what seemed his family's constant struggle to scrape together a bare existence from a hostile environment. It appears that the Rugg family may have had some affiliation with the Congregational church, a family of protestant denominations arising from the nonconformist religious movement in England during the Puritan reformation.

Rugg's mother, Merion Rugg, was remembered as a quiet, rather ineffectual person who was never able to understand or accept Rugg's later liberal leanings. His father held ideas common to the majority in the community and believed that the Republican Party represented the pinnacle of intelligence and the acme of all of the good things in American life. Rugg's father hated Democratic politician William Jennings Bryan and once told his son that he need not come home if he voted for Bryan (H.O. Rugg, 1956). He also spoke to Harold at times about the trends of the day, the industrial revolution, the "new" immigration, and economic imperialism, topics never taken up by his school teachers. Though Rugg clearly admired his father as one of the last of the New England artist-craftsmen, his father was never a strong influence on the development of Rugg's social ideas. On the other hand, the elder Rugg's independent streak seems to have carried over to Harold, probably to a greater degree that it did to his brother or sisters. Harold was raised as the oldest of four siblings. His brother Earle Underwood Rugg was born on March 4, 1892. Harold also had two younger sisters, Doris, born on October 4, 1896, and Charlotte, born January 28, 1899.

As a youth, Harold saw firsthand the stifling effect that difficult economic conditions could have on family life, and later wrote that in lower-middle class homes in Fitchburg, life was directed by "two deep—seated fears—the fear of not having enough and the fear of 'What will the neighbors think?' " (H.O. Rugg, 1941, p. 173). He experienced a "widespread climate of inferiority" created by the hierarchy of neighborhoods in the hills and valleys of the mill city of his youth, a climate of inferiority that held over into adult life, which helped shape Rugg's rebellion against the social order and which would have a significant impact on his persona. In his semi-autobiographical work, *That Men May Understand*, Rugg wrote:

> life in those parental homes was dominated primarily by the quest for food, the benumbing effect of fatigue and an acute class consciousness. The latter, I think, was caused partly by the daily routine of life in an artisan home and

partly by such spontaneous economic symptoms of inferiority as vocal out-
bursts of tired elders. It was fatigue, I think, caused by the attempt to make
ends meet, that lay at the basis of much of the inferiority. The environment
assailed the individual from every angle; home, neighborhood and the town
cooperate in the unceasing endeavor to put each in his place. Young minds
were molded, stamped and labeled—each with an economic and social status. Thus, the sense of inferiority accumulated, and attitudes of conformity
solidified. (H. O. 1941, pp. 173-174)

Later in his life, Rugg reflected on his career as a "rebel" and mused
that he had no real answer to the question of why growing up in essentially the same environment, some individuals in a family become
"rebels," while others do not:

Why do some people in a family, why do some individuals in a family, who
grow up, as far as you can see in essentially the same environment, become
from the beginning, oh, quote, "rebels" about government and economic
life as I was, even as a boy. I was a barbarian, certainly, and certainly ignorant about, but always sort of almost, quote, "against the government," so to
speak. Always very questioning about it all, even though I was very ignorant.
And I don't know why, because it wasn't in the background. My people were
conventionalists in the early 1900s. My father believed that the Republican
Party was the acme of intelligence and all the good things in American life,
and hated Bryan and all his parts. Said that I needn't come home if I voted
for Bryan. It was a background of essential conservative New England
Americanism, old traditional type. Certainly the school education was that
completely. Almost no individualism. (H. O. Rugg, 1956)

School. Long before the 1890s, school had become one of the primary
cultural institutions influencing the development of youth in American
society. From all reports, the schools Rugg attended were rather typical
for the era. Rugg attended Fitchburg public schools which he would later
describe in rather unflattering terms. Rugg's years in the Fitchburg
schools did little to alleviate the mood of inferiority and probably contributed to it. The schools reflected an age when mental discipline and the
classics still held sway, and the curriculum seemed far removed from the
realities of life. The "mass school" of Rugg's youth later became, for
Rugg, a powerful example of what was wrong with education because of
its preoccupation with the dead past, emphasis on drill, and its portrayal
of a static society. Rugg attended a graded elementary school in Fitchburg
and enrolled at Fitchburg High School from 1898-1902. He later wrote:

I can see now that the high school merely continued the regimented curriculum which the rapid rise of the graded school had precipitated. I can see
now that the teachers were not only dull—which I knew then—but they were

uninformed concerning both the problems of modern life and the trends and factors that produced them.... Not only did the school fail to develop understanding and sensitiveness; it thwarted expressive capacity as well. (H. O. 1941, pp. 175-176).

Despite Rugg's rather dismal recollections, Fitchburg High School had a new and beautiful physical plant completed in 1895, and was regarded as one of the better schools in the state (Fitchburg Historical Society, 1972). According to his Dartmouth application, Rugg had successfully completed required courses in English, ancient history, U.S. history, European history, mathematics, French, chemistry, physics, and manual training (Nelson, 1975). Moreover, his admission to Dartmouth belies, to some extent, his stated disdain for Fitchburg schools.

Factory experience. After leaving high school and prior to attending Dartmouth College, Rugg worked in a textile mill and was directly exposed to the realities of modern industry. From 1902 to 1904 Rugg was employed by the Parkhill Manufacturing Company and was engaged in various departments of the cotton manufacturing business, first as a loom operator in the weave room in which he stood, "from before dawn until after dark ... in the din of clacking looms, shoulder to shoulder with a dozen races and nationalities ...," and later as an office boy in the accounting office in which his contact with accounting orders and sales revealed the discrepancy in wages between worker and owner (H. O. Rugg, 1941, p. 176). The work day was from 7:00 AM to 6:00 P.M. with half an hour for lunch. The pay was $4.50 per week (Kay, 1969, p. 55).

As a result of his employment, Rugg became more acutely aware of the class issues of his day. To be sure, Fitchburg was an apt location for awareness. As a mill town, Fitchburg was home to a fairly large segment of working class immigrants. At the time of Rugg's employment in the mill, the majority of workers were most likely Finnish. So many Finns flocked to Fitchburg for factory jobs that the city often called itself "Finnburg." It was at one time the largest concentration of Finns outside Finland, and labor organizing and radical politics were quite strong. The Finnish laborers in Fitchburg were sometimes referred to as "apostles of socialism" (Mehren, 2003). Moreover, the nation as a whole was nearing a time during which socialism had perhaps its greatest appeal to laboring Americans.

TURN ONE, TO DARTMOUTH

Two years of experience in the mill, along with 2 years of encouragement by an unnamed person of greater vision, courage and initiative who, "prodded me to get out of my rut and make something of myself," led

Rugg to enroll at Dartmouth College, even though his family did not want him to go to college (H. O. Rugg, 1941, p. 177). In fact, Harold was the first person in the Rugg family to seek broader horizons outside Worcester County. He was encouraged to do so by an upper class family in Fitchburg, the Frosts, who somehow came to develop an interest in young Harold. Having already passed entrance examinations, Rugg enrolled at Dartmouth in 1904, living during a portion of his college years with another sympathetic family and earning his room and board by working for them.

One family story relates that when Harold first went to Dartmouth and reported to his living quarters he greeted his new roommate by extending a hand and announcing his name, "Harold Rugg." "Yes," the roommate replied. As it turned out, both young men had the same name! His roommate, Harold G. Rugg, would later go on to become associate head librarian at Dartmouth (Alling, 2005).

Admission to an elite college was not as difficult or as competitive as it is today. The vast majority of students did not even attend high school, and few even considered college. The conventional wisdom held that college was for the wealthy or for the exceptionally bright. Despite his parent's misgivings, Harold fit the latter description. Rugg began his work at Dartmouth on September 21, 1904. His first 3 years were made up of the standard liberal arts program required of all students. His senior year focused on the "scientific course" and was taken at the Thayer School of Engineering, an affiliated program on the Dartmouth campus. The "scientific course" included coursework focused on mathematics, graphics, physics and chemistry. Rugg completed a minor in English and a second minor in history and economics for a total of 12 credits, consisting of a year's course in each subject. Given that he was later to become one of the principal thinkers in the social studies this seems at best a modest amount of work in history and the social sciences, with rather mediocre grades. He was, at the time, more interested in civil engineering and so took more courses in mathematics and graphics.

Rugg also gained a brief but very positive teaching experience in the social sciences while at Dartmouth. He served as a tutor in history from 1906 through 1909, making his first attempt at teaching by tutoring sophomores in European history. He wrote a course outline, a Complete Outline of European History, as a junior in college, and "coached" Dartmouth sophomores through professor "Eric's dreaded History I and History II" (Rugg, p. 193). Forty students attended Rugg's first lecture and paid $1.00 each for admission. Rugg proved so popular in this initial venture into teaching that the professor teaching the course threatened to sue him if he did not cease his activities (Elizabeth Rugg, 1965). During his later years in college Rugg also did miscellaneous survey work practicing the trade of civil engineering in New Hampshire (H. O. Rugg, 1919a). Rugg attended Dartmouth from 1904-1908 and graduated in 1908 with a BS degree.

While Harold undoubtedly enjoyed college life, and later described his years at Dartmouth as "superb," he was broadly critical of his college experience, just as he had been of Fitchburg schools:

> the outcome of my nine years of secondary school, college, and technological study was but a superficial smattering of knowledge about a variety of academic things, a fair amount of competence in certain limited engineering skills, almost total innocence of the fundamental forces playing upon the domestic and international scene, lack of acquaintance with the essentials of behavior and a distinct want of mental ballast. (H. O. Rugg, 1941, p. 177-178).

Moreover, his feelings of inferiority were not diminished during these years of self-imposed student poverty. Adding to these feelings of inferiority was a speech impediment with which he had struggled since his youth.

Despite his own later misgivings, Rugg's years in college were remembered fondly by a classmate who noted, "the bull sessions that lasted into the wee hours of the morning on such topics as the difference between fame and notoriety, the Saturday night wet downs, the tobacco shop, 'it pays to advertise' Isaacson, the Hunt club, the burning of the history outlines, the graduate year in the Hunt House, etc. etc." Apparently, his classmates frequently addressed him as "H. O." so as to distinguish him from the other Harold Rugg, who would have been known as "H. G." (Alden, 1951).

After earning his BS degree in 1908 (a member of "the naughty, oughty 8's" as he later joked), Rugg enrolled in the Thayer School of Civil Engineering at Dartmouth and studied civil engineering from 1908 to 1909. He served as a teaching assistant in graphics in the spring of 1908, and graduated with a degree in civil engineering in April 1909. The training at Thayer was to stay with him through an emphasis on precision and "reduction of error," code words for clear and "scientific" scholarship. By this point in his development he had demonstrated a natural affinity for teaching. More importantly perhaps, he had graduated from an elite eastern college. That fact would prove a harbinger of things to come.

TURN TWO, TOWARD ACADEMIA

Following his graduation from the Thayer School, Rugg spent April through October of 1909 working as an assistant construction engineer on the Missouri Pacific Railroad in Missouri and Kansas and beginning to apply the skills he had gained in college, learning, apparently to his own surprise, that the formulas he had learned in college really worked (H. O. Rugg, 1941, p. 179; 1919a). Then, in the late summer of 1909, Rugg accepted a position as an instructor of civil engineering at a small new college in Illinois, James Milliken University in Decatur. Rugg was interested in a teaching position even before he accepted the engineering position with the Missouri Pacific Railroad and applied for, but apparently was not offered, a position as an instructor at the Thayer School in the spring of 1909, approximately the time of his application to Milliken (Nelson, 1975; Winters, 1968). While serving as one of two instructors in civil engineering at Milliken, Rugg was paid $900 per year while teaching courses in civil engineering, directing optional field work classes for freshman and sophomores, coaching a "winning" track team, and managing a fundraising drive for gym equipment (Winters, 1968).

It was during his time at Milliken that Rugg met the woman who was to become his first wife, Berta Melville Miller, of Franklin, Indiana, an instructor in the Department of Domestic Science. They married on September 4, 1912, and later adopted two children, Donald Alan Rugg, born March 16, 1916, and Dorothy Elizabeth Rugg, born December 21, 1918.

Rugg taught civil engineering at Milliken for 2 years. During that time he became interested in the process of education, in questions related to how students learn, the measurement of learning and intelligence, and the sociology of education. His curiosity led him to consider entering school again, but this time in the fields of education and sociology. He applied for and was accepted into a doctoral program at the University of Illinois at Champaign-Urbana, not far from Decatur.

On September 20, 1911, Rugg enrolled in the education department at the University of Illinois as one of the first students in a program leading to the newly authorized doctor of philosophy in education. Rugg spent four years at the University of Illinois. From the time of his matriculation until graduation Rugg supported himself, and in 1912 his new wife, by working as an instructor of civil engineering teaching courses in drafting, engineer drawing, and descriptive geometry to students preparing to become engineers. Toward the latter part of graduate training, he was given the opportunity to serve as an instructor in education during summer sessions, in both 1914 and 1915 (H. O. Rugg, 1919a).

A friend from Rugg's graduate school days at the University of Illinois later recalled an incident which, in its foreshadowing, was "symptomatic" of Rugg's whole career. During those years, Harold purchased his first car and took his "first lesson in driving by taking it on a trip to South Bend and back—120 miles? No timid little turns around the park for you!" wrote the friend (Freeman, 1951).

The education department at the University of Illinois was small, with only five full-time faculty members. Rugg engaged in the graduate study of education with William Chandler Bagley, director of the department, Lotus Delta Coffman, Guy C. Whipple, Edward L. Hayes and their associates. While the shift from civil engineering to education may seem dramatic, both were regarded as technical fields. Rugg later viewed the shift as:

> merely changing the job, the data with which I worked—not my fundamental outlook or interest. Society had made me a technician, and the change from engineering to education left me still a technician—and to a very considerable extent ignorant of the new world order that was being fashioned all around me. (H. O. Rugg, 1941, p. 181)

In the 1910s, the field of education was still under construction. Moreover, at the moment of his turn to graduate school, scholars in education were embarked on a great "fact finding movement." As Rugg would later describe it:

> The new "child accounting" was being born: Thorndike had just published his original studies of the school population. Strayer, Elliott and Cubbberley had question-blanked school finance in cities and states.... The new science of educational psychology was emerging ... the concept of the active school was ousting that of the listening school. Thorndike, Judd and company were producing monographs and articles dealing with the transfer of training ... the infant of the human technologies, "education," was being born. But chiefly because of the infancy of the work, the processes of survey, inventory and rearrangement took precedence over controlled experiment, scientific law, reoriented philosophy and thoroughgoing reconstruction. (H. O. Rugg, 1941, p. 181)

Though Rugg chose to enter graduate training to be a technician in the new and emerging field of education, the choice may not have been an easy one. He had already earned his BA and CE degrees, he had found a steady teaching job at Milliken, and he enjoyed the teaching immensely (Nelson, 1975, p. 20). Moreover, education schools were in their infancy and commanded little respect from the established disciplines. The vast majority of professors of education were teaching in normal schools and training prospective elementary teachers. The teacher of teachers was most often a former teacher who emphasized the drill and practice techniques used in the typical classroom. Nonetheless, with education schools in a growth phase, and becoming more accepted institutionally, Rugg saw an opportunity. He believed that he had an excellent chance to teach at a respected department of education by completing graduate work at the University of Illinois. His brother Earle recalled that Harold "got fed up with engineering" and had found a new interest (E. U. Rugg, 1966). In hindsight, Rugg's drive to seek success and prestige was probably also a major factor in his decision.

Rugg's description of his doctoral training at the University of Illinois as another form of "technical" training is supported by additional evidence. Though the focus on education was new, much of his course work was related directly to mathematical and statistical proficiency. As in his undergraduate work at Dartmouth, there was little to suggest an emerging interest in social studies, though he did complete a 9-hour minor in the field of sociology. During his doctoral studies Rugg took no courses in history, geography, or political science, and only a little work in psychology. The vast majority of his coursework was devoted to courses in school administration, statistics, and research through seminars in education conducted by Bagley and Coffman. He also enrolled in the sociology courses of Edward C. Hayes in which he studied principles of sociology, social evolution, sociological method, and the historical development of the field of sociology.

Rugg's doctoral dissertation, "An Experimental Determination of Mental Discipline in School Studies," was filled with charts, graphs, and coefficients (Rugg, 1915). In it he reported his findings on the extent to which transfer of training occurs in specific situations. The study, supervised by Bagley, investigated the concept of mental discipline, focusing specifically on the notion that ideals, but not habits, were subject to transfer from one situation to another.

During Rugg's time in graduate school he also produced, as second author under Bagley, a study of American history as it was taught in the middle grades. The study, titled, "The Contents of American History as Taught in the Seventh and Eighth Grades" was supported by the National Education Association Committee on Economy of Time of the Department of Superintendence. It involved a content analysis of 23 elementary-level American history textbooks published over the preceding half-century to determine similarities and differences in the topics addressed by the books. The result was an attempt to understand the American history content as it was being presented in textbooks. Bagley and Rugg found that textbook writers emphasized politics and military involvement, at the expense of social and economic issues. Moreover, they concluded, the "influence" of the textbooks was "distinctly toward the promotion of nationalism," an influence which they questioned (Bagley & Rugg, 1916, p. 58). Though Rugg's eventual theory of education was barely in its infancy, this early work demonstrates several insights that foreshadow much of his later work in social studies.

Following completion of his studies in May, Rugg was awarded a doctoral degree in education on June 16, 1915. Following this, Rugg joined

Charles H. Judd and his colleagues at the University of Chicago, receiving an appointment to the faculty in the fall of 1915. At the University of Chicago, Rugg rubbed shoulders with a who's who of educators that no doubt contributed to his growth. During graduate school Rugg had become familiar with the work of Judd and others engaged in the scientific study of education. In fact, Rugg's early work emulated Judd's, even going beyond it in certain ways. Judd and Edward L. Thorndike were, in Rugg's later assessment, the "two main bridges by which experimental, scientific, and statistical techniques were carried over from science and psychology in education" (1947, p. 125). With Judd at the helm the School of Education at the University of Chicago became one of the two major centers for the quantitative and scientific study of education, along with Teachers College, Columbia University.

Rugg joined the faculty of the University of Chicago at the rank of instructor (H. O. Rugg, 1919a). His teaching load was two courses per quarter. During his first quarter at the University he taught two courses with Judd, a survey of educational administration and an introductory course in education (University of Chicago, 1914). In subsequent years Rugg taught a variety of courses in educational measurement, secondary mathematics curriculum, and psychology of secondary curriculum.

The University of Chicago must have been an exciting place to work during Rugg's years there, and many of his colleagues no doubt had a significant influence on Rugg's development. Among the scholars who spent time at the University of Chicago during these years were such luminaries as John Franklin Bobbitt and W. W. Charters, architects of the social efficiency movement in the curriculum, George S. Counts, who would later serve as a close colleague of Rugg's during his years at Teachers College, and John Roscoe Clark, with whom Rugg coauthored a number of publications on the teaching of mathematics. Rugg and Clark also developed and promoted mathematics materials for schools, an experience which would foreshadow Rugg's later developments in social studies (Nelson, 1975; H. O. Rugg, 1941).

Rugg's tenure at Chicago also led to his first contact with another person who would become a lifelong friend. Carleton Washburne, superintendent of schools in Winnetka, Illinois, heard of Rugg through one of his teachers who was taking a course from Rugg. The teacher told Washburne that he must come hear this "wonderful" young professor: "He has energy, enthusiasm, and vision. He inspires us!" Drawn to attend a class session by this accolade, Washburne met Rugg and their friendship began (Washburne, 1960, pp. 176-181).

While Harold was teaching at the University of Chicago, Earle Rugg, Harold's younger brother, taught high school history at Oak Park, Illinois, not far from the University. Earle, who adored his older brother, was an undergraduate at the University of Illinois while Harold was working on his PhD, and later followed Harold to the Chicago area. Earle was active among teachers of history in the Northeastern Illinois Social Studies Round Table and was one of the influences which may have led to Harold's eventual conversion to social studies. In an interview conducted many years later, Earle credited a conversation between the two which occurred in his Oak Park apartment with Harold's gradual conversion to social studies (E. U. Rugg, 1966).

At the University of Chicago, Harold continued to pursue technical studies and established himself as a leader in the scientific study of education. Rugg's early journal publications appeared in the *Elementary School Journal*, which was published by the University of Chicago School of Education faculty, with Judd as editor. Reflecting on his thinking during this period Rugg would later write:

> We lived in one long orgy of tabulation. Mountains of facts were piled up, condensed, summarized and interpreted by the new quantitative technique. The air was full of normal curves, standard deviations, coefficients of correlation, regression equations. I was one of a very large band of intellectuals … proclaiming salvation through fact finding. (H. O. Rugg, 1941, p. 182)

Rugg's major work while on the faculty at the University of Chicago was a textbook on the use of statistics, *Statistical Methods Applied to Education* (H. O. Rugg, 1917), which was soon adopted widely as a graduate school primer. As illustrated by this book, Rugg was thoroughly familiar with the scientific literature in his new field of study and was quickly becoming an emerging star. His text presented statistical methods in a way in which students who lacked an extensive background in mathematics could understand it. In addition, the materials in the text had been developed and field-tested in mimeographed form in classes Rugg taught at the University of Chicago.

Notwithstanding this early success and the notoriety it would bring, Rugg later confessed misgivings about the text, saying, "I hated it and I despised every hour of the writing of it and I felt ignorant when I did it, and I didn't really understand what was in the book and did not understand what I was doing and I left the whole field later for things I felt I could understand" (H. O. Rugg, 1956).

Despite these rather profound uncertainties, Rugg was quickly moving up the educational career ladder and developing a growing national reputation. While serving at the University of Chicago he was promoted from instructor to assistant professor in 1917, after only 2 years, and then to associate professor in 1918, after one more year, a year which included publication of his first book.

TURN THREE, JOINING THE AVANTE-GARDE

When the United States entered World War I in 1917, Rugg was invited by Leonard Ayers, the chief statistical officer for the U. S. War Department, to go to Washington and assist the United States Army in classifying the huge influx of new soldiers drafted and recruited for the war effort. The large scale expansion of the army and the need for specialists in classifying personnel led to large numbers of psychologists and statisticians answering the call to government service. This was the first use of aptitude and intelligence testing on so large a scale. Though it appears that Rugg wavered for a time, and that Judd persuaded him, albeit temporarily, to stay in Chicago, John Coss convinced him that he should join Walter D. Scott, Thorndike, and Walter V. Bingham on the army's "Committee on Classification of Personnel." The Committee was a "handpicked lot of psychologists, educationalists, statisticians and industrial and business personnel executives," who would serve as "fact finders" in support of the war effort (H. O. Rugg, 1941, p. 183). Thus, Rugg left for Washington with a mix of feelings, almost grudgingly it seems. Nonetheless, as we shall see, the experience was to challenge his worldview, and, in a relatively short time, change the trajectory of his life and career (H. O. Rugg, 1956).

Prior to his service on the Committee, Rugg had not really begun to wrestle with the challenges to capitalism, as he noted later:

> Before World War I, I was pro Mr. Theodore Roosevelt. I thought that the big stick was the thing. I thought that the acme of reform in political life was conservation. That was the big thing. If we could just get people to stop wasting, wasting, wasting but ... Free enterprise, that was the way of life, that was the American way of life. That's what you were brought into. And it was right, it was *the* way of life. And the possibility of social control in 1910? No. What do you mean social control. Never could. Yet, I knew something was wrong about the system. I used to say to my father that, "Can't they do something about the system," meaning control it. I didn't know enough to use the word control. And he would say, no, he would say, "Hard times and good times, that's life. You have good times, then you have hard times, then you have good times again. It's a circle." Businessmen believe it. They believed there wasn't anything you could do about the economics system, just let it go. It never occurred to them that man made it.... Then why the dickens couldn't we remake it. (H. O. Rugg, 1956, pp. 4-5)

Rugg's tour of duty on the Army's Committee exposed him to several leading liberal thinkers, thus broadening his views and eventually contributing to his transformation. He was exposed to a new type of thinking by aesthetic intellectuals of the sort he had never come in contact with during his years in school. In the short run, the impact of the new thinking caused him to question the truth of the new science and testing, "the orgy of tabulation" in which he had been engaged.

In Washington, Rugg found himself a close associate of Arthur Upham Pope, a fellow committeeman and a former member of the philosophy faculty at the University of California, and John Coss, an educator at Columbia University in New York. The day after the armistice in 1918, Coss asked Rugg what he was planning to do on returning to Chicago. Rugg replied, "I'm not sure.... Pope has me all stirred up about Van Wyck Brooks new stuff—stirred up and mixed up" (H. O. Rugg, 1941, pp. 169-170).

Through hours of conversation and discussion, spurred by their work together on the committee, Pope introduced Rugg to the writings of America's young social critics, Van Wyck Brooks, Randolph Bourne, and Waldo Frank, much of it contained in the avant garde literary journal, *The Seven Arts*. Rugg found himself associating not only with Coss and Pope, but with Walter Lippman, noted author and associate editor of the *New Republic*, and Fred Howe, political scientist and social critic. During his time on the Committee, Rugg became a confirmed liberal and discovered new "truths" about society. It was a metamorphosis that profoundly changed his outlook, as Rugg later recalled:

> The shock came. I can tell you of specific evenings sitting around there in Washington in those offices waiting for the latest bulletins from Paris.
>
> Walter Lippman would be in the group and at that time Walter was a socialist, not a great world columnist for the *Herald Tribune*. He was really an out and out socialist himself and he would practically spit when news would come that George and Clemenceau had pulled the wool more over Wilson's eyes that night and we could see that Wilson was selling out without knowing that he was selling out. Most of the young men in our group were a generation younger than these leaders. At last I began to say to myself, by golly, there is something called economic imperialism in the world, there are exploited peoples in the world. (H. O. Rugg, 1956, pp. 5-6)

Ruminating again on the origins of his transformation, Rugg said:

> Now I had ... the feeling always for the underdog, because I was one of the underdogs, I suppose. But I also sort of felt, you have to conform, you have to line up, you have to agree, you have to go along with the controlling group. And the community, my community, was a kind of hierarchy. In Massachusetts, not just this town, there was a kind of hierarchy of ownerships and so on. The wealthy people with property lived up on Prospect Hill, and you came down through all the neighborhoods, and when you got down to Wood street, mine ... the highest economic level on my street was the floor walker in Nichols Department Store, a small store. He was the top man in that neighborhood. I suppose he earned maybe 15 or 18 dollars a week.

And we were down the scale. So there was a background of inferiority in all this, you see.

Beyond this sort of rationalizing, I have no clear answers as to what makes you a Lincoln Steffens or Fred Howe or whatever you have. Perhaps if I get to a point where I have to write an autobiography maybe I'll come out with some other answers. I can describe it with great clearness in terms of the bi-level influences, but I still have to say ... groups around me, people who influenced me, and so on. I still have to say there's a great unknown X there in the constitution of the individual. (H. O. Rugg, 1956, pp. 5-6)

Looking backward, from his service on the Army's Committee on Classification of Personnel, the years from 1890 to 1918 had served as years of apprenticeship and preparation for Rugg. Born and raised in a conservative New England mill town, he had witnessed first hand the ravages and inequalities produced by the capitalist industrial system. Years of poverty and the accompanying feelings of inferiority had left lasting marks that adult successes would never completely erase. His early mind set was largely the creation of an age that sought salvation through science, through fact finding and tabulation. Gradually, he had made the transition from civil engineer to educator, but the application of a scientific worldview remained. World War one would change all that.

Prior to the war, Rugg had seemingly been content applying the technical tools of statistical description to the process of education. His service during the war, and the ideas he would come in contact with, challenged his fundamental views on the world, and called him to higher pursuit. Moreover, the academic community, the nation, and the world had undergone a transformation, understanding for the first time the potential horrors and destruction that modern warfare could bring. A new age was beginning. It was to mark a transformation for many intellectuals and a rebirth, indeed a reconstruction of the world view and educational thought of Harold Rugg. His experience while serving in Washington transformed Rugg, and led his turn toward liberal thought, toward social criticism, and toward social studies.

Though Rugg's transformation resulted from a variety of influences, and his service on the Committee on Personnel was chief among them, the literary journal, *The Seven Arts,* was also one of the keys to his makeover. After all, his colleagues on the Committee had introduced Rugg to the journal. This was, apparently, Rugg's first contact with "frontier thinkers" concerned with analyzing contemporary life and its direction. As a civil engineer, and then an educational "technician," Rugg had carved out a comfortable niche in the educational system without giving much thought to the nature of that system or its relationship to society. Perhaps for the first time, he was beginning to challenge the assumptions underlying the system and his own work.

The Seven Arts was an influential literary journal published for only 12 months during the years 1916 to 1917. Despite its brief tenure, *The Seven Arts* shone brightly as a beacon of hope and promise, as a source of sharp social criticism, and later, as an icon of intellectual honesty and vigor. The journal's editorial staff included important young literary figures Waldo Frank and Van Wyck Brooks, who were major American critics. Among its contributors were many of the leading creative thinkers of the day including Robert Frost, Carl Sandburg, Randolph Bourne, Sherwood Anderson, Kahlil Gibran, and John Dewey. The journal combined a call for artistic rebirth with criticism of American culture focused on materialism, the lasting influence of Puritanism, and the lack of meaningful spirituality in American life. Each of these strands was to have a profound influence on the social and educational thought of Harold Rugg (Phillips, 1961).

James Oppenheim, the journal's founding editor, was a freelance poet from the Midwest who had gained some notoriety writing short stories. Grown tired of writing fiction and inspired by the growth of American literature, Oppenheim dreamed of creating a magazine which would publish the work of talented American writers, something similar to *La Nouvelle Revue Francaise,* a French magazine founded in 1909 by a group of French writers and critics who called for artists to take a lead role in creation of an indigenous cultural synthesis. The idea of art playing a lead role in social progress was nothing new, and in America, had been emphasized by Ralph Waldo Emerson and Walt Whitman. In their work, as in *The Seven Arts,* a call for artistic rebirth was combined with criticism of American culture. Emerson's criticisms included the culture's excessive materialism, the dominance of market values, and the overarching influence of these cultural values on American material and spiritual life. In his contributions to *The Seven Arts,* and elsewhere, Walt Whitman also attacked the corruption brought by industrial culture.

The journal *The Seven Arts* got its start after Oppenheim met a young writer, Waldo Frank, at a cocktail party in New York City in late 1915. Frank was something of a boy genius. He had worked for the *New York Times* and *Saturday Evening Post* for a short period before leaving for France in 1913, where he was strongly influenced by writers who had been instrumental in the *Nouvelle Revue.* Oppenheim's idea for a magazine intrigued Frank and the two began looking for financial backing. Joined by another young writer named Paul Rosenfeld, the quest for a financier led to a wealthy older woman named Arlene K. Rankine, who sold her collection of paintings to provide funds for launching the magazine. The trio asked Van Wyck Brooks to join them, and the core staff for *The Seven Arts* was formed. Brooks, the most well known, was deeply influenced by European thinkers, and had grown to associate the European continent with art, and America with a sort of dullness mixed with security. Brooks had authored *The Wine of the Puritans,* published in 1909, which combined an attack on Puritan ethics with the need for a usable past which could be engaged to improve the future. He taught for a few years at Cambridge, then published a book on H. G. Wells in which Brooks emphasized Wells' exaltation of socialism and repudiation of the mechanistic culture of modernity. In 1915, Brooks next book, *America's Coming of Age* combined, again, an attack on Puritan values and a call for artistic rebirth. America was divided, he wrote, between "highbrow" and "lowbrow" culture. Brooks attacked the writers who had succumbed to the commercial, lowbrow strain. His essay combined an indictment of American materialism with optimism for future greatness through art and socialism.

In *The Seven Arts,* these writers expressed a scathing critique of America's emotional and spiritual failures, and saw these failures linked to industrialism, mechanization, materialism, and the Puritan influence. Brooks, in an article titled "Young America" attacked the shallowness of American spiritual life, critiquing its "makeshift art" and "trivial popular fiction" (Brooks, 1916, p. 147). He argued that American life was in a state of arrested development due to the failure of "wise old men of letters" who had been seduced by commercialism. This stagnant culture combined with the triumph of industrialization to create "devitalized men" and "a poor quality of human nature" (Brooks, 1917, p. 662). Waldo Frank offered a similar critique of American culture, writing that "we were smaller than our buildings," and bemoaning the lack of harmony and unity among the American people (Frank, 1917, p. 294).

Though one of the magazine's major themes was the failure of American culture, the solutions offered were usually rather vague, and included calls for greater spiritual and emotional experience, and a raised consciousness through which a new and vital art would lift up the culture. Oppenheim, the editor, issued a call for great national personalities, great creators, great music, and great books to create a stronger national community. In his view, the American past could be coupled with art and socialism to provide a new collective consciousness.

As an idea flows from its source it directly or indirectly touches many minds, who may absorb it or reject it, fully or in part. The ideas embodied in *The Seven Arts* had one of their longest and widest impacts through the work of Harold Rugg. Their social criticism, exaltation of the potential promise of socialism, and their hope of social uplift through art were kept alive and applied to schooling by Rugg.

THE TURNING POINT

When the war ended, Rugg went, dutifully, back to his faculty post at the University of Chicago in late November, 1918. But, he returned a changed man (H. O. Rugg, 1941, p. 170). His wartime experience had opened new vistas, which would lead in significant new directions. Rugg now questioned, more than ever before, the value of the scientific tabulation and description in which he and his colleagues at the University of Chicago School of Education had been engaged. That, combined with his frustrations with the somewhat "domineering" Charles H. Judd, left Rugg ready for a change. The opportunity came in the fall of 1919 when he was offered a position as school psychologist in the Lincoln School at Teachers College, Columbia University in New York. The offer came in October, 1919, from the Director of the Lincoln School, Otis Caldwell, who had been Superintendent of Schools in Decatur, Illinois, when Rugg was on the faculty at Milliken.

Rugg was in New York during the autumn of 1919, considering the possibility of coming to the Lincoln School. During a walk on the long trail from Caldwell's house through Van Cortlandt Park, talking out the possibility of coming to the new modern school at Teachers College, Rugg thought, "I'll come for freedom." Then he told Caldwell:

> I think if I were sure I'd be left really free to work as I wish, I'd come. I'm happy with Judd and his men, although I'm not sure that I'm really free. Judd is pretty dominating, whether he means to be or not. What I need now is a little leisure to study the total problem of America and education and make up my mind what should be done about it. I need to be let alone to choose my job and work at it as I see best. (H. O. Rugg, 1941, p. 187)

Though Caldwell seemed bothered at first, Rugg went on: "When I say 'free to choose my own job,' I mean I should like to select that part of the school's task that I feel I should work on and then be left free to go ahead. I don't want anybody telling me: 'You can't say that,' or 'You can't do that.'" Rugg would later write, "I knew I wished to be free of unspoken pressures as well as word-of-mouth admonitions and interferences. I didn't want to live and work in a climate of opinion which would be forever trying to warp me and label me in its image" (H. O. Rugg, 1941, p. 188).

Rugg accepted the position in the Lincoln School with the understanding that "appointment as a member of Doctor Thorndike's Department in Teachers College will follow this appointment in the Lincoln School in due season—certainly not later than the current year" (H. O. Rugg, 1919b). Also, Rugg agreed to come to New York on two additional conditions: first, he wanted the freedom to experiment as he wished as educational psychologist; second, and perhaps most importantly, he needed time during the spring of 1920, relieved from most duties at the Lincoln School, to read, think, and develop his program of research. Somewhat surprisingly, Otis Caldwell, director of the Lincoln School, agreed to these stipulations. Perhaps this was a reflection of Rugg's growing national reputation, and of the "laissez faire" position of the administration at the Lincoln School.

Rugg and his family moved to New York City and he began his new position at the Lincoln School at Teachers College on January 1, 1920 (Kay, 1969). He would later characterize his arrival in New York as a, "sharp turning point in my life ... (leading to) ... many years of unlearning and an exciting search for understanding.... I have never once regretted it. I became free as probably no other person working on the controversial frontier in America has been free" (H. O. Rugg, 1941, p. 188). On April 5, 1920 Rugg received official appointment as associate professor of education to the faculty of Teachers College, effective July 1, 1920, as he had been promised, appointed to serve with John Dewey and the most prestigious group of faculty in education anywhere on the planet (H. O. Rugg, 1920).

The Lincoln School at Teachers College, which was established in 1917, was recognized as one of the leading progressive private schools in the nation. The establishment of the Lincoln School, as well as other progressive schools of the time, was a reaction against the traditional and fairly rigid educational practices of the typical school. Developed from the ideas of Charles Eliot and Abraham Flexner, and funded by the General Education Board financed by the Rockefellers, the school was proposed as "a laboratory for the working out of an elementary and secondary school curriculum which shall eliminate obsolete material and endeavor to work up in usable form, materials adapted to the needs of modern living" (Cremin, Shannon, & Townsend, 1954, p. 110). Ultimately, the purpose of the Lincoln School was to change the face of American education to a more progressive and modern bent (Buttenwieser, 1968).

Rugg viewed the Lincoln School as similar in purpose to the Dewey School at the University of Chicago:

> it was created first as a "modern school" for the children.... Lincoln is, indeed the only school to be established in the past forty years with a heavy endowment for public school experimentation. (H. O. Rugg, 1947, p. 559)

> The atmosphere of the school was certainly one of freedom of imagination and willingness to experiment. No matter how unworkable a suggestion appeared to be upon first impression it got a hearing.... Everything educational under the sun was tried. (H. O. Rugg, 1941, p. 191)

By 1920, at the time of Rugg's arrival, the Lincoln School was growing rapidly. It had opened in 1917 with a staff of twenty-five and a relatively small student body. By the early 1920s it had grown to a staff of over seventy and a student body of nearly five hundred. Experimentation was the watchword, and both the founders of the school and its administration wanted to create a scientific laboratory that would produce a new and innovative curriculum. No single theory was to be proved or disproved, no particular method was to dominate. The staff responded enthusiastically: old textbooks were thrown out, and by 1921, over 200,000 pages of new materials had been developed (Caldwell, 1926). This context, with support for freedom of thought and freedom to experiment, provided the perfect setting for Rugg's new career direction and for his work in social studies to proceed.

CONCLUSION

To revisit the question posed earlier, How did Harold Rugg come to be who he was? Gradually, as we have seen, Rugg became increasingly independent in his thinking. Always something of a rebel, he was driven to succeed by the powerful combination of a Puritan work ethic and an inferiority complex created by his modest beginnings in a conservative Yankee New England mill town. His drive for success led him first to Dartmouth, then through what turned out to be a rather brief career as a civil engineer. However, that sojourn imbued him with a technical and scientific training that would serve him well, and it opened the possibility of wider vistas, and a career as an educator. His doctoral training opened new doors, and led in a fairly short time to some notoriety as an authority on use of statistics. That led in turn to his call to serve on the Army Committee on Classification of Personnel, to contact with a remarkable group of thinkers who spent many late nights talking, dissecting the issues of the day and opening Rugg to a whole new world of ideas. That experience led, most directly, to Rugg's transformation to social studies education. His appointment to the faculty at Teachers College, Columbia University, culminated a rapid rise and evolution to a position of prominence that suited his interests almost perfectly. He was bright and hardworking, and his ambitions knew no boundaries. As a "brash young man" (H. O. Rugg, 1956) he had a strong faith in his own abilities, a new career direction, time to plan his next steps, and a young family to provide for, a family that undoubtedly provided him with the requisite emotional support.

The stage was now set for Rugg to make major contributions to education, and to develop what remains one of the most innovative social studies programs ever created. With a seat on the faculty of the most prestigious college of education in the world, and the freedom that he wanted, the conditions were ripe for the full flowering of Rugg's creative imagination. A young man from a mill town in Massachusetts was now on the cusp of greatness, of making innovative and legendary contributions to his field, and of stirring the passions of both critics and defenders as no other social studies educator ever has, before or since.

REFERENCES

Alden, A. G. (1951). Alanson G. Alden to Harold Rugg, April 15, 1951. *Harold Rugg: Letters in appreciation of his frontier work.* Unpublished manuscript, Teachers College, New York.

Alling, K. (2005, January 20). Interview with Katharine Alling of Rochester, NY, step-daughter of Harold Rugg, conducted by the author.

Bagley, W. C., & Rugg, H. O. (1916). *Content of American history, as taught in the seventh and eighth grades* (Bulletin # 16). Champagne-Urbana: University of Illinois School of Education.

Brooks, V. W. (1909). *The wine of the puritans: A study of present-day America.* New York: M. Kennerley.

Brooks, V. W. (1915). *America's coming of age.* New York: B. W. Huebsh.

Brooks, V. W. (1916, December). Young America. *The Seven Arts,* 144-151.

Brooks, V. W. (1917, April). The culture of industrialism. *The Seven Arts,* 655-666.

Buttenwieser, P. L. (1968). *The Lincoln School and its times, 1917-1948.* Unpublished doctoral dissertation, Teachers College, Columbia University.

Cremin, L. E., Shannon, D. A., & Townsend, M. E. (1954). *A history of Teachers College.* New York: Columbia University Press.

Caldwell, O. W. (1926). The Lincoln experimental school. Curriculum—Past and present. In H. O. Rugg (Ed.), *The foundations and technique of curriculum construction: Curriculum making past and present.* Twenty-Sixth Yearbook of the National Society for the Study of Education, Part I (pp. 272-273). Bloomington, IN: Public School Publishing.

Fitchburg Historical Society. (1972). *The city and the river.* Fitchburg, MA: Fitchburg Historical Society.

Frank, W. (1917, January). Vicarious fiction. *The Seven Arts,* pp. 294-303.

Freeman, F. N. (1951). Frank N. Freeman to Harold Rugg, April 9, 1951. *Harold Rugg: Letters in appreciation of his frontier work.* Unpublished manuscript, Teachers College, New York.

Kay, G. A. (1969). *Harold Rugg: Educational pioneer and social reconstructionist.* Unpublished doctoral dissertation, State University of New York, Buffalo.

Mehren, E. (2003, December 15). Dispatch from Fitchburg, Mass.: 'Invisible' Finnish community still has one proud voice left. *Los Angeles Times,* p. A27.

Nelson, M. R. (1975). Building a science of society: The social studies and Harold O. Rugg, doctoral dissertation, Stanford University.

Phillips, M. (1961). *The Seven Arts and Harold Rugg.* Unpublished masters thesis, Columbia University.

Rugg, B. E. (2005, January 13). Interview with Brian E. Rugg, of Albany, California. Grandson of Earle Rugg and great nephew of Harold Rugg, conducted by the author.

Rugg, E. (1965, October 12). Interview with Elizabeth Rugg in Bearsville, NY (as cited in Kay, 1969, p. 55).

Rugg, E. U. (1966). The Earle Rugg tape. Prepared by Earle U. Rugg in response to questions posed by George A. Kay and Elmer A. Winters, May 5, 1966. Tape and transcript in the possession of the author.

Rugg, H. O. (1915). *An experimental determination of mental discipline in school studies.* Unpublished doctoral dissertation, University of Illinois, Champaign-Urbana.

Rugg, H. O. (1917). *Statistical method applied to education.* New York: Houghton Mifflin.

Rugg, H. O. (1919a). Biographical notes for Dr. Caldwell, "Harold Rugg" folder, box 58, William F. Russell papers, Gottesman Libraries, Teachers College, Columbia University.

Rugg, H. O. (1919b). H. O. Rugg to James E. Russell, "Harold Rugg" folder, box 58, William F. Russell Papers, Gottesman Libraries, Teachers College, Columbia University.

Rugg, H. O. (1920). "University Appointment Cards," Biographical files, Columbiana Collection, Columbia University Archives.

Rugg, H. O. (1941). *That men may understand: An American in the long armistice.* New York: Doubleday, Doran.

Rugg, H. O. (1947). *Foundations for American education.* Yonkers-on-Hudson, NY: World Book.

Rugg, H. O. (1956). Rugg speaking engagement at Cold Spring Geriatric Society, Cold Spring, New York, June 15, 1956. Transcript and tape in the possession of the author.

University of Chicago. (1914-1915). *Annual register* (as cited in Nelson, 1975, p. 33).

Washburne, C. (1960). Eulogy to Rugg. *Educational Theory, X,* 176-181.

Winters, E. A. (1968). *Harold Rugg and education for social reconstructionism.* Unpublished doctoral dissertation, University of Wisconsin, Madison.

CHAPTER 2

RUGG ON SOCIAL STUDIES

Following his appointment to the staff of the Lincoln School as educational psychologist in the winter of 1920, Rugg's first task was to measure and chart the abilities of every child in the school. By developing and organizing this data, he provided the school with its first system of psychological records. For the first time in his new career in education he was in regular contact with the student population of a graded school, forced to come to grips with the "intimate problems of child growth," and afforded the opportunity to employ his newly acquired skills in administering intelligence tests (H. O. Rugg, 1941, p. 188). The freedom which Rugg had negotiated as part of his transition to Teachers College was definitely not apparent during that first winter in New York.

"A NEW VISTA OF POSSIBILITIES ..."

However, as promised, during the spring of 1920, Rugg was relieved of most of his duties as psychologist for the Lincoln School to devote time to reading and reflection. He was, as he later described it, "free to put my heels on the table and read and think" (H. O. Rugg, 1941, p. 193). This rare opportunity, especially unusual during the early years in a new position, came at a crucial point in Rugg's intellectual development. He had been introduced to the works of Van Wyck Brooks, Waldo Frank, Randolph Bourne and other social critics, especially those of *The Seven Arts*

This Happened in Ameica: Harold Rugg and the Censure of Social Studies
pp. 25–54
Copyright © 2007 by Information Age Publishing

group. That exposure was transforming his politics and kindling his interest in the social world. As he started his program of reading he already had some familiarity with nineteenth century social philosophers such as August Comte and Herbert Spencer, William Graham Sumner and Lester Frank Ward. He also had some acquaintance with the work of social psychologist Thorstein Veblen and the progressive "new history."

Given time to read and think, Rugg now had freedom to explore the recent works of leading scholars in history and the social sciences and to read seminal works published in the late nineteenth and early twentieth centuries (H. O. Rugg, 1941). Among these were works by historians such as Frederick Jackson Turner's "Significance of the Frontier in American History" (1894) and Charles A. Beard's *Economic Interpretation of the Constitution* (1913); books by recent social theorists such as Veblen's *Theory of the Leisure Class* (1899), and Cooley's *Human Nature and the Social Order* (1902). He read new scholarship from economists including John Maynard Keynes' *The Economic Consequences of the Peace* (1920) and others such as Norman Angell, Bertrand Russell, and E. D. Morel who had predicted that rapid industrialization and a mad race for resources, markets and colonies would lead to disastrous ends. He read the works of Fabian socialists such as Frank Podmore, Bernard Shaw, and Beatrice and Sidney Webb who had built a reconstructive faith through the Fabian Society.

He read works on the evolution of industrial society such as John A. Hobson's *The Evolution of Modern Capitalism* (1906), R. H. Tawney's *The Acquisitive Society* (1920), and Leon Marshall's *Readings in Industrial Society* (1918). He read works in political science such as Charles E. Merriam's *American Political Ideas* (1920). And, he read the "new" historians of the United States in greater depth and in new editions, including John R. Commons' *History of Labour in the United States* (1918), James Harvey Robinson's *The New History* (1912), and the broader economic and historical interpretations of Charles Beard. Though his personal library was in its early stages of development, several of Rugg's intimate associates and former students testified that he "maintained an extremely large library and that he had read and studied all of the books" (Winters, 1968, p. 27).

All of this reading was to have a profound impact on Rugg's thinking. He started "to piece together, bit by bit, a mosaic like picture of increasing industrialism around the world ... (and) began to see the intricate ramifications" including both the positive: partial freedom from primitive work, production of large quantities of material goods; and, the not so positive: overcrowding, colonization, and subjugation of "backward" peoples.

As Rugg would later describe it:

A new vista of possibilities as well as problems of man and his civilization opened before me. The very discovery of the deeper-lying trends and movements of the modern industrial world ... (inspired me) ... to master the chief concepts and generalizations of economic, political and social life and to phrase the fundamental problems and issues of our time. (H. O. Rugg, 1941, p. 201)

While all of this was quite stimulating, at the same time it produced "a good deal of mental and emotional discomfort" because it was in conflict with his longstanding attitudes and beliefs. While Rugg had always "temperamentally" rooted for the underdog, he had also believed that "the machinery of industrial civilization was essentially admirable and that capitalism was to be accepted on its proved merits and not really to be challenged" (p. 202). Gradually, for Rugg, a more knowledgeable, more refined and more critical perspective on industrial civilization emerged. That critical perspective lay behind his work from that time forward and served as his greatest touchstone of inspiration.

THE APOSTLE

Following this time for reading, Rugg's conversion to social studies was more or less complete. Though he remained a scholar broadly interested in society, education, and curriculum, social studies was to be his major focus for the next 2 decades, the prime generative years of his career. Though he later wrote that the spring of 1920 afforded him time to think through what he wanted to do in the field of education, he had already found his primary interest.

Though at first glance his record does not seem to indicate a strong interest in history or the social sciences prior to 1918, at least a few of his associates have offered insights that may help to explain the switch. His brother, Earle, believed that the move may have been carefully planned (E. U. Rugg, 1966). Certainly, from the time of his discussions with Pope, Coss, and others on the Committee on Personnel, and after his initial exposure to the work of Brooks, Bourne, and Frank, his interest in the contemporary social world had been piqued. Rugg was ripe for the conversion. The son of a technician who created designs in wood, he had followed his father into a technical trade with promise of a steady income. During his service on the Committee on Personnel, he was awakened to a new world of ideas, which shook him out of his newfound middle-class complacency. He had been exposed to some social theory earlier, during graduate school. Moreover, Earle had been urging his brother Harold to get involved in social studies. By the time of Harold's return to the University of Chicago, he was, it seems, no longer very interested in playing a hand in the continuing "orgy of tabulation."

Monetary factors, the status anxiety rooted in fear of not having enough, may also have been part of the decision. Kenneth Benne, a protégé of Rugg's and a longtime close personal friend, believed that Rugg may have been influenced by the fact that social studies was a relatively new field. The newness opened the possibility of substantial financial rewards for commercial publications which would be virtually assured of a market (Benne, 1967).

Much earlier, while an undergraduate at Dartmouth, Rugg had tutored students in European history and written and published a study guide for that course, suggesting an aptitude and interest in the field. However, given his upbringing, a career with strong and immediate financial rewards was a priority, and civil engineering seemed a good initial fit. The same could be said for his tenure at the University of Chicago. Though he was clearly skilled in his work as an educational technician, and his textbook on the use of statistics in education won him wide recognition, it appears that an interest in social issues, history, and the social sciences may have been simmering on the back burner, just waiting to boil over into a major career shift.

By the fall of 1919, during his job interview at Teachers College, Rugg was plainly stating his interest in social studies. In fact, he later recalled, by the time of his reading interlude in the spring of 1920:

> I had already made up my mind about what I was going to work at—the social studies. My decision was due in part, no doubt, to the hang-over of the talks with Pope and Coss and my reading of the new social criticism.... Others had predicted that I would turn back to my first intellectual love— history and the social sciences. (H. O. Rugg, 1941, p. 193)

During that interview at the Lincoln School, Rugg attempted to define "social studies" in response to his prospective employer's query:

> Caldwell and Flexner had asked me in our first interview: "Social studies? What is that?"
> I didn't know exactly myself. "In general," I said, "all the materials that have to do with how people live together."
> "You mean the facts of history and geography and civics?"
> "Yes, and economics and sociology and anthropology—everything that has to do with social life."
> Rugg reminded them of the 1916 Report on Social Studies, "But even that" he said, "is merely a general caption to group together under one name the existing materials of history, geography and civics. It represents essentially no change in content."
> "What changes would you make?" One of them asked.
> "I don't know—yet. But I'll try to find out in the half-year of leisure you're going to give me.... There will probably be two kinds of changes:

first, the new content will deal with conditions and problems of modern civilization that have never been in schools at all and second, there will be a new organization of the materials—probably a kind of ... 'unified' social studies."

"We need a new principle.... Something like this: that all the facts, ideas, and generalizations needed by a child's mind or an adult's mind, for that matter, should be brought into close relationship with one another. This would necessitate going straight across the boundaries of the academic subjects whenever the indispensable facts for understanding are needed." (H. O. Rugg, 1941, pp. 193-195)

And so, in the fall of 1919, Rugg sketched out a skeletal framework of his initial thinking on the curriculum. It was to cut across, yet not obliterate, the traditional disciplinary boundaries. It would unify the field in light of contemporary needs, and would bring all the relevant materials together for pertinent and clear social thought about contemporary society, something the school was not then attempting.

In his interview at Teachers College, Rugg suggested some of his differences with the 1916 Report on Social Studies (U.S. Bureau of Education, 1916). From his re-creation of that interview conversation it is clear that he viewed the Report as too traditional, as a mere umbrella for previously existing courses. The social studies curriculum created by the 1916 Report was something of a compromise among contending forces, largely made up of previously existing courses, trimmed and tailored to a more modern and progressive vision. Though his comments seem to ignore Community Civics and Problems of Democracy, these new courses, created by the Committee on Social Studies, were innovative reorganizations of material that had found its way into schools in previous iterations in courses of a different name. Rugg wanted to go further, to introduce more new materials dealing with current conditions and problems and to create a unified, integrated curriculum.

In 1920, Rugg was appointed to serve on the Social Studies subcommittee of the National Education Association's Commission on the Reorganization of Secondary Education, a continuation and modification of the original committee responsible for the 1916 Report. The subsequent sub-committee, chaired by J. Montgomery Gambrill, a colleague of Rugg's at Teachers College, was charged with reviewing, and possibly revising, the 1916 Report. As we shall see, Rugg's developing vision for social studies went so far beyond the 1916 Report, that it may have been difficult for the subcommittee to reach agreement. In any case, a revised report was never published.

Though he had spent several years in technical fields, first civil engineering, and then as a quantitative researcher in education, from the spring of 1920 Rugg would devote most of his professional attention to his new focus. He would soon develop a design for social studies, which would burst upon the scene in the form of his pamphlet series and text-books, gaining unprecedented popularity and having a wide influence on both theory and practice in education.

A DEVELOPING THEORY

Many of Rugg's new ideas on social studies began to emerge in the early 1920s in monographs written by Rugg and his research associates and in publications in journals and books. Full development of Rugg's social studies theory occurred in relative synchronicity with the writing and pub-lication of the Rugg Social Science pamphlets. Though Rugg did not pub-lish a single, unified statement of his theory during the early years of his career at Teachers College, his writings provide strong evidence of a developing theory. As it emerged over time, the skeletal frame remained relatively constant. Yet, Rugg's continuing intellectual growth at Teachers College and in the cultural richness of New York City led to the evolution of a more fully developed theory and rationale.

Rugg's first published articles to describe his vision for a new and inno-vative social studies began to appear not long after his arrival at the Lin-coln School. In two similar articles which were published in *Historical Outlook* and *The Elementary School Journal*, in May of 1921, Rugg critiqued the work of the Committee on History and Education for Citizenship, known as the Second Committee of Eight, of the American Historical Association. Though he defended the need for national committees in developing curricula, he was extremely critical of the Eight for failing to take a "scientific approach" and for neglecting to provide the necessary national leadership. He described curriculum making by committee as "a method of the most unscientific sort" in which "the opinion and apriori judgement of a small group of specialists in subject matter have predomi-nated." In Rugg's view the Committee of Eight had failed to provide a rationale for its choices or to delineate its criteria for selection of courses, topics and materials. The Committee, he wrote, offered "no fundamental discussion of the basis of selection and of the placement of materials" (H. O. Rugg, 1921a, p. 186; 1921b). In Rugg's view, the committee proce-dure for creating new curriculum proposals had "failed to bring about sci-entific … reconstruction" of the curriculum. Perhaps its most egregious deficiency was that it had, "failed to acquaint children with the develop-ment of current institutions and problems" (H. O. 1921a, p. 185).

Rugg proposed that future committees "sweep the board clean" and start anew, developing "carefully thought-out hypotheses of selection …

based upon the principle of social worth." He went on to suggest specific guidelines for selection of topics and materials:

> My own procedure would be to ignore the fact that we have today a curriculum in history, geography and civics; and start afresh and define clearly the scope, functions and objectives of the course by this criterion of "social worth." This criterion necessitates that to be included in the course the material must contribute: to a grasp of the great economic, social and political relationships or "laws"; to an understanding of established modes of living; (and) to an interest in and appreciation of the outstanding "problems" and "issues" of contemporary civilization. (H. O. Rugg, 1921a, p. 189)

Later, in the same article, Rugg critiqued the "encyclopedic presentation of facts, with little or no emphasis upon application of these facts to the understanding of great fundamental relationships." He proposed that, "to develop a real power of thought" we should give students "constant practice in generalization" with the aim of helping students understand great movements and causal connections, acquiring information by "gradual accretion" and through "the making of many interconnections— not mere drill upon isolated topics, events, conditions, personages, etc." (H. O. Rugg, 1921a, p. 189). These were pointed criticisms of the common curricular and classroom practice of the day that went right to the heart of its deficiency.

In his next publication, which appeared in the *Historical Outlook* for October, 1921, Rugg presented a more fully developed and cogent statement of his emerging theories on social studies, which he set forth in seven "hypotheses" that his newly formed research team was setting out to either confirm or refute:

> I. All units of work shall be presented definitely in problem-solving form (as contrasted with the narrative, factual, compartment method, with questions at end of chapter which courses now employ). Factual settings are grouped around problems stated so as to force an attitude of further inquiry. One of the most important implications of this principle is that all economic, industrial, social and political material shall be woven together in one course, as contrasted with three or more in current practice.

> II. It is one of our central theses that there should be one continuous social studies course from the first grade to the twelfth.

> III. Problems shall be based (not solely on the spontaneous interests of particular pupils) but on: 1. Common experiences of children of that metal and social age; 2. Personal appeals where possible, e. g. "What would you do if— etc.?"; 3. Alternative proposals where possible, to force comparison and systematizing of facts; 4. Intellectual opposition to obtain interest; 5. Much concrete human detail to obtain interest.

IV. Constant practice shall be given in analyzing, generalizing and organizing, as material that pertains to the "problems" is collected and studied....
The important generalizations in each field must be discovered (excursions,
collecting facts, making maps, making notes of observations, writing
reports, etc.).

V. Problem-situations shall be presented first through current affairs. Only
those historical backgrounds shall be developed which specialists ... decide
are crucial for clear thinking about contemporary matters. Thus, history is
not regarded as a "content subject";--only geography, government, economics, industry, anthropology, sociology, (and) psychology are that.

VI. Historical backgrounds, involving a grasp of "time sequence," "continuity," or "development" of contemporary institutions and activities, are presented through "sharp contrasts."

VII. Problems, or the examples of generalizations and organization which
contribute to them, should recur in many grades, organized on an increasingly mature level (through) ... some form of "layer" scheme. (H. O. Rugg,
1921c, p. 252)

So, by October, 1921, Rugg had developed the core ideas which were at
the heart of his vision for social studies. It was, in essence, a progressive,
issues-centered vision, and an innovative form of curriculum integration.
It focused on issues and "problem-situations," appeal to the interests of
the child balanced with social need, and a curriculum which was to be
designed in advance of instruction. It also contained a theory on the use
of historical material as background to contemporary understanding
rather than as content per se. These were innovative ideas which provided
a foundation for the further development of Rugg's vision and offered a
potent challenge to traditional practice.

Throughout the articles, Rugg made frequent reference to his use of
"scientific procedure" as contrasted with the Committee's "armchair opinion." Critics and opponents responded, resulting in a lively discourse in
Historical Outlook. Of course, Rugg's approach wasn't really "scientific"
either, but borrowed heavily from common procedures in activity analysis
used by leaders in the curriculum field. Rugg transposed activity analysis
into a process for divining the key issues as defined by leading "frontier
thinkers" of the day. All of this was clothed in the much-hyped language
of scientific inquiry in education. In responses to Rugg's "open letter,"
defenders of the committee procedure and the AHA Committee of Eight
strongly challenged Rugg's claim of "scientific" objectivity (Schafer, 1921).
Their central criticism was that although Rugg claimed scientific objectivity, in reality his procedure was no less biased than the work of previous
committees, despite his claims to the contrary.

Rugg's response to the criticism was to argue that the two main points in the scientific method required the scientist to exercise "creative imagination" in the construction of hypotheses, followed by the "collecting and sifting of evidence" (H. O. Rugg, 1921c, p. 249). In this case, the sifting of evidence relevant to selection of the relatively permanent problems and issues on which he proposed to base his curriculum involved examining the work of specialists and canvassing their best thinking regarding the problems of contemporary society.

Rugg's notion of a composite or "unified" course in social studies was not an entirely original idea, though it was a relatively new development and undoubtedly received its greatest boost from his work. In Rugg's case, it was an idea for the transformation of the social studies curriculum instigated by his old friend, John Coss, with whom he served on the Army's Committee on Classification of Personnel. Coss planned to develop a unified course in Contemporary Civilizations at Columbia upon his return to his teaching post after the war, and had discussed this intention with Rugg. It seems that Rugg and Coss were walking one day in Rock Creek Park, in Washington, DC, the day after the Armistice in November, 1918, and discussing their personal post-war plans. Coss was apparently a man on a mission. When Rugg asked, "What are you going to do?" Coss replied, "Well, I'll tell you. I am going to put through just one job—if it's the last one I do. I am going to help make a big orientation course for the undergraduate students in Columbia College" (H. O. Rugg, 1941, p. 170).

Rugg was quite impressed. "Here was a new idea," he wrote, "to bring the social sciences into one overview 'introduction to contemporary civilization' course required of all freshmen." He viewed the central idea, which called for "integration of the college curriculum," as a concept of "enormous importance" (H. O. Rugg, 1941, p. 170). Rugg attributed many of the core ideas which led to his unified social science course to Coss with Rugg adapting them to the secondary level (Coss, 1923). Moreover, the idea for a unified curriculum had some currency in progressive circles and had been tried in a number of schools. Judd and some of his colleagues at the University of Chicago were working on developing such a course during the war, and Daniel Knowlton, then a teacher at the Lincoln School, was also building a similar course (Judd, 1923). A good deal of additional momentum for creation of unified courses came from the American "Herbartians," especially Charles DeGarmo and the McMurry brothers who had created correlated courses with similar subject matter.

Rugg would later argue that the entire social studies curriculum should be organized around problems of contemporary life. Though not the only experiments in unification in social studies at the time, these ideas were clearly ahead of their time, and were later to become central guiding principles for reflective and issues-centered social studies. Philosophically, the vision of social studies as an integrated, issues-centered field was directly linked to the progressive movement in education. Proponents of this definition for social studies envisioned a unitary field of study, fusing or integrating materials from the disciplines and organizing study around societal issues or problems. Historically, this vision embodied the highest hopes of progressive reformers and represented the flowering of the meliorist impulse for societal reform in the curriculum. The most influential progressive, John Dewey, viewed the school as a focal point in preparation for citizenship with the aim of guaranteeing a society "which is worthy, lovely, and harmonious." This cast the school as a lever for social change, for as soon as the goal of a "worthy, lovely, and harmonious" society is defined, educational theory becomes social theory, and the educator becomes an agent for social change, a social reconstructionist (Evans, 2004).

At its root, the reform impulse which led an educator like Rugg to propose a "unified" social studies program, and to advocate a problem-centered approach to courses, was rooted in the small town pietist values held by members of the progressive educational trust. Many of the leaders of the "educational trust" were sons of Protestant clergy. Others testified to the importance of their early evangelical training in their later careers. Their religious upbringing left them with the conventional stress on hard work, thrift in time and money, and a pietist imperative to set the world straight. Reformers made a partial transfer of redemptive power from religious to secular institutions, developing a view of social evolution which held that people could control and improve their world by conscious means. Thus, the reform vision underlying creation of the Rugg social studies program, and the meliorist camp, partly owed its being to the social gospel of Protestant religion which inspired faith in the crusade to redeem society through rational planning and piecemeal reform (Tyack & Hansot, pp. 114-17). In the case of Harold Rugg, his origins in conservative, pietist, small town New England gave him a similar outlook.

Several additional strands of explanation may help us understand the content and direction of the Rugg social studies program. The intellectual roots of Rugg and many other key progressives may be traced to statements contained in *Cardinal Principles,* the seminal National Education Association (NEA) report, which were drawn from Herbert Spencer (NEA, 1918). The reform Darwinism of Rugg's work was influenced by the work of early sociologists such as Lester Ward and Albion Small, Franklin Giddings, and George Vincent, and through the competing though related educational visions of John Dewey and David Snedden. Its disciplinary forbears included advocates of the "New History" such as James Harvey Robinson, Carl Becker, Charles Beard, and other progressive historians. In the truest sense, Rugg's vision for social studies was progressivism writ small, an application of progressive ideas within the context of early twentieth century schooling (Cremin, 1961).

THE PROBLEM WITH THE OLD ORDER

At the time of Rugg's arrival at Teachers College, much of the design work in curriculum building and experimentation was being conducted by members of the National Society for the Study of Education (NSSE). The yearbook of the organization achieved a fairly wide readership and gave contributors the opportunity to reach an audience composed of some of the most influential scholars in education. The general editor for the yearbook at the time was Guy Montrose Whipple, a professor at the University of Illinois during Rugg's latter days in graduate school. Several leaders in NSSE were personal friends of Rugg's. Because of his reputation from his earlier textbook, *Statistical Method Applied to Education* (1917), Rugg was asked to contribute a chapter on statistics in education to the Twenty-First Yearbook of the NSSE (1921). With his newly developed interest in social studies, he was then asked to direct the development of the Twenty-Second Yearbook, which was devoted entirely to the social studies field. Editorship of the Yearbook provided Rugg with a prime opportunity, and gave him a prestigious national platform from which to expound his vision of social studies.

The yearbook, titled, *The Social Studies in the Elementary and Secondary School*, was divided into four sections. The first described the current situation, offering a critique of current curricular practice. The second, third and fourth sections described several "new" reorganized courses, discussed how the new curricular materials were being constructed, and offered an overall appraisal of proposed reorganization schemes. Aside from serving as editor of the volume, Rugg contributed three chapters which provide a more detailed and significantly enhanced glimpse of his emerging vision for social studies.

In the first chapter of the yearbook, Rugg asked, in his title: "Do the Social Studies Prepare Pupils Adequately for Life Activities?" He answered that "they do not," and then set out to describe, and critique, the present curriculum in some detail. First, Rugg argued that the vast majority of our people rarely deliberate thoughtfully on political and social matters. He hypothesized that "critical judgement, instead of impulse, must be the basis upon which our social and political decisions are made," and that it was the primary responsibility of the social studies curriculum to provide students with "knowledge about the issues of contemporary life and how they came to be what they are ... translated into tendencies to act intelligently upon them" (H. O. Rugg, 1923a, pp. 1-2).

"History instruction," Rugg wrote, spans "six or seven school years" from fourth through twelfth grade. He summarized the present focus of historical study as "international, legalistic, and militaristic" with students expected to learn a great deal of "minutiae" of the past. The history deals, he wrote, "with the growth of our nation as a legal and political organization" but largely ignores the "social, industrial, and intellectual aspects" (p. 5). Geography from the fifth grade on exhibits a focus on "countless facts ... learned by rote" from textbooks which are "veritable encyclopedias" organized by continent and country, containing "a multiplicity of detail" and trying to "cover too much territory" (pp. 5-6).

While acknowledging improvements and innovations contained in the new and rapidly growing course in "Community Civics," including a focus on community welfare and conditions in cities, Rugg lamented the fact that "few such innovations" had reached the elementary or junior high school. In those years, and in most government courses at higher levels, the schools continued to "drill students" on the Constitution, and the branches and powers of the federal government (pp. 6-7).

Rugg followed this introductory critique by discussing six important questions and raising several additional criticisms:

1. Does the present curriculum treat adequately the pressing industrial, social, and political problems of the day? It does not (pp. 10-13).

2. Are problems of government adequately treated by the histories and civics books? (No.) ... pupils cannot obtain a grasp of the critical problems of contemporary life from current school histories (pp. 13-14).

3. Do the new school histories pay more attention to industrial and social matters than the older ones did? They do ... (they) deal more definitely with industrial and social matters ... attention to "economic and social aspects of history" has increased to more than one-third of content. Still, 60 percent of the content of high school books is political.... I would say that not more than 30 percent of the total school time devoted to social studies should be given to political and military matters (pp. 14-15).

4. Do social science textbooks furnish backgrounds rich enough for constructive interpretation? *The textbooks do not furnish enough detail* to give students a real depth of feeling and comprehension for the matters under consideration. Social science textbooks are veritable encyclopedias. They are reference books. They devote a half page to this and ten lines to that.... What is needed in place of the brief and isolated paragraphs we now give children to read? *A wealth of*

anecdote, narration, and description about a few worth-while matters ... (including) *rich human episodes....* Instead of being books of texts they must become reading books (containing) *rich reading material.* (Texts should also make full use of) graphs and statistical tables. *Furthermore, maps should be used in reading books,* and closely connected to the discussion of the point under consideration. (Texts need to use) the episode, the long story, and more graphic, statistical, and pictorial matter in social science materials (pp. 15-19).

5. Are social science materials so organized as to give thorough practice in deliberation? They are not. Furthermore, it is difficult to believe that they even promote practice in deliberation.... Much of the organization of current geography texts ... would inhibit thinking rather than encourage it.... Not the learning of texts, but the solving of problems is what we need. Our materials must be organized around issues, problems—unanswered questions which the pupil recognizes as important and which he really strives to unravel ... he must be mentally blocked ... until he is obsessed with a desire to clear up the matter ... he must have at hand the data, facts on all sides of the issue ... he must be practiced in deliberation (pp. 19-20).

6. Does the present division of social science materials into the separate subjects of history, geography, civics, and economics, aid or hamper the teacher and the pupil? Personally, I am confident that the present organization ... hampers the teacher.... The curriculum maker ... should assemble around definite problems and issues those illustrative materials that the mind imperatively needs to deal with the matter in hand ... (gathered) from whatever school "subject" tradition may have housed them (pp. 21-22).

7. What dominates our social science instruction: reading about life or participation in life activities? The social science curriculum is primarily a reading curriculum. Reading and answering teachers' questions about the reading engages nearly all the time of our elementary and high school students ... our social sciences are dominated by reading courses which stress the acquisition of information *about* life. The schools are following the easiest way, the path of least resistance.... What theories is this practice based upon? No theories at all, I fear. The present practice wasn't born— it just grew. The practice implicitly assumes, however, that clear thinking and right conduct will issue from the mere acquiring of information (pp. 22-24).

Rugg also addressed, in his concluding paragraphs, three additional issues and critiques of current practice regarding the use of chronology in the teaching of history. The first contrasted the standard, chronologically segmented curriculum, "broken up transversely," in which all the various threads of development in one time period are discussed before moving on to the next period, and contrasted it with a "longitudinal" organization (a strand approach) via which the entire development of a particular problem, institution, or activity is discussed without interruption, from the earliest times to its present manifestation. In the traditional scheme, the story tends to move very slowly, with too much detail, and never reaches the present, closely tying earlier times with present day matters.

The second concerned the question, "How much of the history shall be taught at any one time?" Rugg framed this question somewhat differently than the first, asking, "Shall history be taught by a continuous account which fills in practically all of the detail, or would it be better to use a scheme of sharp contrasts which bring out a particular epoch sharply against another one, say the present period?" Rugg argued that experimentation with the scheme of sharp contrasts showed promise, made the history move rapidly, and made the "unfamiliar and remote situation stand out sharply against a more familiar and more recent one" (pp. 25-25).

This did not imply neglect of chronology, Rugg was careful to point out. When historical understanding required sequence, continuity, and historical development to be learned, "pupils must study them in chronological order." The underlying issue, he postulated, was "the question of how much of the detail of history is going to be told at any one time." Rugg believed that students too often lost sight of the important issues and became mired in voluminous detail in the traditional scheme.

A third and final issue related to the "present means of organizing history and geography" which lead to "a very *diffuse* (scattered) type of material" in which "matters to be comprehended as a whole are not tied up together in naturally related units." To remedy this, he reiterated his proposal for a "problem" organization (p. 26).

Remarkably, Rugg's description of the standard practices in social studies of the 1920s bear an eerie resemblance to the modal practice today. Moreover, his criticisms and remedies continue to resonate, and may serve as a potential source for reflection and new directions. "The charges against the present order" now fully explicated, the Yearbook turned to illustrations of reform alternatives from a variety of like-minded educators. These illustrations included chapters by Judd, Leon C. Marshall, Earle Rugg, Carleton Washburne, John Coss, and others. Rugg's additional contributions included an overview of the Rugg social studies program for the junior high school, which he and his collaborators were in the early stages of constructing; and, a description and rationale for making problems of contemporary life the basis for the social studies curriculum.

KEY PRINCIPLES OF RUGG SOCIAL STUDIES

Rugg's proposed course in the social sciences for the junior high school as described in the NSSE Yearbook for 1923 was built upon eight "hypotheses." These hypotheses elaborated upon and refined his statement of principles which had appeared in the *Historical Outlook* in October of 1921. An overview of Rugg's "hyotheses" illustrates both the continuity and refinement in Rugg's thinking. Moreover, it is important to remember that Rugg's vision and rationale were receiving the benefit of simultaneous and in-depth practical application through development and field trials of the social science pamphlets and a supporting program of research. An overview of Rugg's "hypotheses":

> *First: Current modes of living, contemporary problems and their historical backgrounds can be learned more effectively through one unified social science curriculum than through the separate school subjects.... It is not an attempt to merge the established subjects....* It completely disregards current courses.
>
> *Second: Each major topic of the course must be of established social value to the rank and file of our people.* Unless a topic can be proved to contribute definitely to an understanding of current modes of living and problems and issues of contemporary life, it can find no place in such a course. Hence, much of the content of present school courses is not found in this proposed curriculum ... a wealth of new material is included.
>
> *Third: An objective analysis of social needs facilitates the assignment to each of the major phases of life, its proper amount of attention in the curriculum....* The permanent problems and issues of our generation are being determined by analytical methods.
>
> *Fourth: Each topic and sub-topic of the course shall be illustrated by detailed episodes and by a wealth of maps, graphs, and pictorial material far in excess of the present use of them....* The *episode*, that is, the anecdote, the story of some actual human happening, is employed to illustrate a particular matter.
>
> Fifth: The reading materials and the exercises should be set so as to stimulate analysis and reasoning.
>
> *Sixth: Only that historical background of a particular problem, institution or activity shall be taught which is necessary to an adequate understanding of the problem; probably the most effective way to teach is by a series of sharp contrasts.* History is to "move rapidly" in these grades. Only a part of the story is to be told the first time over, more being added in successive years.... One era, one condition, one stage of a movement is to be sharply contrasted with another and especially with the current order of things.

> *Seventh: Historical backgrounds will be clearer if the history of only one set of related topics is traced at one time....* In the junior high school we should teach history longitudinally instead of by periods, or transversely.... We should trace directly to the present day, the development of a particular activity or group of activities.

Regarding this seventh point, Rugg acknowledged the criticism "that this leads to learning historical movements in isolation—that it is 'compartment learning' and that children will not get a feel for the total life of our people at any one time." In response, he stated that he had met this objection by "weaving into any discussion the important facts and relationships ... which should be present in the pupil's mind."

> *Eighth: One problem or topic, or at most one restricted group of problems and topics, should be considered definitely and thoroughly at one time.* (Note: This was an admonition to go for depth, an early foreshadowing of more recent theory.) (Rugg, Rugg, & Schweppe, 1923, p.187-191)

While some of these principles were a restatement of earlier ideas, several demonstrated refinement, or an adjustment based on criticism or new thinking. They were clearly set forth in the NSSE Yearbook as an antidote for the problems of the typical social studies curriculum delineated in the opening chapter of that volume.

BEHIND RUGG'S THEORY: A RATIONALE

Rugg's final contribution to the Yearbook presented the rationale for an issues-centered curriculum and described the research and rationale building work which was taking place at Teachers College, largely performed by graduate students under his direction. Rugg began this chapter with a re-statement of his regular plug for an "objective" and "scientific" approach to curriculum building. "In order to determine the critical issues of the day" a multi-pronged analysis was conducted which went beyond the "activity-analysis" promoted by many curriculum theorists of the time (H. O. Rugg, 1923b, pp. 260-261). Rugg expressed an ambivalent view of activity analysis. He intimated that it could tell the curriculum maker "a part, but only a part" of what children needed to know. His central critique was that it would focus on "life as it is to-day," assuming a static society and ignoring the rapidity of change.

He argued that social studies should prepare students to participate in life activities (a socialization function) and "equip them to be constructively critical" of contemporary society (counter-socialization). To do this, he hypothesized, we need expert opinions on which "current modes of living should be changed;" definition of contemporary problems and issues; and, the most likely emerging problems and issues with which the growing generation "will have to grapple" (p. 261).

At the heart of his rationale Rugg posited that development of a curriculum for "a troubled society" required confronting young people with "the most critical problems of that society." Rugg viewed our society as "troubled" and "faced with big and insistent problems." He argued that society was also "dynamic" and that the curriculum must be dynamic as well. Hence, there were two fundamental mandates in creating a curriculum: first, selection of "insistent and permanent problems"; second, to continuously adapt the curriculum to "the problems which experts predict will continue to be insistent in the adult life of the growing generation." Finally, Rugg held, even at this early date, that the school is "our most important agency for the improvement of society" (pp. 261-262).

Rugg and his colleagues at Teachers College were engaged in developing a curriculum and materials for students and teachers, which would not only address persistent issues, but "anticipate" changes and "use the curriculum to prepare children to meet them." In essence, the "problems and issues of contemporary life" would control the curriculum. In the twelfth grade, students would "study and discuss ... the problems and issues of industry, politics, and social affairs." Direct study of problems and issues was the central focus for twelfth grade because "the students are as old mentally and socially" as they would become during their time in public school. Nonetheless, students at earlier grades should "experiment" and become familiar with "problems and issues" so that they would be fully prepared for a focused study in eleventh or twelfth grade. Students in earlier grades "shall have read episodes, historical narratives, studied and made maps, dealt with graphic and pictorial matter, solved problems, and debated questions" appropriate for their developmental level, so that they would be well prepared for the "problem" study in the later grades. Thus, the curriculum he envisioned was geared to the developing maturity of the student.

Rugg also emphasized the fact that he did not expect students to "solve" the problems and issues, after all, adult society had not solved them. Instead, what he expected was that students would review "the evidence which is necessary for the consideration of all aspects of a given problem." This would entail "an unpartisan, open-minded review of the evidence on both sides" of the question (p. 267).

Rugg summarized the procedure:

First, find the problems and issues of modern social life; second, find the particular questions which have to be answered in order to consider all angles of the various problems; third, select typical "episodes" which illustrate the more important points to be made, collect the facts, in narrative, descriptive, graphic, pictorial or statistical form, that are needed to discuss the questions and problems; fourth, to clarify and fix the essential matters, discover the basic generalizations that guide our thinking about society. (p. 266)

To determine the "insistent problems" Rugg argued that no one was better equipped than the group of writers he labeled, "frontier thinkers." These frontier thinkers included scholars in a variety of fields "out on the firing line of social analysis." Rugg and his research assistants drew on the "matured statements" contained in more than 150 books of several score of these frontier thinkers. The books were selected using a four-part procedure. First, drawing from *Book Review Digest*, they selected only those works referred to as "books of distinct merit, irrespective of economic or political faith"; second, they chose books characterized as "important" in book reviews of six weekly and several monthly journals; third, the list was supplemented by "a canvass" of several thousand books held at Columbia University Library; and, fourth, eighty specialists were queried for "a list of ten books in his own field ... which he would use to obtain statements of problems in his field," reflecting "deep insight and balanced vision" and chosen "irrespective of economic or political faith" (p. 267).

Thus, for the first time in a published work, Rugg stated his plan for divining the "insistent and permanent" problems of the day. Each book was to be critically analyzed "by tabulating the space (in quarter pages)" devoted to each problem the author discussed (p. 268). The results of these ongoing investigations, conducted by graduate students under Rugg's supervision, were to be reported in monographs at a later date.

Rugg's vision for social studies also contained both social theory and psychological theory, though the social theory was dominant, even early on. The social theory held that social studies subjects in schools existed in the context of a troubled society and that by becoming aware of issues and problems students would develop a commitment to active citizenship aimed at social improvement. Social value would be the litmus test for selection and inclusion of topics in the curriculum, and social improvement was to be the teleological goal.

The psychological theory held that students were interested in present life conditions and its related issues and problems; that persistent and relatively permanent issues and problems should be at the heart of the curriculum; and, that history and much of the other social science content should be taught in such a way that these traditional sources of knowledge helped to interest and illuminate students lives in the present. Most importantly, Rugg theorized, a focus on issues and problems would prepare students for lives as active and concerned citizens who would help to improve conditions in a "troubled society." Thus, while the interests of the child were an important part of Rugg's theory, he clearly subordinated student interest to social need and the larger goal of social improvement.

Rugg's thinking, as expressed in the teacher guides he developed in the late 1920s to accompany his textbooks, also emphasized the importance of active learning and student participation that would go far beyond a passive "reading" curriculum. The "active" school would replace the traditional "listening" school, though this was stated more forcefully in some later publications (H. O. Rugg, 1929). Learning through active participation meant that the course would involve a stream of activities rather than students simply reading a textbook, answering questions at the back of the chapter, and listening to the teacher talk. Participation would involve a wide range of activities and formats including student research in books, magazines, and newspapers; discussion through open forums and debate; preparation of outlines, briefs, and critiques as needed; and, use of new tools of graphic and pictorial display. As Rugg put it, the materials had to be arranged in "thought provoking form." The student must not only gather and "absorb facts" but must be given constant practice in "making decisions with facts" (H. O. Rugg, 1929, p. 5).

Active learning was, in Rugg's mind, to be predicated on interest and generated by a course that was "real and dramatic." This meant, in part, first hand experience whenever possible: observation, field excursions, and a range of experiences outside the school. Also, dramatic and vivid portrayals of social issues and problems or antecedent historical episodes would make reading as interesting as possible. In either case the teacher and textual materials were to play a lead role in developing student interest.

Rugg viewed learning as a cumulative process in which student knowledge and understanding grew incrementally. The new course in social studies would therefore be based on sequential experiences which would take account of the knowledge and understanding of students, moving from the simple to the more abstract and complex. Rugg believed that schools should provide students with a "wealth" of materials, so that students could learn from as many sources as possible, and through multiple senses: travel, film, pictures, graphs and statistics.

The Rugg course also made provision for the use of drill and repetition to assist students in learning factual data. Geographic locations, reading and writing skills, map work, and knowledge of chronological sequence were all considered important, and the course provided systematic training in each of these areas.

In order to make learning most meaningful, Rugg emphasized selection of a relatively small number of problems, studied in depth, rather than the superficial treatment of many topics. Accordingly, Rugg emphasized the concentration of student attention on one topic at a time and one particular task (Rugg, 1929).

That Rugg's theory would have a psychological side was not surprising, after all he had been hired at Teachers College to be Director of Psychology for the Lincoln School and to serve in a department headed by Edward L. Thorndike. During his first four years as a professor he worked primarily in this area. Also, he had gained experience and expertise in psychology during his graduate school days at the University of Illinois, and with the army's Committee on Classification of Personnel.

Moreover, Rugg's balance between student interest and social need closely fit his support for a curriculum largely designed in advance of instruction, rather than the more spontaneous approach supported by Kilpatrick and many other "child centered" progressives. As Rugg so aptly stated in a monograph published with one of his graduate assistants, "centering attention upon the interests and activities of children has always been important, nevertheless it has grave limitations.... If growth is to be properly directed, the curriculum-maker must be oriented so as to have his eyes constantly on the society in which the child is growing" (Rugg & Hockett, 1925, pp. 19-20).

Though Rugg may have been the leading progressive thinker in social studies, his ideas regarding subject matter and curriculum planning, while innovative, were, if anything, more conservative than many others in the progressive camp. His pamphlet and textbook series, with subject matter organized around contemporary problems and their historical antecedents, represented thoughtful planning in advance of instruction, a relatively conservative approach to pedagogy, more in line with Dewey than with Kilpatrick or others who tended to discount its importance.

LATER DEVELOPMENTS

By 1923 Rugg's theory for the social studies curriculum was largely fleshed out in the form it would take and hold, with a good deal of constancy, for the remainder of his career, though his thinking, the manner in which he framed his proposal, and the rationale underling his vision would continue to deepen and evolve. In part, his evolution and growth were a result of reading and writing and his interaction with colleagues and associates at Teachers College. But, his continuing evolution was also a reflection of the rich cultural context in which he lived. Residing in New York City during the early 1920s was an exciting experience for Rugg, and he was exposed to new ideas and many creative individuals from outside the ranks of professional educators that were to have a profound impact on the direction of his interests and intellectual growth. Given this stimulating environment, Rugg's place on the cutting edge of a new era continued.

In 1924 he spent a portion of the summer at Fred Howe's School of Opinion on Nantucket Island. He shared long walks and conversations with Waldo Frank discussing *Our America* as well as the ideas of Brooks and Bourne. He spent days with musicologist Max Merz and Gertrude Drueck, watching Isadora Duncan's dancers at work and discussing their principles, and listening to Merz's talks on Spengler's *Decline of the West.* He listened to the latest work of the "new" scientists, Conklin, a Princeton biologist, and Shapley, a Harvard astronomer. He met psychologist Everett Dean Martin, who opened new vistas in social psychology, and Horace Kallen, who lectured on individualism. He had long talks with Andre Sigfried, the French publicist.

During the ensuing years Rugg met and was deeply influenced by many new personalities and ideas in New York. He was especially influenced by the avant-garde of the Greenwich Village area. He discovered Alfred Stieglitz' group, studied his photographs, and listened to him discuss his work. He met and talked with Stieglitz's "painter wife" Georgia O'Keeffe.

As Rugg later recalled:

> The library and all the frontiers expanded enormously as I was pushed out across the boundary of the social, economic, political regions into the exciting fields of social criticism and the arts—painting, poetry, architecture, the theater and the dance. It was a tremendous new orientation, this discovery of a whole new world of exciting personalities and new ideas. (H. O. Rugg, 1941, p. 321)

There were, undoubtedly, many important influences on Rugg's social thought and curricular ideas. The dedication page of *Culture and Education in America* (1931) lists several of the main influences. He dedicated the book "to a company of creative students of American culture" including:

> John Dewey, for phrasing clearly the experimental method of knowing; Charles Beard, for his documentation of the interrelationships of economic, political, and social life; Louis Sullivan, integrator of American culture; Alfred Stieglitz, the voice of the creative American, exemplified in "291," "303," and an American place; Randolph Bourne, Waldo Frank, and Van Wyck Brooks, for launching a creative analysis of American culture; Frederic Howe, for his school of opinion—a pioneer attempt to build a true cultural group. (Rugg, 1931, p. v)

These thinkers were to prepare the way for Rugg's development of a curriculum oriented not just toward educational reform, but aimed at the larger project of reconstructing the nation. Rugg's notion of a social studies course developed around great principles or generalizations in history, economics, industry, and the social sciences and aimed at the goal of social improvement was strongly influenced by, and consistent with, the avant-garde ideas he came in contact with in New York's stimulating intellectual environment during the 1920s.

Reconstructing the School Curriculum. By 1926 an article appeared in *Teachers College Record* in which Rugg, for the first time, used the word "reconstruction" in relation to the curriculum. Portions of the article were drawn from a draft manuscript on the school curriculum later published as *Culture and Education in America* (Rugg, 1931). The article was by far the most cogent, succinct and thoughtful presentation of Rugg's ideas to that time. In the article Rugg depicted the "critical need" of teaching youth to understand American life given the nation's "great experiment in democratic government under the most hampering conditions" (H. O. Rugg, 1926a, p. 603). He described numerous groups "ablaze" in conflict: proletarian worker and capitalist owner; Protestant and Catholic; producer and middleman; black and white; industrialist and farmer. As he saw it, a lack of understanding was at the root of each conflict. This was where the schools were to come in, with the goal of educating a generation who would be, "informed about and interested in the American drama, who tend to settle matters of controversy on the basis of reflection rather than prejudice" (p. 604).

In the article Rugg summarized his critique of the curriculum, arguing that "the method of the encyclopaedia" dominated, that its treatment of critical matters was "inadequate and brief," and that it tended to emphasize "form and structure" rather than "the driving forces of American life." He called for a "sweeping reconstruction of the organization" of the entire curriculum, arguing that American society cannot be understood through the piecemeal study of conventional "subjects" because the subjects are "narrow academic compartments of knowledge, representing bodies of technical facts and principals ... assembled for school use by specialists in subject matter ... by experts in research, documentation, authentication." He suggested that curriculum makers should ignore "the conventional barriers between the existing subjects" and that the "starting point" should be the "social institution, or the political and economic problem—not the subject" (p. 607). Later in the article he called for development of "dramatic, vivid, compelling" materials of instruction and argued for greater use of "the dramatic episode" (p. 610).

In what was perhaps his most well argued statement on classroom thoughtfulness, he cited "the power of critical questioning" as the best hope for producing tolerant, thoughtful and open-minded citizens. In order to stimulate thinking, the curriculum would need to confront students with issues that "block the smooth passage of thought." The student must be "mentally thwarted" until he or she is "obsessed with the desire to clear up the matter." Rugg contrasted a problem-posing, issues orientation with traditional textbook learning as the contrast between "the method of exposition" and "the method of alternatives." He called for the "intellectual work of the school" to be focused around "definite, clean-cut issues," with no solutions given by teacher or reading materials, and with group discussion organized by the "open forum." The teacher would repeatedly ask, "What do you think?" (pp. 612-613).

Despite the continuing refinement of his vision, Rugg was not without his critics. One early reviewer of Rugg's work complained that the material was too technical or difficult for the junior high school grades (Goodier, 1926). Another, Robert S. Lynd, a well known social scientist, suggested that Rugg focused on public issues at the expense of the skills needed in everyday social life, and argued for a broader unification across the social and natural sciences (Lynd, 1927). Moreover, some critics referred to most any scheme for curricular unification with the derogatory label, "social stew."

Foundations of the Curriculum. At about the same time, Rugg was involved in working on the 1926 Yearbook of the NSSE, and was again appointed to edit the volume, but this time with a broader focus on the general curriculum. As chair of the committee appointed to create the volume, Rugg was given free reign to select committee members. He selected leading advocates of both the child-centered curriculum, and representatives of a society centered approach to curriculum building. The roster of committee members included child-centered luminaries such as William H. Kilpatrick and Frederick Bonser; relative conservatives William C. Bagley and Charles H. Judd; advocates of education for social effiency such as Franklin Bobbitt and W. W. Charters; and society-centered reformers such as George S. Counts and Rugg himself. Rugg was unquestionably the dominant voice in committee meetings (Mendenhall, cited in Winters, 1968).

The work of the committee offered an opportunity for dialogue on the popular choices for curriculum development among multiple alternatives. The traditional, subject centered curriculum, in the grip of "mental disciplinarians" was well established in the majority of schools at the time. Child-centered advocates had gained some notoriety as reformers, but offered a rather extreme choice. Society-centered theorists offered another emerging possibility. What was needed was a new synthesis of these frequently opposing views. As it turned out, the new synthesis developed by the committee bore the unmistakable stamp of its chairman, Harold Rugg.

The statement of the committee, published under the title, *Foundations of Curriculum Making*, was reached through a series of meetings for which each of the participants prepared a written statement in advance. Individual statements were then discussed in round table meetings. After some rather acrimonious discussion, tentative agreement was reached on major problems and issues, and from this, a general, though extremely vague statement evolved on the view of the entire committee. The committee dealt with several key issues. First, on the question of whether the curriculum should be centered on child life or preparation for adulthood, the committee's synthesis suggested that the school curriculum should prepare the child for "effective participation in social life" via "present life experiences" that would gradually move the child more and more in contact with "social life as a whole." So, the interests of the child were combined with preparation for adulthood. On the need for scientific curriculum making, the committee statement reflected Rugg's position that a scientific analysis of the problems of society should lead to development of a reconstructed curriculum, in which the "school was a conscious agent of social improvement." In a compromise statement, reflecting the competing viewpoints of its members, the committee supported selection of subject matter determined by the scientific study of the needs of society, with consideration given to the needs of the child. It also supported Rugg's position that the curriculum should be organized along more general lines, going beyond the mere fusion of courses. In addition, the committee implied that materials should be constructed without regard for traditional subject matter boundaries, and offered strong praise for general or fused courses in science, math and social studies (H. O. Rugg, 1926b). Despite this attempt at developing consensus, spearheaded by Rugg, the work of the committee was remembered comically, and somewhat caustically, as an ill-fated effort by "the most incongruous committee you ever saw" (Kilpatrick, 1951; Kliebard, 1986)

During the following year, 1927, Rugg gave a speech at the annual meeting of the NEA Department of Superintendence in Seattle, Washington, in early July. The speech explicitly illustrated the influence of the arts on Rugg's thinking, and demonstrated his considerable, and growing, skills as an orator. Moreover, the speech offered insights into Rugg's developing critique of American society. Rugg argued that in a society in which the "economic, exploitative, mercenary" tend to dominate, in which "*things* are in the saddle and ride mankind," schools have produced a kind of education that inhibits thinking and creativity. He suggested that schools were contributing to "standardization of the processes of imagination and of thinking," in a culture in which "independent thinking has been stamped upon" and "understanding of the fine and beautiful has been crushed." He called for a reconstruction of the curriculum focused on developing "critical judgment" and creativity. He argued that the creative artist is the best example of a "disciplined man" because he "recognizes his problem in a great sweep of vision" then proceeds to develop "technic" (H. O. Rugg, 1927, p. 776). He called for the high school to launch into "the effort of reason and the adventure of beauty," and to "reconstruct our materials ... to train children in independent thinking." Finally, in a compelling conclusion to his talk, he asked:

> Can the school produce understanding? I don't know. Can the school produce happiness? Not with the regimented curriculum. It can't produce tolerance unless it sets up its material in such a fashion as to give the children constant practice from the first grade to the twelfth in the confrontation of problems.... And it cannot produce happiness unless its sets up an environment in which each child in America, of the 23,000,000, will be permitted to say what is on its mind; to create with its hands in metals, wood, on canvas, to paint, with the body in rhythmic dance, with music, with words oral and written. Every child in America, I.Q. what it may be, can produce something, and your job and mine is to find the way to let him do it. (p. 776)

The Child Centered School. During the mid-1920s Rugg was devoting much of his time and energy to production of his pamphlet series for school social studies, but still found time to write on the curriculum. *The Child Centered School*, coauthored with Anne Shumaker, which appeared in 1928, proved to be one of Rugg's most widely read and noteworthy volumes. By the phrase "child centered school" Rugg and Shumaker were referring broadly to the progressive schools of the 1920s. Having spent more than a decade in education, and having been closely involved in the Lincoln School for a number of years, Rugg was well positioned to co-author the book. The major purpose of the volume was to bring together, describe, and critically examine the many separate experiments in child-centered progressive education. The authors argued that the schools had historically lagged behind during development of the new industrial culture, and that something of a reorganization in thinking had occurred as a group of educators led by Francis Parker and John Dewey introduced new educational ideas in the 1890s. The child centered schools emerged, placing new emphasis on psychology, practicality, and the fine arts. As compared to traditional schools, with their emphasis on conformity, the new schools focused on development of creativity and individuality, and emphasized "creative self-expression" (p. ix). The "articles of faith" which these schools shared included: freedom over control, child initiative over teacher initiative, the active school, child interest as the basis of the new educational program, creative self-expression, personality development and social adjustment.

In describing the programs of the new schools, Rugg and Shumaker drew heavily on the program at the Lincoln School, but included several other well-known progressive schools such as the Walden School, the City and Country School, the Francis W. Parker School, and the Ojai Valley School. Following this description, the authors offered several pointed and constructive criticisms of child centered schools. Among their criticisms: a lack of design in the program as a whole; failure to plan in advance; the need for greater intellectual rigor; the need for increased use of repetitive learning; and, the general failure to keep systematic records of procedures and outcomes of experimental activities (Rugg and Shumaker, 1928).

In their conclusion Rugg and Shumaker offered a sympathetic critique of the new school movement. Many of the schools, they wrote, lacked continuity in their programs; they failed to visualize the whole of the educational program and the need for design; they tended to emphasize a rather extreme individualism; they lacked self-criticism; and, they displayed "an absence of clear thinking about the psychology of the creative act." Moreover, in committing themselves so fully to the school as life, they ignored the preparatory function. Finally, Rugg and Shumaker lamented, they do not apply any of the child centered philosophy to the high school grades (pp. 314-318).

Despite these criticisms, the book provided an upbeat portrayal of the new schools through its tone of high praise and through its unifying themes. These were "pioneers on a new educational frontier" aiming at the "reconstruction" of the schools (Rugg & Shumaker, 1928, p. 314). The picture it painted depicted "a blazing educational revolution" whose defects were relatively insignificant (Phillips, 1961, p. 59).

For the most part, the theoretical and practical discussion in the book, including both praise and criticism, reflected Rugg's previously developed stance favoring design of instruction in advance, attention to child interest, and active learning over a reading curriculum. Moreover, the book clearly reflected his growing affinity for the arts. It also embodied Rugg's call for a reconstruction of schooling which would balance creative self-expression with education for the improvement of society. The book was, nonetheless, significant because it provided the new schools with "an ideological blanket," and a unifying "cosmic theory,'" which helped popularize the child-centered label (Phillips, 1961, p. 60).

CONCLUSION

Though Rugg's theories on social studies were largely fleshed out by this time and would take root in his social science pamphlets and textbook series, as we shall see in remaining chapters, changes in the context of American society would lead Rugg to a new and pointed emphasis on social studies for social reconstruction, but with little modification in his practical vision for the field.

As it turned out, Rugg's vision proved a viable and popular alternative for quite some time. First, his critique of the social studies practiced in schools was pointed and accurate. Students were asked to read encyclopedic textbooks written by subject matter specialists in which little attempt was made to connect the content with student interests or, in the case of history, with the modern world. For the majority of students this meant that school history and social science was horribly irrelevant and detached, a reading curriculum of little interest.

Second, a unified social studies curriculum, centered around topics selected on the basis of social value, had strong appeal during Rugg's time, and was an extension of mainstream progressive social studies thought. The criteria of "social worth" was a powerful notion that held promise of developing a viable and forward looking framework for social studies instruction, one that would continue to have considerable appeal for many years, and that could still see a revival.

Moreover, Rugg's focus on social issues and problems, his application of a thought provoking, problem-centered method of teaching and learning, his innovative support for a range of discussion and research based activity on the part of students, his call for interestingly written materials employing vivid anecdotes and dramatic episodes, and his appeal for depth of study all combined to offer a vision for social studies teaching and learning that was pedagogically innovative, far ahead of its time. Rugg's vision for a revised social studies program was a reflection of many influences, but clearly owed much to Dewey, Beard, and other frontier thinkers of the modern era. It was a new and avant-garde application of progressive ideas to social studies instruction in schools.

On the other hand, while pedagogically innovative and potentially generative of a strong and well-connected social studies program, his vision was also more than a little grandiose. Rather than modify existing materials and practices, he called for sweeping away and ignoring much of current practice. This rather apocalyptic stance, combined with his call for the longitudinal organization of history, using a topical rather than a chronological scheme, undoubtedly cost him potential support among historians and social scientists. Traditional history had staying power, its support built upon a conservative, patriotic and nation-building impulse, to be ignored only at great risk. Moreover, Rugg's rather stubborn insistence that his vision was "scientific" and "objective" probably cost him some support as well, at least among scholars.

Despite these flaws, Rugg's curricular vision, practical acumen, and his vivid writing style were so powerful that their appeal was instant and overwhelming. As we shall see, as Rugg translated these developing ideas into social science pamphlets, then a best selling textbook series, their influence would reach far and wide, well beyond the walls of Teachers College and the few experimental progressive schools.

REFERENCES

Beard, C. A. (1913). *An economic interpretation of the constitution.* New York: Macmillan.

Benne, K. (1967). Kenneth Benne to Elmer A. Winters, June 6, 1967. Cited in E. A. Winters. (1968). *Harold Rugg and education for social reconstructionism.* Unpublished doctoral dissertation, University of Wisconsin, Madison.

Commons, J. R. et al. (1918). *History of labour in the United States.* New York: Macmillan.

Cooley, C. H. (1902). *Human nature and the social order.* New York: Charles Scribner's Sons.

Coss, J. (1923). A collegiate survey course in the social sciences. In H. O. Rugg (Ed.), *The social studies in the elementary and secondary school.* National Society for the Study of Education. Twenty-Second Yearbook, Part II (pp. 208-215). Bloomington, IL: Public School.

Cremin, L. E. (1961). *The transformation of the school: Progressivism in American education, 1876-1957.* New York: Knopf.

Goodier, F. T. (1926). The Rugg plan of teaching history. *High School Conference, 1926,* 323-327.

Hobson, J. A. (1906). *The evolution of modern capitalism: A study of machine production.* London: W. Scott.

Judd, C. H. (1923). Introducing social studies into the school curriculum. In H. O. Rugg (Ed.), *The social studies in the elementary and secondary school.* National Society for the Study of Education. Twenty-Second Yearbook, Part II (pp. 28-35). Bloomington, IL: Public School.

Keynes, J. M. (1920). *The economic consequences of the peace.* New York: Harcourt, Brace, and Howe.

Kilpatrick, W. H. (1951). Speech on the occasion of Rugg's retirement from Teachers College, Rugg Retirement Banquet Tape. In the possession of the author.

Kliebard, H. M. (1986). *Struggle for the American curriculum, 1893-1958.* Boston: Routledge & Keegan Paul.

Lynd, R. S. (1927). What are "social studies." *School and Society, 25,* 216-219.

Marshall, L. C. (1918). *Readings in industrial society: A study in the structure and functioning of modern economic organization.* Chicago: University of Chicago Press.

Merriam, C. E. (1920). *American political ideas: Studies in the development of American political thought, 1865-1917.* New York: Macmillan.

National Education Association. (1918). *Cardinal principles of secondary education: A report of the Commission on the reorganization of secondary education.* Washington, DC: U.S. Government Printing Office.

Phillips, M. (1961). *The Seven Arts and Harold Rugg.* Unpublished masters thesis, Columbia University.

Robinson, J. H. (1912). *The new history: Essays illustrating the modern historical outlook*. New York: Macmillan.

Rugg, E. U. (1966). The Earle Rugg tape. Prepared by Earle U. Rugg in response to questions posed by George A. Kay and Elmer A. Winters, May 5, 1966. Tape and transcript in the possession of the author.

Rugg, H. O. (1917). *Statistical method applied to education*. New York: Houghton Mifflin.

Rugg, H. O. (1921a). How shall we reconstruct the social studies curriculum? An open letter to professor Henry Johnson commenting on committee procedure as illustrated by the report of the joint committee on history and education for citizenship. *Historical Outlook*, 7, 184-189.

Rugg, H. O. (1921b). Needed changes in the committee procedure of reconstructing the social studies. *Elementary School Journal*, 21, 688-702.

Rugg, H. O. (1921c). On reconstructing the social studies: Comments on Mr. Schafer's letter. *Historical Outlook*, 7, 249-252.

Rugg, H. O. (Ed.). (1923a). Do the social studies prepare pupils adequately for life activities? In *The social studies in the elementary and secondary school*. National Society for the Study of Education. Twenty-Second Yearbook, National Society for the Study of Education, Part II (pp. 1-27). Bloomington, IL: Public School.

Rugg, H. O. (Ed.). (1923b). Problems of contemporary life as the basis for curriculum-making in the social studies. In *The social studies in the elementary and secondary school*. National Society for the Study of Education. Twenty-Second Yearbook, National Society for the Study of Education, Part II (pp. 260-273). Bloomington, IL: Public School.

Rugg, H. O. (1926a, March). A preface to the reconstruction of the American school curriculum. *Teachers College Record*, 27 (7), 600-616.

Rugg, H. O. (Ed.). (1926b). *The foundations of curriculum-making*. Twenty-Sixth Yearbook, National Society for the Study of Education, Part II. Bloomington, IL: Public School.

Rugg, H. O. (1927). American culture and the reconstruction of the school curriculum. *Proceedings of the National Education Association* (Vol. 65, pp. 771-776). Washington, DC: The National Education Association.

Rugg, H. O. (1929). *Teachers guide to accompany A History of American Civilization*. Boston: Ginn.

Rugg, H. O. (1941). *That men may understand: An American in the long armistice*. New York: Doubleday, Doran.

Rugg, H. O., & Hockett, J. A. (1925). *Objective studies in map locations*. New York: Teachers College.

Rugg, H. O., Rugg, E. U., & Schweppe, E. (1923). A proposed social science course for the junior high school. In H. O. Rugg (Ed.), *The social studies in the elementary and secondary school*. National Society for the Study of Education. Twenty-Second Yearbook, Part II (pp. 185-207). Bloomington, IL: Public School.

Rugg, H. O., & Shumaker, A. (1928). *The child-centered school: An appraisal of the new education*. New York: World Book.

Schafer, J. (1921). The methods and aims of committee procedure: Open letters from Dr. Schafer and Mr. Rugg. *The Historical Outlook*, 7, 247-249.

Tawney, R. H. (1920). *The acquisitive society.* New York: Harcourt, Brace and Howe.

Turner, F. J. (1894). *Significance of the frontier in American history.* Annual Report of the American Historical Association for 1893 (pp. 197-227). Washington, DC: Government Printing Office.

Tyack, D., & Hansot, E. (1982). *Managers of virtue: Public school leadership in America, 1820-1980.* New York: Basic Books.

U.S. Bureau of Education. (1916). *The social studies in secondary education* (Bulletin No. 28). Washington, DC: Government Printing Office.

Winters, E. A. (1968). *Harold Rugg and education for social reconstructionism.* Unpublished doctoral dissertation, University of Wisconsin, Madison.

CHAPTER 3

THE PLAN

By the late spring of 1920, Rugg had decided to launch a program aimed at developing a unitary social studies program for the schools and to begin via experimentation with colleagues and students in the Lincoln School at Teachers College. He decided to begin the effort to put his ideas into effect by creating and piloting actual materials for use with school age children. After discussions with his brother Earle, he began planning the development of a course of study to be tried out in the Lincoln School and later expanded to the public schools.

The first step in the new venture was to find teachers at the Lincoln School who would be willing to work with him on the new and innovative project. One problem, which Rugg apparently did not anticipate, was finding kindred souls who supported the notion of a unified social studies curriculum. Most of the teachers he approached at the Lincoln School were willing to participate, but several were less than enthusiastic about a project that would cut across disciplinary boundaries.

During the spring of 1920 Rugg persuaded four teachers to join his experimental team, to begin work in the fall. This first team included the historian in the high school, Daniel Knowlton (who had been a member of the AHA Committee of Eight), a geography teacher, two teachers from the elementary school, a history teacher and a "room" teacher. One of the elementary teachers was Emma Schweppe. Though he had recruited a team of volunteers, it seems that Rugg's plan was rather nebulous and lacked specific detail. The original plan was to begin the experimental

This Happened in Ameica: Harold Rugg and the Censure of Social Studies
pp. 55–106
Copyright © 2007 by Information Age Publishing
All rights of reproduction in any form reserved.

course, teaching history and geography along with contemporary community life, in September 1920, in one long class period each day with the fifth and sixth grades. However, by the time the school year began, the project was little more than an idea. As later Rugg recalled:

> My plan wasn't too clear, even to me, and to the teachers it was utterly nebulous. We were certainly not equipped to do the difficult task of assembling new reading and study and work materials in a vast field where there was almost nothing. It meant mimeographing and graphing, making bibliographies, planning excursions for the children to various parts of the city, keying in the work of the "arts" teachers, the "science" and "industrial arts" teachers and others to see our new program, holding round-table discussions, providing for sufficient practice on the "skills," and what not. I had never taught in the elementary school—and yet had to teach, to illustrate to the other teachers what I was talking about, improvising a good deal of it as I went along. The elementary teachers had never worked at research problems; neither had they acquired a clear conception of the "new history" or of my theories of integration of "the social studies." And the high-school history man was downright opposed to the whole idea. He is to this day, I think (H. O. Rugg, 1941, p. 205).

Materials for the first year of the course were developed on an ad hoc, day-to-day and week-to-week basis. Rugg's only previous teaching experience had been at the college and graduate school levels, yet during that first year he frequently taught fifth and sixth graders to demonstrate what he wanted done. The year proved to be a continuous and at times contentious struggle among the "prima donnas" of the Rugg team, a year of crude trial and error (p. 206). At the end of that first year, in the spring of 1921, the team disbanded. Only one member stayed on for the following year, Emma Schweppe, who remained with Rugg for several years. Daniel Knowlton, the "history man" who was "altogether opposed to the idea" of the unified social studies course went on to become a professor of social studies education, but from a different perspective. Rugg himself described that first year as a failure, though it did provide the groundwork and experience for what was to follow, and gave Rugg new insights into the many difficulties that came with such a grand project (p. 206).

Though the first year of experimentation proved disappointing, it also provided for the further gestation of Rugg's notion for a unified social science course and an alternative to the frankly nationalistic view of history contained in most American history textbooks. Some of these ideas may have been fermenting in Rugg's mind since his graduate school days at the University of Illinois when Rugg and his mentor William Chandler Bagley surveyed 23 American history textbooks then in use in the junior high schools. As noted earlier, Bagley and Rugg found that the texts placed a heavy emphasis on political and military history and gave far too little attention to social and economic issues. The texts, they wrote, focused on "promotion of nationalism" by giving students a common grounding in national development and failing to include many other matters. "The important question," they wrote, centered on:

> the desirability or undesirability of making the development of nationalism the primary function of seventh and eighth grade history. This is an issue that is fraught with consequences. (Bagley & Rugg, 1916, pp. 58-59)

During the summer of 1921 Rugg assembled a new team with his younger brother Earle U. Rugg as a key member. Earle had come to Teachers College in the fall of 1920 at Harold's urging, to a position at the Horace Mann School of Teachers College. The position would allow him to pursue his own doctorate and to work with Harold in developing the new materials. With Earle's full presence on the Rugg "team," the plan was "recast." Harold, Earle, and Emma Schweppe examined the materials that had been produced during the first year, and began assembling more new materials, this time for the fifth, sixth, and ninth grades. Many of the materials developed during the first year were deemed unsuccessful and were discarded. The new "team" began to rewrite the entire course. They assembled nearly one thousand mimeographed pages, some of it original, but much of it excerpted from printed sources. Nonetheless, compared to what would come later, these early materials were later described as "pretty bad" (Rugg, 1965). The materials that were produced were again piloted in Lincoln School classrooms, shared with other teachers and colleagues, and reviewed in Rugg's college classes until they began to take a "more definite form" (H. O. Rugg, 1941, p. 206).

During the 1921-1922 school year, the second year of experimentation, the materials were still in mimeographed form and produced as the need arose. Also, experimentation with the fifth and sixth grades proved limiting and the decision was made to refocus the entire effort on the junior high years. Rugg decided to focus on developing materials for use in the junior high school partly because intelligent fifth and sixth graders found the materials difficult and partly because of the confused state of social studies in the junior high. Also, he realized that a well-written series of social studies materials for the junior high years would have a good chance of being adopted across the entire country. While he saw the potential for personal gain, even more enticing, he viewed his materials as a vehicle to make a difference in the education of democratic citizens (Nelson, 1977).

By the winter of the 1921-1922 school year it became obvious to Rugg that wider experimentation with the plan in public schools would not occur so long as the materials were mimeographed. They were, in hindsight, "hard to read and generally uninteresting" (Rugg, 1941, p. 206). Moreover, the use of photographs, graphs and illustrations was out of the question, as was production of the large number of copies necessary for use in the public schools. Given this dilemma, Rugg proposed to Otis Caldwell, director of the Lincoln School, that published pamphlets be prepared for distribution. Caldwell said that he approved of the project, but also indicated that neither the Lincoln School nor Teachers College could afford the cost. So, some other means of financing publication had to be found.

Rugg approached several foundations for money to support publication of the pamphlets, but his requests were turned down. It seemed for a time that the whole idea might die. At this point Rugg again approached Caldwell, but with an alternative means of financing the project, a plan of "public school cooperation."

"How will you do it?" he (Caldwell) asked.

"I think I can get school men whom I know to 'underwrite' small editions of these pamphlets."

"Underwrite them? What do you mean?"

"I mean, ask a number of superintendents and teachers to subscribe for enough copies to supply one experimental class for each school" (H. O. Rugg, 1941, p. 207).

The plan, which Caldwell eventually agreed to, mirrored what Rugg and his colleague John Roscoe Clark had done with a mathematics course while Rugg was at the University of Chicago (H. O. Rugg & Clark, 1917; H. O. Rugg & Clark, 1919). And so, in the spring of 1922 Rugg sent a short mimeographed announcement of a proposed printed edition of a new social science course for the junior high school to over 300 persons. The recipients, most of whom were former students of Rugg's, now serving as superintendents, principals, and teachers, were asked to subscribe to the new "social science" pamphlets, "sight unseen," for use in one, two, or three of the junior high grades (7, 8, and 9). The response to Rugg's announcement was immediate and astonishing. By June of 1922 over 4,000 orders were received with the proviso that all of the pamphlets must be received on time (Rugg, 1941, p. 208). Even considering the rapid growth of the junior high school and the need for social studies materials at that time, the response was a tribute to Rugg's reputation with his former students.

Rugg was a bit overwhelmed by the response, and had not anticipated such high demand for all three grades, originally planning to develop one-year's series at a time. Faced with the task of producing the full pamphlet series during one academic year, and with 4,000 orders for each of the pamphlets in the series, Rugg faced a daunting task (Rugg, 1941, p. 208).

The production of the pamphlets was to be the work of a new Rugg "team" consisting of Rugg, his brother Earle, Emma Schweppe, and Marie Gulbransen, an experienced editorial assistant and a former student of Rugg's in Chicago. Harold did most of the writing, much of it with Emma Schweppe's assistance; Earle did research, documented material, and prepared suggestions for teachers; Marie Gulbransen revised, edited, and rewrote for printing. Faced with an imposing deadline of his own creation, Rugg and his team set to work. Rugg and his family lived in a house in Yonkers at the time, not far from the Hudson River, and the pamphlets were printed nearby, at the Gazette Press. As he described it later:

> We *had* to come through. So with Earle Rugg as assistant and several stenographers, I assembled a library, isolated myself completely and started to write—what was to be the first of three editions of the social science pamphlets.... We girded ourselves for the task; Earle did the research and documented the material; I wrote, and Marie revised and read proof. By the end of summer (on time) we sent the co-operating schools … the first pamphlet.... Thereafter, every two months they received another; while they tried out one, we wrote another (Rugg, 1941, pp. 208-209).

The original plan was to develop and send eight small pamphlets per year for each grade. Because the schools responded that they would have difficulty handling so many separate items, Rugg and his team instead produced four larger pamphlets per year for each class.

Earle later recalled a rather frenetic pace:

> We wrote 2200 pages and printed it in Yonkers, New York during the year 1922-23. Harold and I wrote rough drafts, then a trained editorial worker, Marie Gulbransen, rewrote it for printing. She averaged fifteen pages per day (including Saturday and Sunday) to the printer and sometimes we were barely a day ahead of her. I wrote exercises, tests and the like in the print shop. We lived there at the time. We also handled the shipping, but the volume was so great that Harold finally hired a man to ship the pamphlets (E. Rugg, 1965).

In April, 1923, the final pamphlet was shipped, and "the first siege was over" (Rugg, 1941, p. 209). So began Rugg's struggle "with a blank sheet of paper" (p. 36). It is important to note that the Rugg social science pamphlets and the course which he and his associates had been developing so feverishly during the preceding year was only one of a number of similarly unified social studies courses being developed throughout the country during that time. However, it was, according to J. Montgomery Gambrill, who surveyed experimental courses in social studies, "the most comprehensive and ambitious that had yet been prepared" (Gambrill, 1923, p. 12).

THE RESEARCH TEAM

By April of 1923, when the writing of the first published pamphlets was finished, Rugg paused to reflect on the progress of his social science program. The published pamphlets were certainly an improvement over the mimeographed materials which preceded them. Yet, there was still a great deal of room for further development. Moreover, the research studies, which were to support construction of the new curriculum were far from completed and had exerted only an informal influence, at best. Rugg's plan was to revise and rewrite the pamphlets, one at a time, over the next few years. The research group was, by this time, fully organized, and their work was providing a continual source of new materials. Rugg also asked the teachers and schools using the experimental materials to submit feedback and criticism so that later editions could be revised and improved.

After some time had passed Rugg received feedback from those using the materials and devoted sufficient time for further study and reflection. During April and May of 1923 Harold and Earle began planning for the second printed edition of the pamphlets. Feedback from the schools suggested that the pamphlets had done a reasonably sound job of describing material civilization, but had failed to adequately consider aesthetic and cultural development. Though this failing may have reflected the rush to publish the first edition, it was also influenced by Rugg's own development. In 1922 and 1923 he was just beginning to develop an interest in the arts and an enlarged view of the process of society's growth and development. However, he did feel more at home in the areas he described as the "social" and "psychological frontiers." He concluded that the main problem of the pamphlet series was that it failed to provide a complete and honest portrait of our social order. The challenge was to provide "a total word portrait of contemporary society" that would include all phases of culture, going beyond the portrayal of "the obvious material civilization" which was the focus of the first edition (Rugg, 1941, p. 211). All of this led Rugg to a stronger focus on the world of ideas and their influence on social trends and societal institutions.

A quote from Auguste Comte, which stayed with him from his graduate school days in Urbana, summed up Rugg's thoughts on the matter: "Ideas rule the world or throw it into chaos." From this he theorized, "the whole social order would fall into a clear picture if we could organize it around the great ideas" (Rugg, 1941, pp. 210, 213). These fresh insights led Rugg and his team of researchers on the "documentary trail" of what he termed the "good concepts," the ideas which were "absolutely indispens-able to understanding the modern world and to living in it as informed, tolerant and co-operative participants" (p. 213). He focused initially on scholars working on the social frontier, scholars of the "social scene," but gradually, over the next decade, enlarged the focus to include work on "five frontiers," the educational, social, personal, psychological, and esthetic (p. 214).

The research projects which Rugg had spoken of in 1921 had barely gotten off the ground at the time and contributed little to the first edition. However, they would soon play a larger and more significant role. An inherent part of Rugg's theory of a "scientifically" derived curriculum was the notion of prolonged and detailed investigation as the basis for deter-mining the "insistent problems" which were to provide the foundation for curriculum building. Four times a year, for the next three years, a new, enlarged and revised pamphlet was sent to the cooperating schools: sev-enth grade pamphlets in 1923-1924, eighth in 1924-1925, and ninth in 1925-1926. This time, Rugg's team of researchers would contribute sub-stantially to the process of rewriting the pamphlets. As results of the research studies became available they were channeled back to the group for analysis and incorporated into the new materials as the pamphlets were once again recast. By June, 1926, the second edition of the Rugg social science pamphlets was complete.

As Rugg would later describe it, the research program developed along a two-fold plan. The first part involved technical investigations aimed at describing the "content and historical development of American culture" along with organization and grade placement of materials. The second part involved assembly of materials for use in the social science pam-phlets. The research program had its beginnings in 1921 and would con-tinue well into preparation of the first commercial textbooks in the latter 1920s. The technical investigations included three studies which exam-ined the current status of the field as well as recent developments. These included a study of existing curricula in history, geography and civics; a historical study of the various national committees from 1892 to 1921; and a study of student abilities and achievement. A second group of thir-teen studies included divining the "problems" of contemporary life to form the basis for the curriculum, describing the main trends of civiliza-tion, and discovering the most significant concepts and generalizations that scholars had developed for understanding the world. Three addi-tional studies examined the grade placement of materials and the sequen-tial development of student thinking abilities. Finally, six studies examined the process of learning and the organization of curricula. Rugg and his associates were launching an impressive, expansive, and seemingly logical program of research, given the goal of a "scientifically" derived curriculum (Rugg, 1941).

With the financial success of the first published pamphlets, and assuming that demand for the new materials would provide additional funds, Rugg borrowed several thousand dollars to enlarge the research team and hire additional stenographic help (Rugg, 1941). Over the next decade more than 20 people would participate in the various projects of the Rugg research team, though not all would be working at the same time. Most of the research assistants were graduate students working on advanced degrees. Not all were Rugg's students.

The major tasks for the research team included (1) finding the insistent problems and issues of modern social life; (2) finding the particular related questions which needed to be answered; (3) selecting dramatic and illustrative episodes, collecting the necessary facts in narrative, descriptive, graphic, pictorial, or statistical form; and, (4) discovering the basic generalizations that guide our thinking about society.

Tasks were broken down into specific research problems for each participant to tackle. Harold Rugg, Earle Rugg, and John Hockett worked on determining the problems of American life as the basis for the school curriculum. Harold Rugg and John Hockett examined map studies. Hyman Meltzer and Neal Billings studied basic concepts and generalizations. John Washburne, Chester Matthews and Laurence Shaffer conducted research on problems of learning, grade placement, and organization of materials. In addition, an attempt was made to coordinate the studies, to simplify procedures, and to assure objectivity.

The entire process was built around a procedure aimed at determining what the basic problems and questions were, along with key concepts and generalizations. Rather than derive such a selection himself, or leave it to his assistants, Rugg decided that the best way to determine the "insistent problems" of the day was to consult the "frontier thinkers," scholars on the cutting edge of each relevant field. Moreover, the best way to determine what they thought were the most significant problems was to analyze their written work, rather than polling them directly. So, a master list of books was chosen using the following specific guidelines:

1. First, books in the social science field were listed from the *Book Review Digest* for the years 1915-1922; only those books were listed which were referred to as books of distinct merit, irrespective of economic or political faith.

2. Second, the book reviews of six weekly and several monthly journals were read for three years. All books which the reviews characterized as important were purchased and analyzed for their statements of "problems."

3. Third, this list was supplemented by a canvass of several thousand books on the shelves of the Columbia University library.

4. The fourth lead—one of the most important ones—was to secure from each of some eighty specialists a list of ten books in his own field (industry, population, national government, world politics, and the like) which he would use to obtain statements of problems in his field. It was stressed that the statements must represent deep insight and balanced vision and that the books likewise should be chosen irrespective of economic or political faith (Rugg, 1923, p. 267).

As a first step in the research program, Rugg wrote letters to 150 specialists, describing his goal of constructing curriculum materials through "only the most objective and reliable methods" and asking for "a selected list of books which represent in the highest degree, penetrating insight and critical analysis of contemporary life and problems. Will you help us in this enterprise?" (H. O. Rugg, 1924). Each scholar was then asked to submit a short list of books which "dig deepest into problems and issues" in the specialist's field of study. One hundred replies were received, and from the responses a composite list was developed.

Following this canvassing, a few of Rugg's colleagues apparently made an effort to contribute their additional thoughts and criticism to the project. On the evening of November 16, 1925, a meeting was held at which criticisms of the pamphlets were offered, apparently in the hopes that Rugg's "monumental undertaking" could "stand all tests which might be applied to it." Following the meeting Dean James E. Russell of Teachers College wrote to Rugg offering both praise of his work to date, and his "hope you will make use of the suggestion offered for getting the judgment of experts in the several fields" (J. E. Russell, 1925). Much of the concern apparently focused on the perceived need to beef up the level of discipline-based knowledge in the pamphlets' coverage of key topics. Rugg responded that the criticism was "well founded" and that he would "act in close accordance with it" (H. O. Rugg, 1925).

The work of Rugg's research team began with a number of studies conducted concurrently. Rugg and Hockett used the master book list to generate an inventory of the major social problems of American life. Using quantitative methodology, Hockett identified approximately 3,000 problems, which he culled to a master list of 300, which were, in turn, eventually written into the social studies materials (Hockett, 1927). At the same time, Billings and Meltzer were using the same master list of books to determine the basic concepts and generalizations the specialists thought were necessary for understanding contemporary life. Billings identified some 4,600 generalizations, which he condensed to 880 for incorporation into the materials (Billings, 1929). Other studies included Earle U. Rugg's semiscientific examination of the social studies curriculum to determine what was currently being taught and to what extent it met the needs of students (1928); Chester Matthews examination aimed at determining the difficulty of written and graphic materials for appropriate grade level placement (1926); and, Laurence Shaffer's similar study of student understanding of cartoons used in the first edition of the pamphlets (1930). Other studies examined map locations, methods of presenting materials, and the use of questions (H. O. Rugg & Hockett, 1926; Washburne, 1927). As results from the studies became available they were read by the research group and then incorporated into the revision of the pamphlet series, and later into the commercial edition of the textbooks.

The work of the research team produced what can reasonably be assessed as a highly skewed interpretation of American society. Perhaps Rugg's most grievous and fatal mistake was that he and his research team failed to sufficiently include competing or dissenting ideas. Moreover, presenting a biased collection of liberal thought without competing ideas or a declaration of value was one thing, but to clothe his procedures in quasi-scientific robes was contradictory and ultimately raised many doubts.

Throughout preparation of the published pamphlets, Rugg's theory held that the findings of his research team would determine the development. The extent to which this actually occurred is a subject of some dispute. It may be more accurate for the later revisions of the pamphlets and for the development of the textbooks. How much of the research work made it into the pamphlets, and at what point the research may have influenced either the pamphlets or the commercial textbooks remains somewhat unclear. While Rugg claimed the mantle of science and a research base for his materials from the start, several sources question the extent of the influence and to what degree the linkage really existed (Nelson, 1975). Given the relatively short timelines between editions, Rugg's attention to other works, his professional commitments, and the apparent similarities when pamphlets and texts are examined, it is likely that the research influenced the materials somewhat sporadically and largely informally. However, the role of the findings, materials, and advice of the research team may have been much greater on later editions of the pamphlets and the commercial textbook series as evidenced, in part, by Rugg's inclusion of generalizations developed by Billings in his treatment of the "great war" in the textbook series (Kliebard & Wegner, 1979).

THE RUGG SOCIAL SCIENCE PAMPHLETS

Because of their importance to what came later, and because of their high quality and groundbreaking nature, it is important to examine the Rugg pamphlet series in some depth. The pamphlets were original in design, content, format, and style, and they were written in what we might call today, a high interest writing style. Despite the frequent criticisms of Rugg's ideas, there was no doubt that he could write with flair. Moreover, the pamphlets were pedagogically innovative. Rugg and his associates made a gallant attempt to frame the content of their new unified course in social studies around problems and issues. Though some of the materials are more obviously framed by present day controversies than others, in virtually every pamphlet an attempt was made to create a problem in order to give students an interesting framework, a vantage point, from which to take in and work with the social science topics they were studying.

The first version of the published pamphlets filled 11 booklets, 200-300 pages each in length, 6 × 9 inches in size, and incorporated hundreds of pictures, maps, charts, graphs, reading lists, test questions, and so forth. Titles of the 11 pamphlets included the following:

- Seventh Grade Series:
  - Town and City Life in America
  - Resources and Industries in America
  - Resources and Industries in Modern Nations
  - The American People
- Eighth Grade Series
  - The Westward Movement and the Growth of Transportation
  - The Mechanical Conquest of America
  - America's March Toward Democracy
- Ninth Grade Series
  - Americanizing Our Foreign-Born
  - Resources and Industries in a Machine World
  - Waste and Conservation of America's Resources
  - How Nations Live Together

The second published edition, revised from 1923 through 1926, and influenced by the ongoing studies of the Rugg research team, included the following topics in this sequence:

- Seventh Grade Pamphlets
  - Town and City Life in America
  - Resources, Industries and Cities of America
  - Industries and Trade Which Bind Nations Together; Part I, The Great Industrial Nations
  - Industries and Trade Which Bind Nations Together; Part II, The Changing Agricultural Nations
- Eighth Grade Pamphlets
  - The Westward Movement and the Growth of Transportation
  - The Mechanical Conquest of America
  - America's March Toward Democracy, Part I
  - America's March Toward Democracy, Part II
- Ninth Grade Pamphlets
  - America and Her Immigrants
  - Problems of American Industry and Business
  - Problems of American Government
  - How Nations Live Together

An additional note appeared in the preface to the pamphlets:

> The authors need co-operation and criticism from the public schools. They will welcome inquiries and suggestions about the pamphlets and the experimental work through which they are being constructed.
> Address all inquiries to Harold Rugg, The Lincoln School, 425 West 123rd Street, New York, N. Y.

Though there were some modifications to the titles and to the sequence of topics, the general outline remained constant. The seventh and eighth grade pamphlets focused on geographic and historical content, making it relevant to contemporary concerns and connected to the child's life. The ninth grade material focused directly on insistent problems including immigration and relations among peoples, problems of business, and problems of government. Unlike the earlier grades, in which problems and issues form a frame around content from history and geography, in the ninth grade problems and issues are the main content emphasis, with an explicit focus on different races and cultures, economic problems, and current issues in government.

Among the more notable aspects of the pamphlets were pedagogical innovations focused on key questions, content innovations centered on inclusion of difficult and controversial topics, and creative sequencing for understanding and connectivity. As promised, the pamphlets used a topical and problem focused organization rather than being strictly chrono-logical; they used material drawn from history, geography, economics, political science, anthropology, sociology, and other fields. Sometimes questions, issues, and problems were used as a rhetorical or framing device to make the expository material more interesting; sometimes they were used by directly posing a contemporary or historical problem. Combined with use of the "new history," this meant that Rugg's treatment of topics such as corporate America or the founding fathers typically raised many questions that some people didn't want introduced in schools.

Throughout the pamphlets history was treated in topical fashion, in strands of development presented in chronological sequence. This meant that the history of only one topic or one group of related topics was treated at a time, in a topical strand from the earliest relevant episode to the present day. Rugg made a serious attempt at organizing all material using a problem-solving framework. He made repeated use of the "dramatic episode" to enliven topics, build interest, and provide human insight. He also made frequent use of sharp contrasts in history, between the way things were in the past and the way they are they are in the present. All through the pamphlets there was a focus on contemporary problems including: immigration, natural resources, industry and business, transportation, the American city, education, the formation of intelligent public opinion, government, social problems, and world affairs.

Pedagogical Innovations. Pedagogical improvements were numerous. In an effort to facilitate thoughtful use, the pamphlets included guidance in critical thinking in a, "Forward to the Pupil," which posed questions such as: What are the true facts about this matter? Is there another side to the question I have not considered? Are the facts … reliable? Which side of the question is supported by the most important facts? (H. O. Rugg, Rugg, & Schweppe, 1923, p. v).

More than simply a reading text, Rugg's materials called for students and teachers to actually discuss matters, and to become emotionally engaged in dramatic stories and episodes or hard-hitting source material. They made frequent use of open forum discussion. To encourage such discussions, a framed box appeared in the text, with instructions to the teacher and students to hold an open forum discussion on the question(s) that followed. Many chapters also included a framed section labeled, "Class Discussion," which contained interesting questions aimed at getting students thinking and talking about what they had read, a study guide with questions for understanding and activities, and frequently, a map exercise. Typically, the mood of the writing was interrogative rather than expository.

Stylistic Advancements: The pamphlets were written in a very lively and readable style, in a highly accessible outline form with frequent heads, subheads, questions, photos, cartoons, charts, statistics, and primary source material. In short, the authors used a variety of interesting ways of presenting information. Each pamphlet was written to lead naturally into the next pamphlet in an attempt to provide the continuity that Rugg felt was lacking in the traditional curriculum. Moreover, the pamphlets had an attractive feel with a rich mix of high interest and highly readable materials.

Framing: As mentioned above, the pamphlets were innovative in the way they framed materials from the social sciences, using thoughtful open-ended questions or story-problems as an interest building technique that encouraged student problem solving, thinking and further reading. Most began with a present life-interest problem that framed the remaining content on that topic. For example, the first pamphlet for the eighth grade course, titled *Explorers and Settlers Westward Bound* (1926), began with a photo essay portraying different scenes from American cities, towns and farms. The text asked, "Do You Know How People Live in Your Own Country?" and "How many of the scenes do you recognize?" Captions asked, "Where is it located?" and "What does this scene represent?"

The text then posed the overarching problem for the year, "Your problem in the social studies this year is to learn how this amazing country of ours became what it is" (Rugg, Woods, Schweppe, & Hockett, 1926, p. 8). In a similar fashion, Rugg framed many chapters with contemporary concerns, then used a flashback to the relevant strand of historical development to examine how it got that way.

Presentation and Use of Evidence: The pamphlets made use of a large quantity of first person evidence and eyewitness accounts through dramatic episodes or selections from primary source materials. For example, some chapters began with a story or dramatic episode aimed at capturing students' interest. This was usually followed by a set of questions or exercises. Some pamphlets also made frequent and creative use of rhetorical questions, cartoons, illustrations, photographs, and so forth, to get at the facts and to make the facts seem both interesting and relevant to students. Moreover, they were often used to raise a question or problem. The materials presented a great deal of first person evidence, eyewitness accounts, and descriptions of past and contemporary social conditions and made voluminous use of source materials, facts, and quotations.

Conceptual Qualities: Conceptually, the pamphlets presented a unified social studies curriculum offering nothing less than an overview of modern industrial civilization, its historical development and continuing dilemmas. Though much of the content presentation was in narrative form, similar to more traditional texts, selection of content frequently cut across disciplinary boundaries. And, the pamphlets offered Rugg's openness to feedback and criticism, unlike any other textual materials this author has ever reviewed. Thus, Rugg put himself on the line, opening the door to criticism and illustrating his belief in interactive and problem-centered learning.

Content Innovations. The Rugg pamphlets also contained a great deal of content that did not make it into the typical textbook. They raised troublesome issues and questions in a frank, matter-of-fact, and pointed manner, questions and issues that most texts didn't touch, some of which were quite controversial. They made use of the latest scholarship from the "frontier thinkers." For example, in *America's March Toward Democracy, Part 1* (1926), treatment of the constitutional convention drew on Beard, that is, "they wanted a strong central government; and they did not want too much democracy."

He followed that introduction with a look at problems in political life today, which he described as "threads through the political history" discussed in subsequent pages. Among the problems, each illustrated by a cartoon: political parties, the history of voting, freedom of speech, public education, growth of the constitution, extension of government services, regulation of business, tariffs, methods of taxation, control of government by business, addition of territory, and world affairs. In each case the problem was briefly introduced by a central, hard-hitting, and difficult focus question. For example: "What control does the government have over business? Is this old or new? Is the Government effective in controlling business for the benefit of the masses of the people?" (p. 12).

In his discussion of the constitution Rugg asked, "Which classes of people were in favor of the constitution and which opposed it? Why?" (p. 120). Moreover, he clearly framed Bacon's Rebellion as class conflict, "The First Conflict," of "Aristocracy v. Lower Classes" (p. 37).

In another pamphlet, *America's March Toward Democracy, Part II* (1926), he raised difficult questions regarding the functioning of American democracy. An "Open Forum" question, box-framed at the end of the chapter was titled, "The Extension of Services by the Government" and read:

An Open Forum

Do you think more services should be added to those performed by the government?

If you do think they should, what services do you think would be useful? (p. 145)

Another boxed-set of discussion questions in the same pamphlet read:

An Open Forum

Do you think there is any way to limit the power of business in government?

Do you think that power should be limited? (p. 188)

In these passages and elsewhere, Rugg gave attention to topics that got little or no treatment in the standard curriculum: the role of government in business; the role of business in government; extremes of poverty and wealth; the rights of labor; Columbus' mistreatment of the Indians; and, the wealth of the founding fathers. He also confronted issues of race and human diversity in an advanced manner, given the times. The ninth grade pamphlet, *America and Her Immigrants* (1926) devotes significant space to multicultural issues and offers a relatively forward looking treatment of those issues, asking "What solution to the race problem do you suggest?" and posing an open forum on the topic: "Resolved, that race hatred can be eliminated," followed by alternative solutions for racial issues (pp. 184-185).

In sum, the Rugg pamphlets and subsequent textbook series gave full treatment to topics and issues on which most textbooks were silent. This was history and the social sciences with all the warts on. The reverse was also true. Rugg purposefully omitted a few topics which traditional textbooks covered extensively, leaving out military history, the lineage of kings, and other topics that could be found in traditional textbooks.

Simply put, the Rugg social science pamphlets were the most advanced materials of their day for teaching history and the social sciences. They compare favorably, in style, content, readability, and interest level with materials of any subsequent era. It is little wonder that they were well received and led to development of a best selling textbook series.

Rugg at Dartmouth, c. 1906 (Dartmouth College Library)

2. Rugg's Parents, Edward and Merion Rugg (Courtesy of Brian E. Rugg)

Harold Rugg, c. 1924 (Special Collections, University of Northern Colorado)

Rugg family at Earle's graduation from Teachers College, Columbia University, 1923; l. to r., Earle, his wife Cena, Edward, Merion, Doris, and Harold (Courtesy of Brian E. Rugg)

Harold Rugg, c. 1932 (Dartmouth College Library)

Harold and Berta Rugg home in Yonkers, New York (Photo by the author, 2003)

The Rugg Social Science Series (Buckingham, *The Rugg Course in the Classroom*, Ginn, 1935)

The Rugg home in Woodstock, New York (Photo by the author, 2003)

Rugg's semicircular desk at home in Woodstock (Courtesy of Bruce Bodner)

Rugg's desk and fireplace at home in Woodstock (Courtesy of Bruce Bodner)

Thor at Rugg home in Woodstock (Courtesy of Joan Van Dyke)

Harold and Louise in Woodstock, 1938 (Courtesy of Joan Van Dyke)

Louise Krueger, headmistress, Walt Whitman School, New York (Courtesy of Joan Van Dyke)

Harald "Hal" Rugg in garden at home in Woodstock, 1938 (Courtesy of Joan Van Dyke)

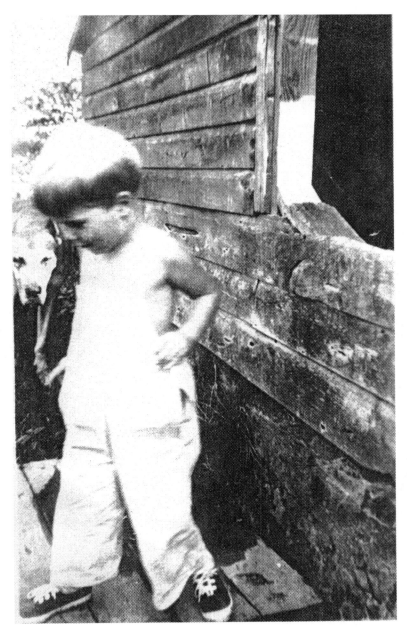

Hal and Thor (Courtesy of Joan Van Dyke)

Harold and Thor (Courtesy of Joan Van Dyke)

George S. Counts, 1889-1974 (Morris Library, Southern Illinois University, Carbondale)

William H. Kilpatrick, 1871-1965 (*Progressive Education*, January, 1940)

Howard Scott, founder of Technocracy, Inc. (Courtesy of George Wright, Technocracy, Inc.)

"Engineering Our Way Out of Depression Trenches" (Dartmouth College Library)

"The Changing World" (Gottesman Libraries, Teachers College, Columbia University/ National Education Association)

Harold O. Rugg, c. 1939 (Dartmouth College Library, photo by Mary Morris).

THE TEXTBOOKS: FROM CONTRACT TO FRUITION

By the end of June, 1926, after the revised second edition of the social science pamphlets was completed, and about 100,000 copies of each pamphlet printed and distributed to schools, Rugg had planned to shift his focus to writing for an adult audience in an effort to publicize and explain his social studies program and the work of his research group. According to Rugg's own account, the costs of his work on the series, the "lavish use of pamphlet income on educational research," and the constant grind of writing and revising had depleted his financial resources, leaving him with a "large" deficit (Rugg, 1941, p. 222). Though the size of Rugg's financial deficit as of the summer of 1926 is somewhat unclear and subject to dispute, it is clear that the pamphlet series had very appealing commercial possibilities and that Rugg always appeared interested in finding new ways to make financial gains. A number of his associates believed that a desire for wealth was a prime motive for his conversion to social studies. From all appearances, Rugg liked to live "the good life" and money made that possible (Winters, 1968, p. 89).

By the end of 1926 the second edition of the pamphlet series was in use in more than 300 schools and was receiving increased national attention. Their success led to multiple expressions of interest in developing a commercial edition from "a dozen publishing houses" with several larger publishers asking Rugg for "the opportunity to discuss contracts" (Rugg, 1941, p. 223). Despite these offers, there was apparently little doubt in Rugg's mind to whom he would turn in an effort to publish the books. He had long been a friend of Henry H. Hilton, Dartmouth, 90', who was a Ginn and Company partner and "a kind of elder-brother adviser" to Rugg. However, according to representatives of the company, it was another partner, Mr. Charles H. Thurber, who was instrumental in convincing Rugg to sign a contract with Ginn and Company. The agreement was finalized in August, 1926. Under terms of the contract, the social science pamphlets would be renamed *Man and His Changing Society* and would be issued as six, 600 page textbooks, two per grade level from grades seven through nine. This meant combining, reorganizing, and incorporating new material, then re-writing what had been a four part series for each grade level into two books per grade. The research team continued its work, producing a steady stream of new materials to be considered for inclusion in the books, and Rugg again postponed plans for other projects to focus on preparation of the texts.

The first volume in the series, *Introduction to American Civilization*, was distributed to schools in August, 1929. Every six months thereafter, another text in the series emanated from the Ginn and Company press and the Rugg team. Each text was accompanied by a workbook and teacher's guide.

The success of the books was immediate. In the remaining four months of 1929, over 20,000 copies of the first volume were sold, with nearly 60,000 copies sold the following year. During the decade of the 1930s, sales of Rugg's textbook series literally skyrocketed. Each volume of the series averaged over 20,000 copies per year until 1938. During the ten-year period to 1939, the series sold 1,317,960 copies at approximately $2.00 each, and over 2,687,000 workbooks. According to a sales agent for Ginn and Co., the books were the easiest to sell of any that he handled. Rugg and his associates had created a unified social studies program and his books attracted worldwide attention and imitation. He had clearly become the leading social studies educator in the United States (Winters, 1967). Considering the fact that these remarkable sales took place during the height of the depression, their success is all the more impressive.

As in the pamphlet series, the content organization of the Rugg text-books was centered around guiding principles distilled from the frontier thinkers including the growth of modern cultures, development of loyal-ties and attitudes for decision-making, and the synthesis of knowledge through social studies. The methodology for introducing this content included the dramatic episode, planned recurrence of key concepts, prac-tice in skills of generalizing, and learning by doing. The six volumes of the Junior High School program were "designed to provide a comprehen-sive introduction to modes of living and insistent problems of the modern world," with the purpose of "introducing young people to the chief condi-tions and problems which will confront them as citizens" through a uni-fied course in social studies. Rugg defended his development of a "unified" course by alluding to students need to "utilize facts, meanings, generalizations, and historical movement" in understanding modern institutions. He cited the need to tie various factors "closely together in their natural relationships" to help students understand the modern world. As he wrote in the introduction to the texts:

> Whenever history is needed to understand the present, history is presented.
> If geographic relationships are needed to throw light upon contemporary
> problems, those geographic relationships are incorporated. The same thing
> has been done with economic and social facts and principles. (H. O. Rugg,
> 1931, pp. vi, vii)

Though the books contained a great deal of historical narrative, not unlike many other texts, the overarching aim was to make the study of his-tory and the social sciences relevant, interesting, and meaningful to stu-dents. As in the pamphlets, material from history and the social sciences was framed with issues and problems of present concern. In addition, the writing was engaging and down to earth. For example, the narrative for one text began with an imaginary meeting of the Social Science Club of "George Washington Junior High School of Anystate, U.S.A.," in which members of the club discussed the problems and issues to be taken up in group study (H. O. Rugg, 1931, pp. 3-10). The description is lively and engaging, and undoubtedly helped to interest many students in the remainder of the text.

Over the course of its development the organizational scheme for the pamphlet series and the textbooks remained relatively constant. The text-book series, *Man and His Changing Society,* included six titles: *An Introduc-tion to American Civilization, Changing Civilizations in the Modern World, A History of American Civilization*, and *An Introduction to the Problems of Ameri-can Culture*. The final volume of the first edition was published in January, 1932. Not only was the organizational scheme relatively constant, the con-tent and format of the textbook series was more or less the same as that of the pamphlets, despite Rugg's assertion that the materials were completely rewritten. Rugg and his team apparently did a good deal of cutting and pasting, moving content from one section to another. There were significant revisions, updates, and additions including adding a teachers guide and workbook. Many of the innovative pedagogical features of the pamphlet series such as the open forum questions were moved out of the text and into the teachers guide or student workbook, yet the lively writing, dramatic episodes, and problem-centered format remained. Though the pamphlets were massaged and rearranged for publication as textbooks, many other unique or innovative features were retained including the frequent use of statistics, graphs, charts, cartoons, maps and photographs. Many new photographs and other graphics were added. Though the extensive bibliographies were retained, the new volumes cited sources less frequently, making it appear that Rugg had written more of the material. Rugg claimed that the series was written at a lower reading level due to studies showing the reading level of the pamphlets was difficult for many junior high students. Of course Rugg took full credit for rewriting the material, though on the whole, very few of the sentences or paragraphs were altered (Nelson, 1975).

After years of perseverance in his struggle "with a blank sheet of paper" Rugg's major work was complete. From his arrival at the Lincoln School in January of 1920, to the publication of the final volume in the textbook series in 1932, he had devoted large segments of his time to production of the social science pamphlets and the subsequent conversion of the pamphlets to the textbook series. His research team and most of his professional writing were aimed at supporting the creation, dissemination, and marketing of his vision for the social studies, and in bringing that vision to fruition in classrooms via his materials. During a twelve-year period, Rugg and his associates had created a unified social science program for the junior high school. It was truly a major achievement, one that attracted worldwide attention.

Not only were the books a commercial success, they were used by a relatively high percentage of junior high students during the time. According to one survey completed in 1930, the Rugg course was required in all three grades of over half of the junior high schools surveyed (Wilson & Erb, 1931). Through his path breaking work, Rugg was influencing a rising generation of American citizens.

Though Rugg was very pleased with the popularity of his books, he was concerned about the way they were being used. In some cases, reports suggested, teachers were ignoring the main ideas of the texts and merely requiring students to memorize the factual material. Moreover, in many more classrooms, students were not being challenged sufficiently in the kind of inductive reasoning that Rugg intended the texts and teachers to help instigate. By the time of the textbook controversy in the late 1930s, Rugg thought of his work as being, at least partially, a failure (E. U. Rugg, 1965).

Nonetheless, Rugg's full vision of a reconstructed curriculum went far beyond the junior high school. The plan was to include a cradle to grave introduction to the world of ideas. The junior high series was, in Rugg's mind, only "a fragment" of what he envisioned as a "library of materials appropriate to every stage of intellectual maturity" that would appeal to every level "from the primary school to the adult forum" (H. O. Rugg, 1934, p. 8).

Following completion of the first edition of the textbook series, Rugg and one of his principal long-term collaborators, Louise Krueger, began work on a set of textbooks for the elementary schools aimed at grades three through six. The texts were planned as an introduction to the junior high series, and like that program, they were designed as an integrated whole. The elementary series consisted of eight books, two for each year, averaging over 400 pages in length. According to the introduction to the first volume, the series was built on principles of "curriculum integration" similar to the junior high series, with "geographic facts and principles ... woven around their indispensable historical themes. The geographic facts, historical facts, economic, social, anthropological, and aesthetic facts (which are needed for understanding), are put together in close relationships" (H. O. Rugg & Krueger, 1936). As in the junior high series, the books were permeated with the aim of understanding the problems of American life. They were published by Ginn and Company from 1936 through 1938, and were, likewise, very successful, though not as pervasive in schools as the junior high series. According to an undated memorandum found among Rugg's papers, approximately 750,000 copies of the elementary texts were sold by 1945 (H. O. Rugg, undated).

Prior to publication of the elementary series, members of the Rugg research team were also preparing a series of reading books for the primary grades. This series was largely the work of Louise Kruger and Arensa Sondergaaard. Though Rugg was not listed as a coauthor of these books, he was their publisher, distributed the books from his office, and was closely involved in their production. He considered them part of the overall plan of the Rugg social studies program.

During the latter 1930s the junior high series was revised, partly because of the usual number of misprints and errors, but also, in response to several critical attacks on the series. Coupled with the fact that the elementary series covered much of the same material, Rugg and his editors decided to make a fairly thorough revision. This revision led to two completely revised books under new titles, and substantial changes to the other four books.

Rugg's overall plan also called for a series of texts for the senior high school. He began work on this project during the late 1930s, but dropped the idea after the junior high series came under severe attack. A final portion of the plan was to include adult forums for discussion of national and world problems and issues. Though this did lead to at least one publication, to be discussed in the next chapter, like the senior high texts, its full development never reached fruition.

RUGG THE BOHEMIAN

During the decade of the 1920s, as work on the pamphlet and textbook series continued at a nearly frantic pace, Rugg came into increasing contact with New York intellectuals and artists who's influence continued to lead Rugg's career transformation from engineer to social prophet. The social and cultural criticism of *The Seven Arts* editors, Waldo Frank, Randolph Bourne, and Van Wyck Brooks, meshed nicely in Rugg's evolving intellectual outlook with artistic trends and advances by innovative artists like Georgia O'Keefe and Alfred Stieglitz who were among the Greenwich Village "bohemians" who influenced Rugg's thinking, and with whom Rugg had come in contact (Kliebard & Wegner, 1987). Not only did the bohemian culture influence his career, it would also have a profound impact on his personal life.

Writing some years later, Malcolm Cowley, also a part of the New York intellectual scene of the 1920s, defined bohemia as "a revolt against certain features of industrial capitalism" (1951, p. 55). By the 1920s Greenwich Village had become a counterculture mecca permeated with a host of liberating ideas. The Village was "not only a place, a mood, a way of life," but was also "a doctrine." The doctrine included the idea of "salvation by the child" through child-centered forms of education, the notion of creative "self-expression" as a means to the realization of full individuality, paganism and the idea of free love, living for the moment, personal freedom and the crusade against Puritanism, female equality, psychological adjustment, and the value of expatriation to better and freer cultures (p. 60-61). The bohemian culture also embraced various stripes of socialism and social criticism, though not always in earnest. The bohemianism of Greenwich Village was, in many ways, Cowley wrote, a revolt against the "business-Christian ethic," as represented by the *Saturday Evening Post*. According to this mainstream production ethic, the great virtues were "industry, foresight, thrift and personal initiative" (p. 61).

The new bohemianism in Greenwich Village presaged a revolution in morals that affected the entire nation in the decade of the 1920s. The war had relaxed all moral standards. Freudian psychology "made it unfashionable to be repressed," and later "the sex magazines and the movies, even the pulpit, would advertise a revolution that had taken place" as the Greenwich Village standards began to spread throughout the country. It was a period when young women bobbed their hair and quit wearing corsets. It was time in which women were suddenly:

> not very self-conscious when they talked about taking a lover; and the conversations ran from mother fixations to birth control while they smoked cigarettes.… People of forty had been affected by the younger generation: they spent too much money, drank too much gin, made love to one another's wives and talked about their neuroses. Houses were furnished to look like studios. Stenographers went on parties, following the example of the boss and his girl friend and her husband. The "party," conceived as a gathering together of men and women to drink gin cocktails, flirt, dance to the phonograph or radio and gossip about their absent friends, had in fact become one of the most popular American institutions … it developed out of the "orgies" celebrated by the 1830s French romantics, but was introduced to this country by the Greenwich Villagers—before being adopted by salesmen from Kokomo and the younger country club set in Kansas City. (Cowley, 1951, pp. 64-65)

The influence of Greenwich Village ideas and their many cultural permutations created something of a culture war between those who embraced the old Victorianism and those who were swept up in the new cultural freedom. The changing scene led Rugg to increasingly embrace the new social criticism and to combine it with a growing appreciation for creative artistry and an openness to personal change, in his professional ideologies and writing, and in his personal life.

By the fall of 1929 Rugg had been married to Berta Melville Miller for 17 years. They had two adopted children, Donald Alan Rugg and Dorothy Elizabeth Rugg, and lived in a modest but comfortable house on a tree lined street at 59 Edgecliff Terrace in Yonkers, New York, and had lived there since 1922. There is little doubt that the exciting climate of ideas in the 1920s, the new bohemia, the liberating influences present in Greenwich Village and the cauldron of New York City had its impact on Rugg's personal life. At some point in the late 1920s Rugg's professional relationship with Louise Krueger apparently grew into something more. Shortly after the first text in the commercial series was published in August of 1929, a scandal broke over Teachers College, as witnessed by the following anonymous note to Dean William F. Russell, received on September 23, 1929:

> Is Harold Rugg the kind of man you want on your teaching staff? Is the kind of a man who will desert his wife for his secretary the kind of a man Teachers College should support?

Students and teachers alike are gloating over the scandal? How is it reflecting upon the college? (Anonymous, 1929)

Rugg himself seemed to acknowledge the scandal in a confidential letter to Dean Russell, dated September 16, 1930:

My dear Dr. Russell:

I am writing to tell you that the personal problems which I confronted in the Spring have been adjusted satisfactorily. The matter was arranged with care, quietly, and so far as I know without public announcement or discussion.

I want you to know also that after careful consideration I decided to remarry at once. This was done without any public announcement. Although we want to have our close friends informed of the marriage now, we consider it wise not to have any general discussion of it.

There were many interesting phases of the summer's experience which I shall be glad to tell you about in some moment of leisure. I regretted intensely the enforced absence from the College during the summer session....

I have returned with improved health and look forward eagerly to taking a more active part in the development of the College. (H. O. Rugg, 1930)

Rugg was divorced from Bertha Miller during the summer of 1930 and married Louise Krueger on August 25, 1930. A research associate and member of the Rugg research and writing team from 1926, she had been an assistant at the Lincoln School, and later served as a teacher and as founder and director of the Walt Whitman School in New York. Dean Russell responded to Rugg's letter with a brief acknowledgement, dated September 22, 1930:

My dear Professor Rugg:

This is to acknowledge your personal and confidential letter of September 16 which came to my desk.

Yours faithfully,

William F. Russell (Russell, 1930)

This was not the first nor would it be the last time that one of Rugg's administrators received a complaint about one of his leading faculty members, Harold Rugg. However, and to his credit, it appears that Dean Russell took no additional action. Perhaps this was a sign of the changing times.

REFLECTIONS ON THE TEXTBOOKS

Numerous reviews of the Rugg textbooks were published by educators and other observers in both academic journals and in the popular press. Most reviewers discussed the Rugg social studies program of research and development that lay behind the books, then turned to the specific volume at hand. The majority of the reviews were generally complimentary, but made little attempt to analyze Rugg's theory in any depth. A few, who had their own competing textbook series, or an alternative vision for social studies, were critical of Rugg's approach. Bessie Pierce found the material too heavily laden with statistics for the junior high school and overly didactic. Moreover, Pierce, a historian, thought that Rugg tried to do too much, and had too limited an understanding of history and the social sciences (Pierce, 1930). Several of the reviewers found factual mistakes or errors of interpretation but still found the books excellent. A few offered very critical comments or attacked the books.

One reviewer in particular offered a thorough and scholarly analysis of the books and of Rugg's attempt at curricular fusion. Howard E. Wilson, a professor of education at Harvard, offered a thoughtful counterpoint to Rugg's arguments for curriculum integration in a book-length treatment of curricular fusion. First, in response to Rugg's claim that the subjects were rigid and inflexible, he argued that history and the social sciences were evolving continually and that each discipline overlapped the others. For Rugg, he argued, the subject boundary line was merely a straw man in constructing an argument for a fused curriculum. Though Wilson accepted the need for a functional curriculum that connected to student's lives, he disagreed with the need for fusion to meet this end. Moreover, Wilson was very critical of activity analysis as promoted by the leading social efficiency educators, Bobbitt, Charters, and Snedden, as a means to scientific curriculum design, and thought that Rugg's approach was basically the same. Additionally, Wilson challenged Rugg's assertion that the research studies conducted by his team demanded a fused curriculum. He closely examined the Billings study to determine whether the basic generalizations were equally applicable to the separate social sciences. Wilson found that of the 880 generalizations uncovered by Billings, only 662 of them were confined to one field, meaning that a good portion (one quarter) of the social science content was naturally fused by this overlap. In a similar vein, Wilson examined Meltzer's work to determine whether the traditional curriculum was excluding key concepts. Wilson examined three popular textbooks, one each from history, geography, and civics, and found that 19 of 25 key concepts were covered in all three fields. Thus, he argued, this additional evidence of overlap among the disciplines did not support the argument for a fused course. Wilson also argued that Rugg's reorganization of material into "units of work" to correlate subject matter from different disciplines offered no advantage. He concluded that the Rugg course did not offer any significant advantages over what could be accomplished in traditionally organized courses. On the contrary, Wilson believed that a curriculum featuring in-depth study of the disciplines offered development of potentially superior student understanding (Wilson, 1933).

As mentioned previously, Rugg's vision for a scientific curriculum in social studies and the plan for research that lay behind it had been challenged as early as 1921 by a scholar from the traditional history camp, Joseph Schafer, who questioned the process that Rugg recommended, seeing it as "merely 'opinion' camouflaged by the cant of a professed 'scientific investigation'" (Schafer, 1921). Rugg's procedure for curriculum development was also questioned, along similar lines, by another scholar during the period when reviews of his textbook series were current. In 1934, J. T. Phinney questioned the representativeness of the books and articles that had been selected as the source of "problems and issues." He concluded that Rugg's work was not really very "scientific." Phinney went on to argue that, "the question of how the curriculum should be organized must remain largely a philosophical question." A glance at Rugg's list of writers and advisors reveals a definite liberal strain. The process was not scientific at all but was an attempt at thoughtful curriculum construction with the aim of raising questions about social, economic, and cultural institutions posed by what Rugg had called "the American problem" (Phinney, 1934a, 1934b).

Were the Rugg textbooks problematic? The books were definitely left leaning and have been described as "new dealish" in orientation, though they were not the communistic propaganda Rugg's critics later claimed. Previous reviewers of the Rugg materials have disagreed over the degree to which the textbooks reflected Rugg's social vision. For example, one writer called the text series "quite moderate," and suggested that they did not reflect his "more radical views" (Stanley, 1982). Another author concluded, "there can be little doubt that the books clearly echo his own socioeconomic orientation" (Carbone & Wilson, 1995, pp. 66-67). My own look at the Rugg textbooks suggests that they were progressive in orientation and relatively moderate in outlook, given the rhetoric of the times. They also contained a great deal of narrative history and dramatic stories well told, as well as stimulating photos and cartoons. They were, decidedly, oriented toward raising serious questions in the minds of students about the social and economic institutions of the nation. Yet in that sense, they were typical of many progressive school textbooks of the era. It is also clear from examining the timeline of their development, and Rugg's other writings, that the textbook series was not created as an explicitly "social reconstructionist" program as critics later charged. During the time in which the textbooks were being developed and up until the series began to be published, Rugg did not speak or write of social reconstructionism, per se, but of "reconstructing" the school curriculum. As we shall see in the next chapter, by the late 1920s that began to change.

The research program conducted by Rugg and his associates that lay behind the Rugg social studies program also had an ideological orientation, despite being clothed in "scientific" language. Throughout the conceptualization and development of the pamphlets and textbook series Rugg argued that he had arrived at a "scientific" procedure for selecting social studies content, partially on the basis of examining key writings recommended by "frontier thinkers" in the social sciences. In 1921, in one of his first published articles in the social studies field, Rugg challenged the "armchair" committee method and offered his own prescription. To reiterate, Rugg's stated procedure for selection of content involved defining insistent problems and issues, organizing appropriate materials into a composite course, and examining the writings of "frontier thinkers" who would be identified via a variety of means. Rugg and his associates then distilled a list of some 300 contemporary problems to be used as the heart of the curriculum. Behind this selection process was a rationale which combined student interest with social worth, a powerful combination that still has appeal.

To what extent were Rugg's curricular scheme and the resulting materials scientific? Schafer denied that it was scientific in any sense whatsoever. He charged that Rugg's plan was:

> a setting up of "opinion"—either your own or that of others chosen by you—as criteria for determining what is "vitally important," "crucial," etc.... Who are the "outstanding thinkers" and how do you select them for obviously you do select them? ... if your investigator is a social reactionary he will collect opinions from a given group of "prominent" men; if he is a liberal he will collect from a group largely or wholly distinct from the first, and if he is a radical he will collect from yet another group ... after all it is merely "opinion" camouflaged by the cant of a professed "scientific" investigation. (Schafer, 1921, p. 248)

By today's standards, Schafer was largely correct. Despite Rugg's protestations to the contrary, his frontier thinkers represented a decidedly liberal and critical strand of social thought. That liberal stance carried over into Rugg's thinking and resulted inevitably in a certain tone and stance in the pamphlets and textbooks. Sometimes Rugg's leanings were revealed in the problems selected or in the way questions were posed. At other times, the treatment and discussion of problems and topics revealed Rugg's opinion.

Rugg sought out recognized authorities doing cutting edge work in each of the fields relevant to constructing a social studies curriculum. However, Rugg's list was far from exhaustive, even as it was expanded and developed by his research team. Another curriculum developer with a different way of seeing might have made more ideologically diverse selections. Curriculum development and the selection of content inevitably involve value judgments as to the importance of certain ideas, topics and materials and the specific treatment they are given. When this is recognized, a curriculum can be constructed which reflects a certain value orientation. In essence, Rugg did this, whether he was fully aware of it or not, yet he continued to clothe the process and his materials in the language of "scientific" curriculum development. Perhaps this was one of his most costly mistakes because it raised doubts about whether his materials fully included dissenting views (Carbone, 1977). With either a direct admission of the value judgments being employed, or a more honest attempt at balance by seeking out alternative voices, perspectives, and evidence even though it may have seemed disagreeable, Rugg might have avoided this conundrum.

My own review of the pamphlets and textbooks suggests that, despite these flaws, they were innovative in both content and form, in style and substance. The overall plan of Rugg social studies, despite its flaws, was far ahead of others at the time. The Rugg course was a monumental achievement from which today's educators can learn many important lessons. Rugg was attempting a massive reconceptualization of social studies, and with the help of his capable entourage, endeavoring to create a set of materials that would transform his avant-garde reorganization of the field from theory to practice. His efforts to revamp the curriculum reached its peak in the publication and distribution of his best selling textbook series, *Man and His Changing Society*. His achievement was the zenith of social studies reform in the progressive era, and stands to this day as a testament to his singular brilliance and perseverance.

CONCLUSION

Harold Rugg held a progressive vision for reconstructing social studies education, aimed at improving a rapidly changing society and helping it live up to many of its often lofty but unrealized ideals. The Rugg plan was to reconstruct social studies education in the United States in order to create a curriculum that would lead to an active and informed citizenry by centering the study of society on social issues. The rationale for Rugg's curriculum led to the goal of social improvement. And, though the direction of social improvement was never explicitly defined, much of the content of the Rugg pamphlets and textbook series left little doubt as to the progressive drift of Rugg's worldview. In October of 1929, the stock market crashed. Fortunes, virtual and real, were lost overnight. The market crash and ensuing economic meltdown set off a chain of events which led Rugg to develop a much stronger, more focused, and more explicit social vision as the goal of social studies, indeed, as the goal of all education. That shift in Rugg's thought, would echo across the land in the coming decade and ultimately haunt the latter portion of his career.

Rugg's personal life also underwent a period of turmoil during the late 1920s. He was a driven, hurried professor, set on transforming social studies education, and then, ultimately, the modern industrial world. The bohemian culture of New York City, and especially Greenwich Village, had a profound influence on the native New Englander. Its influence, combined with the ego-building career success he had found through his long hours at work, led him to forsake his wife and family of 17 years for a new and exciting partnership with his writing collaborator, Louise Krueger.

Because of his textbook series and its success in reaching schoolchildren, Rugg had a real impact on schools. His thoughts and scholarly work influenced several generations of scholars, and his textbook series influenced a rising generation of Americans coming of age during the 1930s. Rugg created an avante-garde social studies program, a prototype for a unified, interdisciplinary curriculum focused on issues and problems and aimed at aiding the cause of the meliorist program. Rugg was a forerunner of education for social justice. Rugg's work and social vision are of great interest to contemporary educators partly because the pursuit of education for social justice remains a possibility filled with great, but largely untapped, potential.

REFERENCES

Anonymous. (1929). "Is Harold Rugg the kind of man...," September 23, 1929, "Harold Rugg folder," box 58, William F. Russell Papers, Gottesman Libraries, Teachers College, Columbia University.

Bagley, W. C., & Rugg, H. O. (1916). The content of history as taught in the seventh and eighth grades: An analysis of typical school textbooks. *University of Illinois School of Education Bulletin, 16*, 5-59.

Billings, N. (1929). *Curriculum studies in the social sciences and citizenship.* Greeley: Colorado State Teachers College, Tribune-Republican.

Carbone, P. F. (1977). *The social and educational thought of Harold Rugg.* Durham, NC: Duke University Press.

Carbone, P. F., & Wilson, V. S. (1995). Harold Rugg's social reconstructionism. In M. E. James (Ed.), *Social reconstruction through education: The philosophy, history, and curricula of a radical idea* (pp. 57-88). Norwood, NJ: Ablex.

Cowley, M. (1951). *Exile's return.* New York: Viking.

Gambrill, J. M. (1923). *Experimental curriculum-making in the social studies.* Philadelphia: McKinley.

Hockett, J. A. (1927). *The determination of major social problems of American life.* New York: Bureau of Publications, Teachers College, Columbia University.

Kliebard, H. M., & Wegner, G. (1987). Harold Rugg and the reconstruction of the social studies curriculum: The treatment of the "great war" in his textbook series. In T. S. Popkewitz (Ed.), *The formation of the school subjects: The struggle for creating an American institution* (pp. 268-287). New York: Falmer.

Matthews, C. O. (1926). *The grade placement of curriculum materials in the social studies.* New York: Bureau of Publications, Teachers College, Columbia University.

Nelson, M. R. (1975). *Building a science of society: The social studies and Harold O. Rugg.* Unpublished doctoral dissertation, Stanford University.

Nelson, M. R. (1977). The development of the Rugg social studies materials. *Theory and Research in Social Education, 5,* 64-83.

Phinney, J. T. (1934a). The objective selection of curriculum material in the social studies. *The Social Studies, 25,* 69.

Phinney, J. T. (1934b). The scientific reconstruction of the social studies curriculum. *The Social Studies, 25,* 108-109.

Pierce, B. O. (1930). Review of *Introduction to American Civilization. Elementary School Journal, 30,* 790.

Rugg, E. U. (1928). *Curriculum studies in the social sciences and citizenship.* Greeley: Colorado State Teachers College.

Rugg, E. U. (1965). Earle Rugg tape: A recording of recollections of the early days of progressive education. Greeley, CO, May 5, 1965. In the possession of the author.

Rugg, H. O. (1924). Harold Rugg to Nicholas Murray Butler, November 24, 1924, "Harold Rugg" folder, Nicholas Murray Butler Papers, Butler Library, Columbia University.

Rugg, H. O. (1925). Harold O. Rugg to James E. Russell, November 25, 1925, "Harold Rugg" folder, box 58, William F. Russell papers, Gottesman Libraries, Teachers College, Columbia University.

Rugg, H. O. (1930). Rugg to Dean William F. Russell, September 16, 1930, "Harold Rugg folder," box 58, William F. Russell Papers, Gottesman Libraries, Teachers College, Columbia University.

Rugg, H. O. (1931). *An introduction to problems of American culture.* Boston: Ginn.

Rugg, H. O. (1934). *Building a science of society for the schools.* New York: Columbia University.

Rugg, H. O. (1941). *That men may understand: An American in the long armistice.* New York: Doubleday, Doran.

Rugg, H. O. (undated). Memorandum in Rugg's handwriting found among Rugg's papers, Rugg Papers, the Rugg home, Bearsville, NY, 1965. Cited in G. A. Kay (1969). *Harold Rugg: Educational pioneer and social reconstructionist.* Unpublished doctoral dissertation, State University of New York, Buffalo.

Rugg, H. O., & Clark, J. R. (1917). A cooperative investigation in the testing and experimental teaching of first-year algebra. *School Review, 25,* 346-349.

Rugg, H. O., & Clark, J. R. (1919). *Fundamentals of high school mathematics*. Yonkers, NY: World Book.

Rugg, H. O., & Hockett, J. A. (1926). *Objective studies in map location*. New York: Bureau of Publications, Teachers College, Columbia University.

Rugg, H. O., & Krueger, L. (1936). *The building of America*. Boston: Ginn.

Rugg, H. O., Rugg, E. U., & Schweppe, E. (1923). *The social science pamphlets*. New York: The Lincoln School of Teachers College.

Russell, J. E. (1925). James E. Russell to Harold O. Rugg, November 17, 1925, "Harold Rugg" folder, box 58, William F. Russell papers, Gottesman Libraries, Teachers College, Columbia University.

Russell, W. F. (1930). Russell to Rugg, September 22, 1930, "Harold Rugg folder," box 58, William F. Russell Papers, Gottesman Libraries, Teachers College, Columbia University.

Shaffer, L. F. (1930). *Children's interpretations of cartoons*. New York: Bureau of Publications, Teachers College, Columbia University.

Schafer, J. (1921, October). The methods and aims of committee procedure: Open letters from Dr. Schafer and Mr. Rugg. *The Historical Outlook*, 7(7): 247-249.

Stanley, W. B. (1982). A reinterpretation of Harold Rugg's role in the foundation of modern social education. *Journal of Thought*, *17*, 85-94.

Washburne, J. E. (1929, May). The use of questions in social science material. *Journal of Educational Psychology*, *20*, 321-359.

Wilson, H. E. (1933). *The fusion of the social studies in junior high schools*. Cambridge: Harvard University Press.

Wilson, H. E., & Erb, B. P. (1931). A survey of social-studies courses in 301 junior high schools. *School Review*, *39*, 497-509.

Winters, E. A. (1967). Man and his changing society: The textbooks of Harold Rugg. *History of Education Quarterly*, *7*, 493-514.

Winters, E. A. (1968). *Harold Rugg and education for social reconstructionism*. Doctoral dissertation, University of Wisconsin, Madison.

CHAPTER 4

SOCIAL RECONSTRUCTION

Education cannot be neutral. It will, inevitably, have ideological influences, through both its form and content. Social reconstructionists believed that schools and educators have a responsibility to play an active role in helping to solve social and cultural problems. Though this notion had appeared in educational thought for many years, it was in the 1930s, during the peak years of the great depression, that it came to prominence and had its greatest influence on both rhetoric among educators and the public, and on school classrooms. That this movement's influence waned does not diminish the power of its ideas, many of which resurfaced in the form of education for social justice during the late twentieth century.

Though social reconstructionists have been critiqued from many quarters, and sometimes displayed a naive faith in the potential of schooling to change society, they were, on the whole, well aware that schools could not significantly alter the social order without widespread public support and the cooperation of other organizations and institutions. Nonetheless, they projected teachers and educators as leaders, the vanguard of what would be a major transformation of society. Beyond the value of their social vision and the general accuracy of their critiques of schools and capitalist society, the social reconstructionists contributed a language and tradition of social criticism which has lasted. They remind us of the importance of including, as far as possible, the full spectrum of ideas in education, both in the curriculum and in our deliberations over educational policy. Additionally, their example has contributed to a

This Happened in Ameica: Harold Rugg and the Censure of Social Studies
pp. 107–142
Copyright © 2007 by Information Age Publishing

reenergized movement on behalf of education for social justice. This is a movement in which a range of ideas and ideologies are considered in discourse on schooling, and in which the various forms and possibilities of democratic and socialist thought are not feared or omitted but are given due consideration.

ORIGINS, INFLUENCES, AND INVOLVEMENTS

There were many influences on Rugg's thinking and development that led to his strong support for social reconstructionism during the 1930s. But, it must be clearly understood, Rugg had reconstructionist leanings at least from the time of his conversion to the liberal viewpoint during his service on the Committee on Classification of Personnel during World War I. His ideas for the social studies curriculum contained a strong reconstructionist strain from the very start. What did change, and it was notable, was his use of the words, "social reconstruction" along with the accompanying rhetoric. Moreover, during the early 1930s he turned explicit attention to writing an analysis of the nation's economic dilemmas and the role that education might play in helping to remedy the situation.

There were many influences on Rugg that led him in the direction of social reconstruction. Among these were the Teachers College discussion group, his colleague George S. Counts, elder statesman John Dewey, the continuing influence of *The Seven Arts* group, the Greenwich Village crowd, and the emergence of the social theories expounded by advocates of technocracy. Moreover, Rugg's personal life had gone through a significant change in the summer of 1930 with his divorce from Berta Miller and his new marriage to Louise Krueger. Rugg purchased, in 1930, a parcel of land in Woodstock, New York. The property was in the area of Woodstock known as Bearsville, and encompassed a number of acres, eventually growing through purchase of neighboring parcels to encompass an estate of 50 acres. Though the initial tract was modest, it was in a beautiful natural setting in the Catskills, along the Hudson Valley, and had a glorious mountain view. As always, even at his new retreat, Rugg was extremely busy, focused on the next writing project.

George S. Counts. In many accounts of the influence of social reconstructionism on schooling, the story begins in 1932, at a meeting of the Progressive Education Association (PEA), when George S. Counts delivered an address titled, "Dare Progressive Education Be Progressive?" Counts oration that day has been described as an "electrifying speech," resulting in a "yeasty" response. The audience was so moved by the speech, they sat in silence, contemplating the prospects and the vision that lay before them (Krug, 1972, pp. 235-6).

"Dare the Schools Build a New Social Order?", the pamphlet created from the 1932 speech, became perhaps the main source of reconstructionist thought in education as Counts' challenge "burst upon the profession." The aim was not simply to save the PEA, but to cast the school as a lever in transforming the society. Arguing against the child-centered tradition, he challenged educators, "to face squarely and courageously every social issue, come to grips with life in all of its stark reality ... develop a realistic and comprehensive theory of social welfare, fashion a compelling and challenging vision of human destiny, and become less frightened ... at the bogies of *imposition* and *indoctrination*" (Counts, 1932a, pp. 9, 12). Arguing that schools cannot be neutral, Counts wrote, "all education contains a large element of imposition ... the real question is not whether imposition will take place, but rather from what source will it come." He did not support the notion that teachers should, "promote particular reforms through the educational system." Instead, he hoped they would endeavor to provide a "vision of the possibilities which lie ahead" and "enlist (students') loyalties and enthusiasms in the realization of the vision." Teachers and students would "critically" examine "our social institutions and practices in the light of such a vision" (pp. 12, 27, 87). Thus, Counts vision held special implications for social studies education, supporting issues-centered study in the vein of Harold Rugg's work.

By the 1930s, in education circles, the idea of social change was already in vogue. The reconstructionists added emphasis on the notion that change was something people could direct. These theories implied a "revitalized" social studies. Reconstructionists called on schools and teachers to lead in creation of social change, and social studies teachers were to be the vanguard. The idea of using schools to change the social order was far from new but was recapitulated by Counts, Rugg and other reconstructionists in such a way and at such an opportune time that it gained currency.

The reconstructionist crusade was centered at Teachers College, Columbia University. Counts was the lead reconstructionist, but the ranks included Kilpatrick, Rugg, Newlon, Childs, Raup and others, and the group had links to Dewey. It was a modern expression of a long "messianic tradition," a new language to express traditional faith in utopian reform through schooling (Bowers, 1969). Though Counts was the figurehead leading the new movement for social reconstructionism, in actuality, Rugg had been arguing for something similar since the early 1920s and had been using the term "social reconstruction" since at least the late 1920s. Moreover, they were close colleagues with many similar ideas who undoubtedly influenced each other's thought.

The Social Gospel. The reconstructionist turn grew out of several key influences. The reform vision underlying social reconstructionism owed its being, at least in part, to the social gospel of Protestant religion. Popularized in the late nineteenth century, especially among Protestant groups, the social gospel movement helped to create the fervor for social improvement and reform that profoundly influenced the creation of social studies (Hopkins, 1940). Rugg, like most progressive educators, was of older stock, not a recent immigrant, and had small town pietist and Republican roots with the concomitant obligation to set the world straight. From the upper-middle class loft by which he viewed the world, this appeared possible through the curriculum.

The Discussion Group. Another major influence on the growth of social reconstructionism, and Rugg, came through the Teachers College discussion group. Founded and headed by William Heard Kilpatrick, the group began meeting regularly beginning on May 8, 1928, at Union Theological Seminary a few blocks east of Teachers College, for dinner and discussion. Among the regulars in attendance were a who's who of progressive educational theorists including Kilpatrick, Rugg, Counts, John Childs, R. Bruce Raup, Goodwin Watson, Jesse Newlon and others. Dewey would attend occasionally. In Kilpatrick's own words, "No limits were placed on the discussion, and talk ranged all over the field of man's experience. As one memoir put it, 'Not only was the sky the limit,' the uttermost reaches of man's changing culture and industrialism were too. And every new angle in the scholars' researches and interpretations in the sciences and arts. These bi-monthly meetings went on for ten years and in the course of these many talks, certain ideas and agreements emerged. They were very interesting. We argued things out right there." The meetings continued from 1928 through the early 1930s, then resumed in the late thirties at Rugg's request, continuing into the early 1940s (Kilpatrick, 1951).

Ideas emerged from the discussions which influenced education. Each man would get a plate full of food and bring it to the separate discussion room. Kilpatrick presided over the conversation, which began after dinner. "We would have each time a man to present a point-of-view. He would present it, and then we would discuss it" (Kilpatrick, n.d.).

"It wasn't anything like anger, but there were different points of view presented. Each man had his own point of view." Rugg played a vital and often provocative part in the meetings. On Rugg, Kilpatrick noted, "I personally seldom agreed with Rugg" (Kilpatrick, n.d.). According to Rugg, the discussions touched on "the roots of every phase of our culture," and included "hundreds of hours of friendly argument" which plumbed "the social foundations of education." By 1932 it had become "a fairly cohesive group, taking our stand together for the general conception of a welfare state, agreeing fairly closely on the constituent of the democratic principle, avoiding membership or participation in political organizations but studying and critically appraising all platforms, creeds, strategies and tactics" (Rugg, 1941, p. 156). A number of collaborations were to grow out of the discussion group including leadership of Teachers College, the founding of the journal *Social Frontier*, the joint experience of a number of participants in team teaching the foundations course at Teachers College, and establishment of the John Dewey Society.

John Dewey. Undoubtedly one of the most important influences on Rugg was John Dewey. In his writings, Dewey synthesized progressive ideas that had been brewing for some time. Dewey wrote little on social studies per se. And, though he made no specific attacks against traditional history, he did offer critiques through euphemisms such as "our present instruction," and the "existing school system." The problem with the system, Dewey charged, was that it attacked the subject matter first and the student second. Dewey held that dogmatic faith in the educational value of the subject matter (i.e., traditional history) ignored the primacy of student interests and needs. He wrote that educators should strive to, "make history functional … by relating the past to the present as if the past were a projected present in which all the elements (were) enlarged" (Dewey, 1897, p. 21). And, he wrote, "Past events cannot be separated from the living present and retain meaning. The true starting point of history is always some present situation with its problems" (Dewey, 1916, p. 251).

Dewey is commonly viewed as the father of progressive education. The new integrated approach to social studies, and the vision of social reconstruction through education, would not have occurred without progressive education, and may not have occurred without Dewey. The progressive education movement emerged out of a general "culture of protest against the ideology of business, cultural uniformity and the lifestyle and idea of a good life" (Krug, 1972, pp. 178-179). Progressive education was part of progressivism writ large, and had grown out of the general response to problems brought by industrialization. In broad terms, it was an effort to cast the school as a fundamental lever of social and political regeneration.

The progressive education movement had its philosophic roots in Herbert Spencer and in the work of reform Darwinists such as Lester Frank Ward and Albion Small, sociologists who argued that the mind is "telic" and that evolution can be directed toward worthy social ends. Thus, education was the foremost activity and a great panacea for curing social ills. John Dewey, a younger colleague of Small, wrote, in 1897, that "education is the fundamental method of social progress and reform," and that the teacher was, "the prophet of the true God and the usherer in of the true kingdom of God" (1899).

Dewey retired from the faculty at Teachers College during Rugg's first decade on the faculty, though he was a continued presence until his death in 1952. On the occasion of Dewey's 90th birthday party, Rugg wrote a moving tribute to Dewey as a contribution to a memory book created by many of Dewey's students and admirers (Rugg, 1949). Rugg's letter makes clear the admiration and esteem in which he held Dewey, who was perhaps the nation's greatest public intellectual during the first half of the twentieth century.

Social Frontier. Another important influence on Rugg's thought was his participation in the journal launched by his colleagues. In 1934, educators sympathetic with reconstructionism, headed by the Teachers College discussion group, launched a new journal, *Social Frontier*, with Counts as editor, to help advance their cause. Over the years of its existence the journal served as a lively forum for debate on social reconstructionism and on the role of schooling in creating a new society. "To exercise educational leadership can only mean to define the issues of contemporary life and to initiate persistently and consistently clear-cut movements, in the school and out, calculated to achieve the goals of a good life," the journal's editors declared . While the most persistent theme of the journal was the evil nature of laissez-faire capitalism and rugged individualism, differences emerged on the efficacy of the class struggle as a means to bring social change. A major evolving focus of the journal was the debate over whether teachers had the right to "indoctrinate" students with perspectives critical of mainstream institutions. Among the most frequent contributors were John Dewey, William H. Kilpatrick, Boyd H. Bode, H. Bruce Raup, Goodwin Watson, Kenneth Benne, George S. Counts, and Harold O. Rugg.

The Commission on Social Studies of the AHA. Another notable impact on the social studies dialogue of the period, and on Ruggs thought, came with the work of the American Historical Association's (AHA) Commission on Social Studies. Social reconstructionism had a profound impact on the work of the commission, on the ideas of social studies educators in several camps in the struggle over social studies, and on the practices of at least some educators. The commission represented a huge contribution of talent, scholarship and funds.

Begun in 1929, the commission was an outgrowth of previous AHA committees on school history. Charles A. Beard and George S. Counts were its most prominent and influential members. But, many other notable scholars were also involved through subcommittees or consultation, among them, Harold Rugg, Boyd Bode, and Franklin Bobbitt.

For his part, as a member of the Committee on Objectives, Rugg emphasized the need for a study in the schools of the problems of society, and the need to educate teachers about those problems. At a meeting of the committee Rugg argued:

In the senior high school, if we are to make this social science course worth its weight in salt, it seems to me we ought to make those problems of contemporary life stand right out to the teacher. Frankly, they don't know what the problems are, and I think we should illustrate in the statement of objectives what those problems are, and I think we should illustrate with a few crucial ones, not surface ones, but the fundamental, crucial ones of industry and agriculture, forms and functions of our political life, of urbanization, the growth of urban groups and so forth (AHA Committee, 1929, p. 182).

As for the notion of a social science course centered on problems and issues, Beard, the single most influential member of the committee, took issue with Rugg. Later, and at some length, Beard discussed his misgivings about a curriculum devoted to social issues or current events. Admitting "grave problems" are "all about us in society," and suggesting that such questions cannot be ignored, he cautioned against "the hasty opinion that the public schools can solve the problems of democracy," or the contention that "the chief purpose of the social studies is to assure a presentation and discussion of current issues." He then went on to provide a detailed argument against the problems of democracy as a guiding framework for the curriculum: problems are temporary; lists of problems are "partial, one-sided ... trivial"; they cannot be solved by "classroom consideration"; discussion of some issues may jeopardize a teacher's position; and, schools are "merely one agency" of information (Beard, 1932, pp. 42-47).

He suggested, instead, an emphasis on "wide knowledge of facts and a discipline in thinking," and went on to write:

To be sure, many facts presented should be immediately germane to problems, and the mind may be whetted on live issues as well as dead issues, but there is something to be said for giving pupils a thorough grounding in the historical records of human experience before they attack the more elusive questions of the living present. (p. 47)

Later, Beard described the tentative nature of knowledge, and expressed a preference for inquiry, not indoctrination in the education of citizens, stating that "no fixed set of dogmas" would be appropriate (p. 95). Then he outlined the knowledge, skills, attitudes, and values that needed to be acquired to allow the fullest possible development of each individual.

The overall findings and recommendations of the commission were diverse, voluminous, and somewhat unclear. The first publication of the commission, *A Charter for the Social Sciences*, written by Beard, appeared in 1932. This introductory volume enumerated several of the key beliefs of the commissioners, and had a strong reconstructionist bent. Beard postulated the need for the disciplines as a powerful conditioning force in the creation of social studies in schools. The commission report rejected a general social science and a curriculum detached from the disciplines, and found a curriculum based on problems of democracy to be insufficient. Beyond this declaration, which may have been aimed at Rugg and others who supported an issues-centered curriculum, the report did little to clarify the relationship among history and the social sciences, or what was to be included in the school curriculum.

Drafted by Beard and Counts, the *Conclusions and Recommendations* of the Commission expressed a "democratic American radicalism" that could only have appeared in 1934, at the height of the depression. The *Conclusions* stated that "the age of individualism and laissez faire in economy and government is closing and that a new age of collectivism is emerging" (Commission on Social Studies of the American Historical Association, 1934, p. 16). It argued that we would see the emergence of a consciously integrated society, in which "individual economic actions and individual property rights would be altered and abridged."

The *Conclusions* gave a good deal of attention to the curriculum, discussing the disciplines, as well as contemporary American life and theories and philosophies designed to deal with the problems of industrial society. Though it did not specify a scope and sequence, the commission did clearly "embrace the traditional disciplines ... including history, economics, politics, sociology, geography, anthropology and psychology," and repudiated "the notion that any general or comprehensive social science has been created which transcends the disciplines themselves" (Commission on Social Studies of the American Historical Association, 1934, pp. 6-7). Though the commission had involved Rugg tangentially, its conclusions would have received, from Rugg, a mixed review. He supported the commission's social vision, but was at odds with some of its curricular mandates.

RUGG ON SOCIAL RECONSTRUCTIONISM

Rugg had been a long-term advocate of social reconstructionism through the schools, but in the 1930s his rhetoric became more strident. During the 1920s Rugg's social thought was influenced in two main directions. He read social criticism and was feeling the thrust of arguments for social engineering. At the same time, he was investigating the views of those who held that artists and writers should lead the way to social improvement. These strands matured in his thinking in the 1930s and stood behind his continuing work on the textbook series and his books and articles calling for reform. Rugg frequently described his social vision as a "thousand year march" of democracy toward a "cooperative common-wealth" (Price, 1983, p. 1). Despite such rhetoric, his social vision was not as radical as his critics portrayed, but placed him somewhere between New Deal liberalism and democratic socialism. Above all, it was a democratic vision.

During his early years at Teachers College, Rugg concluded that teacher education was too difficult and did not work. He decided to attempt to improve education through what he saw as the most influential element, the textbook. In an article published in 1921, he called for a social studies curriculum that would be entirely problem-centered, built around what he called the "American Problem" (Rugg, 1921). Rugg's vision was of a better society, which he referred to variously as "the great society," "the great technology," and "the great new epoch." The reconstructed society was to be created through a combination of large-scale social and economic planning and a new education which would cultivate "integrated" and creative personalities (Carbone, 1977, p. 4). Achieving widespread popular consent for democratic social planning could only take place if the public were made more aware of existing social problems and potential reforms, thus a focus on social problems and issues.

Culture and Education in America. Rugg had long been an advocate of a strong role for schools in leading social change. Long before the depression of the 1930s he believed that education could "coordinate the power of individual teachers to remake the world" (Rugg, 1923, pp. 261-262). However, his main focus during the 1920s was on reform of the school curriculum rather than reconstruction of the social order. By the early 1930s Rugg's focus shifted with completion of two of his most important works. The first of these, *Culture and Education in America*, was first written in 1926 after completion of the revision of his Social Science Pamphlets. Rugg's aim in that original draft was "to prepare a comprehensive description of our changing civilization" (Rugg, 1931, p. vii). The work was, in Rugg's words, "recast three times" in the intervening years, and publication delayed by a host of other commitments and by his own "residue of discontent" with the manuscript. As Rugg's reading and thinking evolved in the 1920s, the "characteristic features of the theory" became more clear and resulted in publication. In this book Rugg set forth his theory of social reconstruction through educational reconstruction in some depth, and discussed several key issues that lay behind his theory. He endeavored to develop an "honest and intelligible description of American society" drawing once again on the frontier thinkers, and seeking deeper understanding of an "acquisitive society" marked by "the desire for things and the tendency to seek individual success through the accumulation of money and power over other men" (p. 4). Rugg described the current social impasse of unemployment and inequitable distribution of material wealth in dramatic terms:

> five to eight million men are walking our streets, starving, ill clad, and unable to find work ... due to a tragically inequitable distribution of our vast wealth, bread-lines and Rolls-Royces, poverty-stricken slums and "gold coasts," keep company in each of our larger towns and cities. (p. 8)

He then clearly outlined the "national need for planned programs of action," and called for development of an "expressive theory of individual and group life" and "a program of collective action—a planned regime for economic, political, and social life."

The new theory of individual life which Rugg had in mind would "plot a clear profile of the integrated personality," with "new loyalties," and a theory of group life "broad enough to deal with every phase of collective life in America" as a basis for development of a planned system for the "production and distribution of physical goods" (p. 10).

Rugg's critique of industrial society and his prescriptions for improvement were built, in part, on the theory of cultural lag. He believed that the period of transition brought by the industrial age required new modes of thought, new values, and new institutions to accommodate a changing technology. However, these new modes of living were delayed by cultural lag. The theory went something like this: scientific breakthroughs lead to rapid technological advances and increases in productive capacity; the increase in production required adjustment by social institutions, but social institutions tended to change very slowly; people "cling to outmoded ideas" while productive capacity exceeds needed social change; and, institutional control becomes ineffective. The end result of cultural lag was a society bewildered, and in chaos, despite the economic capacity to provide security for all. Rugg believed it imperative that social invention and popular consent keep pace with economic productivity and technological change. Thus, a comprehensive educational program was needed, reaching both adults and children, to gain the popular consent necessary for social adjustment. The purpose, in short, to reduce cultural lag. Once again, these ideas were not original to Rugg, though he gave them a fresh spin. They were drawn on the work of William Ogburn and other "frontier" thinkers and social theorists (Ogburn, 1922). Moreover, John Dewey had frequently asserted that schools lagged behind social conditions and social problems.

While Rugg refrained from spelling out his vision in complete detail in *Culture and Education*, and argued that the necessary programs could be constructed only by "the cooperation of many far-seeing and critical minds specially versed in the social sciences," he did provide a broad outline of the type of programs he had in mind, including:

- a program for the wise conservation … of natural resources;
- a program of employment in which all persons able and prepared to work will find it possible to obtain regular employment at a living wage;
- a program which will provide for the planned control and operation of national and international systems of currency and credit;
- a program for the effective concentration of ownership and control over basic industries, resources and public utilities—whether by state or private initiative; and
- a program which will provide flexible government—government delicately responding to changing economic and social conditions (p. 11).

Schools, and the social studies curriculum, would play a lead role in creating support for social action in this new direction by directing study to an understanding of civilization, its issues and problems, and by offering consideration of alternative paths.

In the remainder of *Culture and Education in America*, and in several other works, Rugg explained his theories in greater depth. Rugg imagined the possibility of a new American culture. In order to bring about this new culture the American people would have to overcome the "exploitive tradition" which was represented by the combination of industrialism and laissez faire economic theory. Though the "exploitive tradition" had led to production of great wealth and material goods, it had also instilled an acquisitive attitude that led to unrestrained competition and periodic economic crises. Rugg viewed the American "mass mind" as preoccupied with acquisition of material goods, and dominated by exploitation, acquisitiveness, and conformity.

In Rugg's view, the arts and the development of full and "integrated" personalities had been neglected due to the general public admiration of science, which built industrial civilization. In part, Rugg blamed the pragmatists, including John Dewey, Charles Peirce, and William James, for an overemphasis on experimental inquiry and problem solving with too little attention to feeling, appreciation, and contemplation. Rugg described the pragmatists as "rationalizers" of American industrial culture (Carbone, 1977).

In his review of these ideas, Sidney Hook took Rugg to task for "hasty thinking and a scandalous misinterpretation of the experimental attitude." Rugg, he argued, failed to recognize that "appreciative awareness" was "a presupposition of an intelligent experiment" (1933). Dewey, for his part, believed in the method of intelligence, but parted ways with Rugg and other reconstructionists over imposition of much beyond that.

At the heart of Rugg's critique of pragmatism was his belief that the arts had been neglected by a society that exalted science and technology, a society that overemphasized experimental inquiry and problem solving. Rugg argued that while Pierce, James, and Dewey had made brilliant contributions to science, and to the "experimental method of knowing," they had substituted "no new 'objects of allegiance'" (Rugg, 1931, pp. 119, 141). For Rugg, there were at least four main shortcomings to be found in instrumentalism: too much emphasis on the "preparatory;" de-emphasis of the emotional, creative, and artistic side of education; stress on adaptation to the social group which could deepen conformity; and an underemphasis on development of "happy" individual personalities. Rugg argued that education must have goals that reach beyond the scope of instrumentalism.

Though he gave full credit to the "exploitive" tradition for its technological success and achievement, he drew a sharp contrast between the "exploitive" tradition and what he termed the "integrative" tradition. Ralph Waldo Emerson and Walt Whitman had provided an "organic" view of the individual and group life and presaged the work of recent social critics such as Van Wyck Brooks, Waldo Frank, and Randolph Bourne. After 1900, Rugg wrote, "an increasing host of young creative artists appeared—poets, painters, dramatists, social and literary critics—rediscovering the concepts first affirmed by Emerson and Whitman (Rugg, 1931, p. 164).

These portions of Rugg's work were especially indebted to Van Wyck Brooks whose book, *America's Coming of Age* (1915) had castigated the idealization of business and likewise criticized authors who succumbed to the lure of commercialization. Rugg especially embodied the Brooksian notion of the mass mind focused on materialistic and acquisitive goals, with the consequence that the creative mind was rendered inarticulate, or diverted into technical fields or business. A few literary giants, such as Emerson and Whitman, had transcended this dilemma.

Rugg was extremely optimistic, some might say unrealistic, in his evaluation of the prospects for social improvement. As the following passage suggests, he thought all of the needed ingredients for creation of a great new culture were already present:

As a consequence of these achievements of the scientist and the artist, the constituents with which to bring forth a great culture are at hand. There are vast energy resources, an efficient machine technology and trained technician enough to completely wipe out the economic problem. There are creative leaders on the frontiers of thought and feeling who are equipped to design a centrally coordinated economic-political system, a humane social organization and a regime of beauty. There are many millions of persons who, taken together, constitute a potential informed thinking minority whose opinions can form the supporting intellectual climate for the new designs. These are, indeed, the constituents for a magnificent culture. (Rugg, 1933, p. 284)

Rugg's Plan of Social Reconstruction. Rugg's proposed plan of social reconstruction included several steps. First, he recommended the need to develop a comprehensive description of American society, a sort of definition and framing of the problem upon which his solution would be built. This description of society would be based on the work of the frontier thinkers on whom he had drawn for more than a decade. However, the individual inquiries of scholars on the frontiers of knowledge would have to be "integrated" into a total description outlining the basic characteristics and problems of the current social order.

Second, once a full description was completed, the next step was to educate citizens, both children and adults. This could be accomplished through formal schooling in the case of children (who would use his textbooks, among other sources), and through cultural discussion groups, in the case of adults. These would follow the model of Frederic Howe's Nantucket group. Similar groups would be formed in most every community across the nation. Community organizations, including government, industry, business—and various social agencies—would explore alternative suggestions for social reconstruction. This would all be coordinated as part of a "school-centered community" headed by the school superintendent and an advisory board.

Third, the description and analysis of society would be aimed at developing a theory of individual and group life. Rugg's theory of individual life would be built on pragmatism, but would go beyond it. Beyond the rational and experimental habit, it would also include imagination, contemplation, appreciation, and feeling:

Artists—have given us additional concepts of the good life. Listen to them: self-cultivation … conscious—appreciative—awareness … detached contemplation … the integrity of the natural thing … feeling import … imaginative reason … confident belief in self … the whole self and the whole society. (Rugg, 1931, p. 229)

In sum, the "integrated" individual would meld together "science, art, intellect and imagination." As Rugg wrote: "In the synthesis of pragmatic and artistic concepts we have a sound basis for a description of our society … the marriage of intellect and imagination" (p. 211).

The fourth step in creating a reconstructed society, as Rugg envisioned it, was creation of a group life. The goal of an "integrated" culture would necessitate development of "integrated" individuals. Out of the interaction of these cultured and integrated individuals would come a society "of the highest order of social good.... It will approximate social purity; it will be relatively free from hypocrisy ... hypocritical anti-social competition can then give way to true social cooperation" (Rugg, 1931, p. 255; Carbone, 1977, pp. 34-57).

Many of these ideas were drawn from the social criticism of *The Seven Arts* group. Moreover, Rugg's criticisms of capitalism owed much to the critiques developed by a number of "frontier thinkers" including R. H. Tawney, Graham Wallas, the Webbs, and other collectivist writers in the United States and Europe.

By the winter of 1932 Rugg argued, in an article that appeared in the journal *Progressive Education*, that the laissez-faire approach to economics "had produced enormous inequalities in wealth and social income" and that a lack of central control contributed to the cycles of recession and unemployment as well as unequal distribution of wealth and income. Rugg believed that these difficulties could be avoided and advocated "scientific control of economic activities in the interest of all the people" (1932-1933, p. 13-14).

The Great Technology. The bulk of Rugg's plan was contained in a second major work published 2 years after *Culture and Education in America*, and titled, *The Great Technology: Social Chaos and the Public Mind* (1933). In this volume Rugg explained his vision of the society that could be, and came closest to outlining an explicit program of reform. A poetic description of "The Great Technology" graced the frontispiece of the volume, and framed the choices before Americans in dramatic terms, as the first epoch in which "man can bring forth a civilization of abundance, of tolerance, and of beauty." Rugg wrote that man would no longer "need to be a cringing slave of nature" or a victim of exploitation or greed. He then framed the choice:

We stand at the crossroads to a new epoch: in one direction lies the road to the Great Technology: in others lie various pathways to social chaos and the possible destruction of interdependent ways of living. (Rugg, 1933, p. iv)

For Rugg, the choices were stark and weighted with serious consequences. The core of the volume dealt with what Rugg described as "deeper-lying issues" such as "the continuance or abolition of free competition; the relation between the productivity of machine technology and the return to the worker; the analysis of the ownership and control of the production-distribution system ...; determination of the value of goods

and services; and the ... problem of government by consent." In the fore-
word to *The Great Technology* he asked, "Can interdependent ways of living
be carried on any longer on an irresponsible competitive basis? Must not
central public control be imposed on the warring, self-aggrandizing cap-
tains of industry? Can this control be set up with the intelligent consent of
a large minority of the people ... ?" (Rugg, 1933, p. ix).

In the balance of the volume Rugg offered a description of his societal
vision and a more in-depth and detailed prescription for social reform.
Rugg's central concern continued to focus on his hope that social education could be used to help in the "scientifically designed reconstruction of
society" for the general benefit of all. He called for "a mammoth and creative program of educational reconstruction" facilitated by a program of
adult education which would educate a minority to lead reform (pp. 18,
233).

Rugg's work in *The Great Technology* was profoundly influenced by the
ideas of social theorist Thorstein Veblen (1921) and Howard Scott, leader
of the popular movement for technocracy. Scott, author of *Introduction to
Technocracy* (1933), had been expounding his theories for years in Greenwich Village. Rugg came under Scott's influence through his contacts in
Greenwich Village, and carefully studied Scott's views in the early 1930s.
Both Veblen and Scott proposed that control of the economy should be
placed in the hands of engineers and technicians, removing the financiers
whose decisions were ruled by the desire for profit. Rugg, a trained engineer, called for a similar program in which technological experts would
design and control the economy in the public interest. As Rugg wrote:

> The economic problem, then, is to design and operate a system ... which
> will produce the maximum amount of goods needed ... and distribute them
> in such a way that each person will be given at least the highest minimum
> standard of living possible.... Whether some persons, on account of greater
> creative ability and initiative, should be permitted to take more than the
> minimum ... is more a question that can be answered only by future social
> experimentation. Personally, I should say they should, with definite restric-
> tion of the "ceiling" to a low multiple of the minimum. (Rugg, 1933, p. 106)

Rugg believed that the economic problem was not one of scarcity, the
view held by conventional economists, but one of designing the economy
so that we could take advantage of "abundance." In Rugg's view, "the production and distribution of material goods can no longer be left to the
vagaries of chance—specifically to the unbridled competitions of self-
aggrandizing human nature" (p. 172).

In completing Rugg's vision of social reconstruction there were three
additional steps: design, consent, and technical operation of the economy
under democratic control. By "design," Rugg meant a planned economic

system designed through cooperation among technologists, political scientists, economists, philosophers, psychologists, and artists. "Consent" meant creating a supporting climate of public opinion by educating an informed, intelligent minority. "Technical operation" meant that the economic system would be managed by technicians who would run basic industries and regulate production according to consumer needs. Thus, the design and management of the economic system would be carried out under the authority of elected representatives who would leave details to the experts (Rugg, 1933; Carbone, 1977, pp. 60-61).

Rugg had a rather low regard for politicians who typically gave "grand and golden promises" but frequently had little regard for the truth and were "too often self-seekers" who generally had "no real solutions" for the nation's problems. Thus, he saw it as imperative to create "an intelligent minority" that would lead the change to technocracy. Likewise, he feared a "business oligarchy" and thought that it "would probably put a stop to independent thinking."

As for the question of who would control the system, Rugg suggested "no one group should be in political control, except a great group of millions of thoughtful persons" (Bird, 1932). However, the change to technocracy would require a new and scientific distribution system with "a rigid control at the top in the production of all 'quantity goods,' food, clothing and so on, that can be produced in 'million lots.'" This would necessitate rigid "scientific" control, but would be guided, at least in a general sense, by "democratic representation of the people." For Rugg, this meant it was imperative that "a compact thinking minority must be created quickly." In Rugg's own words:

> The real task is to combine democracy and technology and through swift, nation-wide adult education create a minority that will permit the management of the production of all basic "quantity" goods—food, fibers, fuels, metals—and all basic utilities by designed engineering control. But these would still be under the political control of representatives of the people— some kind of "lay" national council, under "congress."
>
> This compact group should name technological directors of American life as it is today. These engineers would be in charge of production and distribution of quantity goods.... This must mean some kind of group ownership of "quantity" resources and production. We do it now with respect to water supply and many public services (Rugg, quoted in Bird, 1932).

Rugg's statement, as reported in this news article, regarding "group ownership" of large scale resources and production, went further than his subsequently published statement in *The Great Technology*, and seemingly contradicted his stated inclination "that collective control can be exercised without collective ownership" (Rugg, 1933, p. 180).

On the other hand, in Rugg's view, 'quality' goods would be "produced by the creative effort and initiative of individuals," much like his father, the skilled craftsman, and the artisans in his newly adopted home of Woodstock. The individual would still own his residential land, his garden, his creative job, and his craft "in which he would make unique things with his artistic abilities." Rugg's vision was of a society of plenty, made possible by automation and industrialism, managed by public servants in the public interest. All would be made possible by "the new machine technology" if we could only harness it for the good of all. Under this new arrangement, work would become a pleasurable thing, and people would have a new leisure in which to "dance, sing, and play." Most importantly, "we can all be happier … we will no longer be fearful because of economic insecurity." All of this would supposedly come to pass through a "great nation-wide campaign of propaganda for open-forum discussion." It would all be accomplished in the interest of "the production of a humane civilization" (Rugg, quoted in Bird, 1932).

Rugg viewed this proposal as an ideal compromise, which merged democracy and science, and he explicitly described the steps necessary if "democracy is to produce social change without violence." He called for creation of an organized body of minority public opinion to lead the change, and wrote:

> Such a procedure bears both the democratic and scientific sanctions. It is based upon scientific design by experts, the adoption of the design by the true consent of the people, and practical administration by chosen legislators, executives, judges. (Rugg, 1933, p.172)

Rugg later added estimates of the numbers of persons needed to change the climate of opinion in an interview published in 1934 by *Independent Woman*, the organ of The National Federation of Business and Professional Women's Clubs. The essence of the interview is captured in the following passages:

> Just what do I mean by a new "climate of opinion"? Harold Rugg smiled as he tilted back in a rather unprofessorial chair in his pleasant study at Columbia University. "A new climate of opinion is a new set of beliefs held by a considerable number of people in each community … (which) … will in time form an active and intelligent minority of our citizens. This minority will eventually be powerful enough to vote a planned social structure for an economy of abundance into action.
>
> Pausing to light a cigarette, the genial professor … eager and earnest, absorbed in his subject … explained further, "I figure that, among our 80,000,000 persons above 18 years of age, there is a potential thinking minority of 25,000,000. From this number we should be able to weld a group of four or five million … to see that the assumptions of political

democracy become established fact ... our program of adult education must
be concentrated on them.

This magnificent educational plan worked out by Professor Rugg ...
which will bring out the creative impulse latent even in the humblest, is the
glory of the Great Technology. When I voiced my admiration, Professor
Rugg, again with his charming smile, returned, "Education should be the
glory of any state, but especially ... in our new order which plans for a true
civilization of abundance, toleration, and beauty." (Eames, 1934, pp. 53-54)

At the heart of the adult education program were several key generalizations and related choices. In his book, Rugg described "the generalizations which must be available to the public mind if a genuine supporting
public opinion is to be created." Rugg labeled the generalizations, "Axioms for the Great Technology" and described them in some depth in a
chapter of *The Great Technology*. Rugg's "axioms" for the economic system
postulated an economy of abundance, a shorter work week, redistribution
of surplus social income through progressive taxation ("the institution of
income and inheritance taxes in the higher levels of income and wealth"),
regulation of business and industry (a "controlled private capitalism ...
exercised without collective ownership"), and the creation of popular consent for social reconstruction to be achieved via "a mammoth program of
adult education on a nation-wide scale" (Rugg, 1933, pp. 179-181).

I have found little hard evidence that Rugg ever explicitly or consistently embraced any form of socialism, though his proposal for a mixed
economy and expert control of basic industries in the public interest
seems quite similar to the kinds of ideas advocated by many democratic
socialists over the years (i.e.. Eugene Debs, Norman Thomas, Michael
Harrington, Barbara Ehrenreich). Rugg disparaged what he called "the
'isms': Socialism, Communism, Fascism, capitalism," charging that they
were "necessarily prejudiced, because they have something definite and
specific to defend." He called instead for a new age of control by trained
engineers, who would be "disinterested" public servants. However, he
frankly admitted, at least to one writer in 1932, that his plan required
"some kind of group ownership of 'quantity' resources and production"
(Bird, 1932). This was clearly a thin disguise for a rose by a different
name, but still a rose. Perhaps Rugg refused to identify his plan with any
of the familiar "isms" because of the negative baggage they so often carried. Perhaps it was a wise choice, and for a time, it seemed, it may have
helped stave off the kind of severe criticism that ideologues from another
point on the spectrum may have hurled.

However, Rugg's critics later cited evidence of his support for the
"socialist" cause, including Rugg's membership on the Committee of 500
to Support Norman Thomas, socialist candidate for president in 1936,
and his service as a director, in 1934-1935, of the League for Industrial

Democracy (L.I.D.), a democratic socialist organization. It seems that Rugg's name appeared on the letterhead of the L.I.D., along with others, including Norman Thomas and Harry W. Laidler, who were the organization's executive directors. These anomalies, along with Rugg's denial of his reported statements at the 1934 Cleveland convention of the Progressive Education Association, led critics to question Rugg's veracity (Rudd, Hicks & Falk, 1941).

Reflections. Rugg's ideas for social reconstruction had a great deal of merit, especially given the context of the great depression. However, a number of scholars have pointed out several flaws in his arguments. One commonly cited problem is a lack of detail and frequent use of vague terms and generalities that make many of his proposals enigmatic and evaluating them very difficult (Carbone, 1977; Phillips, 1961). Another criticism is the suggestion that his design may be seen as undemocratic because he failed to state any clear limitations to the technocratic planner's authority. Rugg argued that "the basic industries must be taken from the sphere of political manipulation and carried on purely as a scientific and technological enterprise" (Rugg, 1933, p. 175; Carbone, 1977). But, how these industries were actually to be managed, and the extent to which the current political apparatus would exert control was never really clear.

Moreover, his design could be viewed as elitist because it relied on the consent of an "intelligent minority," which would lead the "rank and file" to follow their plans by creating a large supporting body of public opinion (Dennis, 1933). This scheme is somewhat at odds with his view of democracy as government by popular consent because it relied on conditioning, led by an intellectual elite who would mould public opinion in favor of social change, rather than seeking to develop true understanding by the majority of citizens (Carbone, 1977).

Also, as several scholars have pointed out, his social analysis is lacking in originality and is almost entirely drawn from other sources. Rugg's ideas have also been described as overly optimistic, unrealistic, impractical, enigmatic, simplistic, over generalized, and naive. His plan had something of a dreamy, pie-in-the-sky, drawing room quality. And, it is true that many of his ideas were "marred by his tendency to label and simplify" and by his use of "vague terms" (Phillips, 1961, p. 67).

Phillips suggests that many of these flaws can be traced directly to *The Seven Arts* group itself. In "his exuberant acceptance of their ideas" he failed to critically examine their weaknesses. Thus, Rugg's work contains flaws similar to those of *The Seven Arts* group, the originators of Technocracy, and other frontier thinkers on whom he drew. One common critique of *The Seven Arts* group was their emphasis on social criticism with little, if any, concrete detail on alternative proposals to remedy the situation. Moreover, Phillips argues that Rugg failed to anticipate the problems which might result from any attempt to put his plans for schools into action. These difficulties included "the harsh realities of school board politics, economic considerations and questions such as who would train the teachers for the teachers colleges and how they would be converted to his system" (Phillips, 1961, pp. 69-70).

Philosopher Sidney Hook reviewed *The Great Technology* and suggested that Rugg offered "an obviously Utopian approach to the questions of political power" and neglected to indicate how "the influence of existing pressure groups" would be eliminated or how conflicts "between the groups which share his social philosophy and those who do not, are to be negotiated" (Hook, 1933).

Technocracy. Many of these criticisms of Rugg are accurate, and are, in part, a reflection of technocracy, one of the main sources of Rugg's ideas. Technocracy was something of a fad among intellectuals during the great depression. Rugg, Counts and many others among the New York intelligentsia were enamored with the proposal, at least for a time. Technocracy offered "a technological design for an engineered human society in America," one that would provide a technical solution to a technological problem and "an intellectual guidance based on scientific fact finding" rather than relying on theories, credos, or religious and political faiths (Technocracy, 1932). Technocracy did have a certain appeal, though it seemed based on the assumption that technological solutions could be divorced from philosophical and political concerns. However, for Rugg and many other intellectuals it seemed a logical alternative. In Rugg's case especially, as a trained engineer and educational technician, some form of social engineering seemed imminently feasible.

Technocracy developed in the United States early in the twentieth century as a manifest expression of the progressive movement. Its origins may be traced to Frederick Winslow Taylor's concept of efficient scientific management, from which advocates of technocracy developed an all-encompassing engineering worldview. As a utopian theory, it was part of the extensive history of utopian thought from a long line of theorists including Sir Francis Bacon, Saint Simon, and August Comte. During the progressive era in American politics writers such as Henry L. Gannt, Thorstein Veblen, and Howard Scott suggested that businessmen were not capable of reforming industry in the public interest and that control of industry should be given to engineers.

As historian William E. Akin has described it:

By the end of World War I a cluster of "progressive" ideas about technology and the industrial state, planning and expertise, efficiency and social engineering had become current. At the core of this strand of thought was the identification of industrial production, and the technology that made it possible, with society's present interest and future greatness. This belief ... was deeply rooted in nineteenth century thought. Along with the acceptance of technology and industrialism went the desire for national economic planning. Progressives tended to see centralized direction as the only method of abolishing the economic hardships and class conflict associated with industrialization, of achieving social justice, and of assuring that the industrial machine met the needs of society. Planning required the use of experts who alone possessed the professional training, technical skills, and scientific rationality to understand the complex modern industrial machine. Rational planning demanded that experts be freed from partisan politics in order to bring their ideologically neutral rationality and efficient scientific methods to bear on the engineering of social problems. In this separation of administration and politics a certain amount of democratic control would have to be sacrificed, but the benefit would be the common political good ... replacing corrupt political democracy with ... industrial democracy (Akin, 1977, pp. 4-5).

The leading proponent of technocracy during the 1920s and 1930s was Howard Scott. In the winter of 1918-1919, Scott had formed a group of scientists, engineers, and architects that became known, in 1920, as The Technical Alliance, a research organization later incorporated in 1923 as a nonprofit, nonpolitical, nonsectarian, membership organization. In 1932, the much publicized Committee on Technocracy, headed by Walter Rautenstrauch, was organized in New York City, though the committee was dominated by Scott.

Scott proclaimed that all prior economic concepts based on scarcity were invalid because of the potential for technologically produced abundance. He predicted that the price system was due for an imminent collapse, and that it would be replaced with a bountiful technocracy. Scott had come in contact with Thorstein Veblen in New York City during the period from 1918 to 1921 while Veblen was teaching at the New School for Social Research and while Scott was writing for the International Workers of the World, the I.W.W. or Wobblies. Veblen's attempts to understand the relationship between technology and modern society was a key influence in the development of Scott's vision of technocracy, which might be seen as an attempt to elaborate on and concretize a social program, based on Veblen's ideas. Veblen imagined engineers taking over the direction of American society and redirecting capitalism, which he euphemistically referred to as "the price system and its attendant business enterprise." In what might now be seen as a poor choice of words, Veblen imagined control by a "soviet of technicians." Technocracy adopted much of Veblen's analysis of industrial society along with his positivistic belief in science and technology and his faith in the ability of the technical classes to engineer social reconstruction. Scott established himself in Greenwich

Village after the great war as a kind of bohemian engineer. He appeared a flamboyant, engineer-adventurer, his persona adding to the appeal of his ideas. Tall, lean, and rawboned at 6'5" and 200 lbs., with a broad brimmed hat and big leather coat, he looked as if he had stepped directly off command of some hugely important outdoor engineering project.

Scott argued that a system of value based on the amount of energy expended in production should replace the market determination of price. He believed that this system of value would abolish the profit motive, and eradicate poverty through the combination of abundance and efficient industrial production. The general thrust of the technocrat's program was to harmonize the highly technological process of industrial production with social institutions via scientific planning. The planning would be done by experts who understood the industrial machine. It would abolish the dependency of production on the marketplace and free it from the need to maximize profits. Technocrats asked the American public to compare their vision of potential abundance with what seemed impending social chaos. And, for a time, they had the nation's ear.

Rugg studied Technocracy carefully and later stated that he agreed with three of its main concepts: first, that the nation's "abundance in natural and human resources and in technology" was apparent; second, that the social system was not designed nor was it actually working, in either production or distribution, to meet the needs of the people; and, third, that the central task before the American people was one of studying "the problems of design." Though Rugg embraced and adopted much of Scott's vision, he rejected what he saw as an "authoritarian tendency—a dictatorship by technicians" (Rugg, 1941, p. 153).

Later, after the initial rush of popular public interest in Technocracy had passed, Howard Scott's academic qualifications were discredited in the press. He was known as Dr. Scott, but, it turned out, his claim to academic credentials was suspect. Some of the group's data on energy use in production, which they had been collecting for more than a decade, were also critically questioned (Raymond, 1933). The lack of specifics as to what the technocrat's ideal society would look like, and what might be relinquished in exchange for abundance brought more criticisms. Moreover, there were serious disagreements among members of the group over social policy. The Committee on Technocracy broke up within a year and was succeeded by the Continental Committee on Technocracy. This group, in turn, faded in 1936, and was succeeded by Technocracy, Inc., headed by Scott.

In the larger scheme of things, Technocracy was a variant on utopian social theory, and embodied a form of radical social engineering. The movement was marked by its advocates use of theological forms of speech and discourse, a view of the future extrapolated from the past and present, and the language of prophecy, all characteristics of Rugg's social vision. Underlying the technocrats optimism was a profound faith in progress and in the possibility of redemption via technology, a corollary of the secularized social gospel which lay behind progressive and reconstructionist visions for schools and society (Reed, 1975).

During the height of its popularity technocratic organizations sprang up across the United States and Western Canada. But, the technocratic movement was weakened by its failure to develop politically viable programs. Ultimately, its support was lost to the New Deal and third party movements. Technocracy also spawned fears of authoritarian social engineering. Though Scott's organization declined after 1940, Technocracy, Inc. survives to this day (Akin, 1977; Technocracy, Inc., 2006).

As for Rugg, it appears that he was influenced by the ethos of the new generation of progressive-minded engineers who would redirect the engineering profession and create a new role for engineers in the society. Rugg's training as a civil engineer, and as an educational technician, coincided with a transformation in the field of engineering. The progressive interest in reform, and in the new and expanded role of technology, planning, efficiency and rational administration by experts encouraged young engineers like Rugg to see themselves as the ideal type for progressive leadership. During the progressive era the engineering profession literally pulsated with new ideas projecting a greatly expanded social role (Akin, 1977). Much of this new energy was literally embodies in Rugg's social and educational vision.

Despite all the flaws in Rugg's social ideas, the general notion behind *The Great Technology*, that we must take collective action to address the human suffering created by injustices inherent in the current system, was an idea of merit, shared by many. The call for action was especially appealing, because it was a plea to do something about the disaster that had overtaken the nation, indeed the world.

Woodstock. It is also probable that Rugg's home in the arts community of Woodstock, at which he spent a good deal of his time when away from Teachers College, had a strong influence on his thinking and development. As a choice for a second home, Woodstock was an excellent fit. Woodstock lay in the foothills of the southern Catskills, 10 miles northwest of Kingston. Since early in the century, John Dewey had been encouraging his fellow professors to spend summers in the vicinity of Woodstock, especially East Riding, location of Byrdcliffe Arts Colony. Among those who did were historians James Shotwell and Norman Towar Boggs, and later, Harold Rugg. Woodstock had a long and well-earned reputation for exceptional natural beauty, and for being a community in which free-thinking ideas held sway.

In 1902, inspired by the Utopian social philosophy of John Ruskin and William Morris, a small group of refugees from urban life settled in the town of Woodstock, deciding that it was the perfect place for the release of creative energies. Led by Ralph R. Whitehead, who had earlier been a student of Ruskin's at Oxford, they founded Byrdcliffe Arts Colony, an outgrowth of the arts and crafts movement of the latter nineteenth century centered on the notion that workers in the industrial era were deprived of the satisfaction of making products from beginning to end, becoming little more than wage laborers, alienated from their work. The crowding of workers into factories and slums and the heartlessness of child labor, it was believed, could be overcome by a return to the old system of handicrafts.

Whitehead wanted to establish a community in which the arts and closeness to nature would help create a happy and reasonable life. The production of works of art would have a minor place in the life of the community. Instead, the community's main purpose was to demonstrate the possibility of a better life by turning away from the industrialized and urban society, and the pollution of air, land and water which accompanied it. By the 1920s the town became known as an art and cultural center and as home to Byrdcliffe where residents were working to develop a lifestyle that would integrate arts and crafts with advanced social ideas. By the 1930s it had become a mecca for the summer homes of the Greenwich Village Bohemian crowd and was developing a freewheeling image (Evers, 1987).

Much of Rugg's writing was completed at his home in Bearsville. The Rugg property, purchased with money acquired from his textbooks, was located on a hillside overlooking a beautiful mountain valley with views of several Catskill peaks. Rugg decided on Woodstock at the urging of his friend Henry Cowell, lived in the nearby village of Shady. After a visit, Rugg decided to purchase some hillside property on Ohayo Mountain that he spotted during a drive through the hills and valleys around Woodstock. As the story goes, he hired a highly regarded local stone mason, Ishmael Rose, and went to the property to locate the foundation for his new home. He took a chair with him, and sat down on a clearing on the hillside, with a view to the north looking up the valley and east, to the mountains, and said to Rose, "Here. Here is where we begin." The house grew gradually from that point. By the late 1930s Rugg had built, with the help of Rose and his sons, an impressive home in which to reside. The home included a large living space, a dining room and living room joined around a giant fireplace, small bedrooms, several additional fireplaces, expansive picture windows, and a large study with fireplace, floor to ceiling bookcases, picture window, and a huge semicircular desk at which Rugg could survey his domain, and at which he could write, inspired by the grand view and at home in the comfortable surroundings. The desk, which allowed him to have everything he might need at easy reach, came to be known by the Rose boys as "Doc's playpen." The home also had a porch that opened to the view of the valley. In fair weather, Rugg would retire to the porch in the late afternoon to savor the peace of the valley, and to rest and reflect on his day's work (Alling, 2005).

Rugg described the building of his home in loving terms in *Now is the Moment*:

> Into the Valley comes a Man. To a naked plateau on unlived-on mountain-side he comes to work, to produce, to have a family, to build his House. He does part of what he came to do. He settles on his mountain land, just below the plateau ... Then ... he knows. He must build his House. On the plateau it shall be, looking across his farm neighbors' cultivation of the little valley below, presided over by a dozen wooded mountains. His own unique house.... A house appropriate to the terrain and landscape of the wild mountain forest ... appropriate to the geography of the valley.... So he builds his House and cultivates his scene—a room at a time. A house indigenous to the land and the local culture; built by local labor from the stone, sand, and gravel of the man's own hillside.... Thus the Man builds his house and through it help to build a new conception of the House of the American. Not a mere building of sticks and stones, but a harmonious fusion of the land, the site, the setting in community, valley, region, nation, and country. (Rugg, 1943, pp. 36-38)

Peak of Influence? As we have seen, Rugg's complete program for social reconstructionism involved not only child education through the schools but also adult education through forums and discussion groups. This notion, and Rugg's accompanying rhetoric, caused something of a national stir in 1934 when Rugg spoke before the Cleveland, Ohio, meeting of the Department of Superintendence of the National Education Association, which met concurrently with the annual meeting of the Progressive Education Association. Under the auspices of a committee on adult education Rugg had developed a proposal for nationwide study of the economic situation and assisted in the preparation of study materials for adult education (Rugg & Herring, 1933). The outline of the plan included a central planning agency for socioeconomic education; a central publications and information service; regional, short-term institutions for training teachers; and, radio and press services. According to Rugg, executives of over 40 national organizations showed interest in the plan and cooperated in its formulation (Rugg, 1941, p. 148-150).

Rugg presented the plan as the report of the Adult Education Committee at the Cleveland Meeting in early March, 1934. The report focused on social, economic, and political trends and their implications for education of the "new America." It stated much of the reconstructionist ideology in plain language, most of it drawn from Rugg's written work. It also posited many of the basic tenets of technocracy, that "an economy of abundance for all can now be ushered in," wiping out economic insecurity for all Americans. It called for "some other scheme of purchasing power," different from the price and market system. A "new system of control and operation for the production and distribution of goods" would be devised. It called for a new socialized method for handling debt and credit, and suggested that "banks" and "basic industries and utilities" must be "taken from the sphere of private manipulation and carried on as a scientific technological enterprise in the interest of the general social welfare" (NEA Committee, pp. 534-537). The report also called for "government by experts" as part of the effort to correct the "lag of political institutions behind social conditions." In all, it was a forward looking synopsis of the reconstructionist program that Rugg envisioned, with much of the language drawn from *The Great Technology* (NEA Committee, 1934).

At the meeting, Rugg stated that a 3-year "New American" campaign, to be financed by $50,000 per year, would be launched to obtain the support of all intelligent liberals in the nation. The Cleveland *Plain Dealer* and the *Cleveland Press* reported on Rugg's statement that a group of 14,000,000 people would be organized to push President Roosevelt "to the left." The story as reported in the *Cleveland Press* carried the headline and subhead, "School Heads Plan Pressure on Roosevelt, Educators Would Force Move for Radical Changes in Economic System." The story began:

> Within the next three months progressive educators of the country will attempt to force more radical changes in the economic system by organizing 14,000,000 people or more into a closely-knit pressure group.
> This was announced today by Dr. Harold Rugg of Teachers College, Columbia University, one of the leaders in the "left wing" movement among educators....
> Dr. Rugg revealed that funds to carry on the program will be forthcoming "in perhaps three or four weeks." He declined to divulge the source of the financial assistance. He said, however, "we probably will get about $50,000 a year for three years."
> The plan he outlined before the group meeting includes the setting up of a central planning agency, probably in New York City, which will tie together thousands of groups of citizens desirous of seeing a definite left wing movement on the part of the administration.
> "The president," said Dr. Rugg, "will go just as far to the left as we push him." (Renney, 1934)

According to the *The Plain Dealer*'s account, Rugg stated: "A dying laissez faire must be completely destroyed and all of us, including the "owners" must be subjected to a large degree of social control" (Shumaker, 1941, p. 44). Later, in his account of the meeting, Rugg stated that both the report and his speech were grossly exaggerated by reporters, creating a national sensation in the press. Foundations, which had shown interest in the plan, were "scared off" (Rugg, 1941, p. 150). Rugg wrote a small book and two study guides aimed at adult study groups and forums, but the grand plan was never realized (Rugg & Krueger, 1933).

Despite his later denial of ever having made such statements, Rugg's plan for social reconstruction clearly did call for educating a minority whose thought would serve as the vanguard of social reform. In a pamphlet written to promote his textbook series in 1934 he wrote:

> We stand at the crossroads to a new epoch.... A new public mind is to be created. How? Only by creating tens of millions of new individual minds and welding them into a new social mind. Old stereotypes must be broken up and new "climates of opinion" formed in the neighborhoods of America. But that is the task of the building of a science of society for the schools. And the first step is the preparation of an honest and intelligible description of our changing social order. (Rugg, 1934, p. 32)

CRITICS

Criticisms of social reconstructionism appeared at a number of times, directed at targets of choice. Reconstructionists were critiqued from both the left and the right. The left viewed reconstructionists as naive and unrealistic in their hopes that schools could change the capitalist social order. These critics charged that reconstructionists failed to recognize the deep hold of class structure and capitalist ideology (Tyack, Hansot & Lowe, 1985). From the right, David Snedden called reconstructionism, "romantic nonsense," labeled its advocates "utopians, subversive of 'civic decency,'" and charged that its supporters played into the hands of Communists. School administrators were largely alienated from reconstructionism because of "its lack of prospects for success." As one argued, "Schools and schoolmasters are not ... permitted to take the lead in changing the social order." Thus, to many critics, Reconstructionism was a visionary romanticism that "wouldn't work" (Krug, 1972, pp. 238-9). One superintendent reportedly said that the Teachers College oligarchy "should be put in rear seats and muzzled" (p. 251). Another mused, "The stream of words and books about a new social order which has poured over teachers in the last few years seems very much like the proverbial water on a duck's back"(Moseley, 1936).

A good deal of the animus toward social reconstructionism found its way into the reactions to the AHA Commission on Social Studies, in which Counts had a leading role, and to which Rugg had contributed. Hearst newspapers and other sources reacted to Beard and the AHA Commission on Social Studies as a "red menace" in both cartoons and editorials. State legislatures reacted by passing loyalty oath laws, and by requiring patriotic instruction and rituals. Patriotic and business groups reacted as well. The Daughters of the American Revolution listed the NEA as an organization in "sympathy with communist ideals," and the American Legion led a drive promoting loyalty oaths for teachers. By 1936, 21 states had enacted special oaths of allegiance. The National Association of Manufacturers used advertising to improve the image of capitalism and later commissioned a textbook survey that contributed to attacks on textbooks. Anti-Communists vilified many progressive and reconstructionist educational leaders as Communists or sympathizers. Counts, Rugg, and Dewey even came under FBI surveillance (Dilling, 1934; Nelson & Singleton, 1977; Tyack et al., 1985, pp. 63-64).

Despite all the criticism, during the 1930s many publications for teachers reflected a reconstructionist emphasis, though the degree to which social reconstructionism trickled down to the classroom is more difficult to assess. Reconstructionists succeeded in creating a lively debate on the purposes of education, and contributed to increasing attention to the Problems of Democracy (POD) course and an emerging focus on social problems as the high point of the curriculum. Despite this growing attention, course texts for POD continued to embody a somewhat disjointed, piecemeal, meliorist approach rather than looking at the pattern of unequal power relationships which educational reconstructionism called forth. However, on the whole it appears, the impact of reconstructionism on the educational mainstream was somewhat limited. In part, this was because many teachers feared community reaction. One survey found that only 5.6% of superintendents and 11.6% of teachers believed that students should be led to enter discussions on reform and social issues, and 82% of teachers agreed that "educators should avoid partisanship" (Tyack et al., 1985, p. 67). Given these attitudes on the part of the vast majority of teachers, the prospects for success were slim.

As we have seen, Rugg's ideas on social reconstructionism were critiqued for their frequent use of vague terms and generalities, and for their lack of originality. His vision was also described variously as elitist and undemocratic, overly optimistic, unrealistic, impractical, enigmatic, simplistic, over generalized, and naive. In addition, Rugg was frequently criticized for offering a lack of concrete detail and for his utopian approach to questions of political power, which ignored the influence of pressure groups.

One respected contemporary of Rugg's who might have critiqued many of his ideas, and who did offer a progressive counterpoint to social reconstructionism in general, was the father of progressive education himself, John Dewey. Dewey was probably the most influential critic of reconstructionism. It was not that Dewey was totally opposed to the notion that schools should play a role in changing the society, but Dewey's view of the process was markedly different from that of Rugg and other reconstructionists (Stanley, 1992). Dewey advocated "the method of intelligence" as the best means for transforming society, arguing that a failure to develop skills of critical and reflective thought would leave the population "at the mercy of propaganda, and drifting from one plan and scheme to another according to the loudest clamor of the moment" (Dewey, 1935b, p. 334).

Dewey agreed with Rugg that the school should have a social orientation. However, for Dewey, "It is not whether the schools shall or shall not influence the course of future social life, but in what direction they shall do so and how" (Dewey, 1937, p. 236). Certainly, to some extent, Dewey embraced the reconstructionist impulse. However, Dewey did not go so far as Rugg, Counts, and many other reconstructionists in spelling out the kind of social order that was desirable, or in advocating means to that end, beyond the method of intelligence. He tended to limit his statements to broad generalities such as his famous vision of a society "worthy, lovely, and harmonious," (Dewey, 1899) or his statement, with John Childs, supporting, "a better, more just, a more open and straight forward, a more public society" (Dewey & Childs, 1933b, p. 318).

Dewey's method of intelligence was, as he saw it, a process that would help the society clarify and achieve desirable social ends. However, the method of intelligence itself recommended no particular social end except preservation of conditions under which the method of intelligence would itself survive and be applied to a variety of questions. The method of intelligence was grounded in empiricism and aimed at drawing tentative conclusions. Going much beyond that would amount to indoctrination.

Dewey did not agree with reconstructionist critics who attacked his instrumentalism as neutral, aloof, or "purely intellectual." He believed that his method "cannot fail ... to support a new general social orientation" (Dewey, 1935a, p. 9). And argued that the method of intelligence would, if allowed to run its course, lead to an improved social order. In making a case against indoctrination, Dewey wrote:

> The upholders of indoctrination rest their adherence to the theory, in part, upon the fact that there is a great deal of indoctrination now going on in the schools, especially with reference to narrow nationalism under the name of

patriotism, and with reference to the dominant economic regime. These facts, unfortunately, are facts. But they do not prove that the right course is to seize upon the method of indoctrination and reverse its object (Dewey, 1937, p. 238).

Dewey held to a more extreme definition of indoctrination than that expressed by Rugg, Counts or other leading reconstructionists. He defined indoctrination as "systematic use of every possible means to impress upon [students] a particular set of ... views to the exclusion of every other" (1937, p. 238). The only form of indoctrination Dewey supported was to assert that the method of intelligence was the preferred approach to education. He wrote, "If the method we have recommended leads teachers and students to better conclusions than those which we have reached—as it surely will if widely and honestly adopted—so much the better" (Dewey & Childs, 1933a, p. 72).

George Counts, on the other hand, seemed to support a version of indoctrination which was quite a bit stronger than anything Rugg might have endorsed, with his open declaration that schools should seek to impose on students certain values, attitudes, and ways of thinking. Counts believed that some form of cultural and ideological imposition was inevitable, and wrote:

> The real question is not whether some tradition will be imposed by intent or circumstance upon the coming generation (we may rest assured that this will be done), but rather what particular tradition will be imposed. To refuse to face the task of the selection or the fashioning of this tradition is to evade the most crucial, difficult, and important educational responsibility (Counts, 1932b).

If education was to make a significant contribution to the cause of human freedom, to development of democracy, and even more importantly in the depression era, to democratic collectivism, it had to be designed for that purpose. At the same time, Counts shared Dewey's faith in education for growth, supported application of the scientific method in schools, and favored a similar open-endedness in the process of education. Counts, Rugg, and Dewey agreed that the school could contribute to building the new social order, they agreed that the nature of this new social order would be collectivistic, and they expressed their support for the method of free scientific inquiry and consideration of all relevant views and evidence in schools. The nub of difference apparently centered on whether free inquiry could proceed unhampered in light of a prior commitment to democratic collectivism, and possibly, on the extent to which that commitment would discolor creation of a thoughtful and open-ended curriculum.

Rugg never explicitly supported a program of indoctrination and would not have supported any deliberate suppression or distortion of information. He frequently insisted on free and open access, consideration of all available evidence, and deliberation over a range of perspectives. However, Rugg's social science pamphlets and textbook series did not fully live up to his stated ideal and provided a selection based on the work of those Rugg considered to be "frontier thinkers." Some years later, Boyd H. Bode, in a letter to John Dewey, suggested that Rugg sometimes failed to live up to the balance required by free inquiry under the method of intelligence. He wrote that he was "darkly suspicious" of some attempts to develop theory, and wrote, "To quote Harold Rugg: 'Let the facts speak for themselves.' In other words, let us pick out a body of facts in a given area of presentation, and then build theory on these facts" (Bode, 1950).

Somewhat different criticisms of social reconstructionism were voiced many years later by educational historian C. A. Bowers. Bowers offered four central critiques of social reconstructionism. First, he argued that it tended to promote a "ubiquitous sense of mission" which often led advocates of reconstructionism to obscure or overlook the need for critical analysis of certain key issues. Second, he viewed social reconstructionism as naively utopian in its belief that education could reform society and solve social problems. Third, Bowers argued that reconstructionists tended to uncritically assume that the majority of citizens really did seek the good life. Finally, the reconstructionist's view of the potential role of teachers and schools in society was unrealistic, and overestimated both the power and inclination of teachers (Bowers, 1969).

As for Rugg, many of Bower's criticisms are on target. His use of the work of the "frontier thinkers" led him to offer a set of materials that was extensive and well grounded but which lacked full balance. His naiveté was evident in the lack of details contained in the social vision he described in *The Great Technology* and other works, and in the general lack of sophistication revealed in his projections of what was possible via the political process. Finally, Rugg's view of the potential for teachers and schools to serve at the vanguard of reform failed to take account of the facts about teachers lives, that most teachers are overworked, underpaid, and tend to teach as they were taught, in fairly traditional ways.

Despite these rather obvious failings, Rugg's vision set off in a worthy direction and offered hope and inspiration to many during a time in which American civilization was on trial as never before. It is a truism that most educators, if not all, hope that schooling will help to improve society. That truism opens the gateway to many ideologies in pursuit of the goal of social improvement, some more strident than others. Rugg's vision for the future of schooling and society was predicated on hopefulness for a better tomorrow. The many strengths of his ideas, proposals, and materials for improving schools and society have left a lasting legacy, and serve as an inspiration to like-minded educators and as a call to those who would assist schools in fulfilling their ultimate promise.

Rugg's vision, and his highest hope for social studies instruction in schools is perhaps best captured by one teacher who used the Rugg program, who wrote:

> suppose the citizenry of today—the men and women who went to the polls in November, 1934, and who were taught by methods then in vogue, let us say, thirty years ago—had learned in school to reason upon contemporary social matters instead of learning the qualifications of congressmen and the terms of office of state functionaries. Suppose that in school they had become accustomed to examining their prejudices instead of memorizing capes and bays. Suppose that in school they had exercised critical judgment concerning our country's problems instead of accepting the conclusions of a race of historians too jingoistic to be truthful. Then what?
>
> Under such circumstances presumably we might expect a political campaign to be less emotional, but saner and vastly more likely to help in the solution of problems....
>
> These are considerations of some moment. In connection with the social order of the next few years the school-teacher of today is in a strategic position. He has some important decisions to make. Among these not the least important are his decisions with reference to the study in his school of the origin and development of human society. (Buckingham, 1935, p. 84)

RUGG'S PEDAGOGY

The central theme of this chapter has been the evolution of Rugg's social ideas and the flowering of his version of education for social reconstruction. Rugg's pedagogical vision, though largely constant, went through a slight transformation as well, with development of a more explicit focus on education for social reconstructionism. Examining Rugg's social studies curricular ideas and the materials produced during the decade of the 1920s leaves one wondering how they could have eventually generated such controversy. However, much of the controversy regarding Rugg was initially fomented by his scholarly writings and public speeches, rather than his textbooks and materials designed for school children. Nonetheless, Rugg's own statements of his curricular vision demonstrate a subtle shift. After 1930, Rugg's social reconstructionism was full blown, and his depictions of his scheme for social studies, while relatively constant, reflected that shift to some extent. His rhetoric went further than mere "educational reconstruction" and employed the phrase "social reconstruction" with regularity. Moreover, his social studies program went beyond a unified course that emphasized issues and problems and was now focused on "The American Problem" (Rugg, 1939). The aim was encapsulated most clearly and succinctly in Rugg's 1939 statement, "Curriculum-Design in the Social Sciences: What I Believe...." In this article, Rugg stated a clear and explicit goal and rationale:

> As the years have passed I have become convinced that the life and program of the school, like the life of American democracy itself, must be focused and given motive power by a great purpose ... (like) a religion ... a driving purpose so clear and magnetic that thousands of teachers and millions of parents and youth will be energized by it. I have tried many leads but none had been so helpful ... as The American Problem! What is it? To bring forth on this continent—in some form of co-operative commonwealth—the civilization of abundance, democratic behavior, and integrity of expression and of appreciation which is now potentially available. To gather together the makings of the great society that are at hand, and to organize them into a going national concern that will produce economic abundance, democracy and beauty—that is the problem of our times. (Rugg, 1939, pp. 140-141)

CONCLUSION

As we have seen, social reconstructionism was not a new idea when it burst upon the scene in the 1930s. Progressives in education and in the society had held visions of social improvement for many decades and conceived of schools as an institution that would play an integral part in the creation of a better society. However, the brand of social reconstructionism advocated by Rugg, Counts and others among the *Social Frontier* group was a potent mix of ideas, expressed in starker language than the softer reconstructionism that had come before. In the case of Rugg, social reconstructionism was the means by which to transform the industrial world, with all its readily transparent flaws, a world in the throes of conflict, into a new democratic and technocratic collectivist society in which rational order, peace, and social justice would prevail. The abundance now available as a product of increasing automation and growing industrialism would be shared by all in a new tomorrow. Just how this would all transpire remained a bit vague. Moreover, there were unresolved tensions around the nature of social education for social reconstructionism. Were certain social visions to be cast in favorable light, while others would be portrayed in less flattering terms? To what extent would teachers and textbook authors explicitly share their social, cultural, and political ideologies? Was there a preferred vision? If so, how would other alternatives, including the present system, with all its problems, be portrayed? How would the method of intelligence be used in the classroom? Was it contradictory to frame inquiry within any particular social vision, no matter how general?

The ultimate answers to these questions go right to the heart of the process of education, its meaning and purposes. Tension, and open conflict swirled about these questions during the decade of the 1930s, instigated by progressive and reconstructionist visionaries such as Rugg, Counts, and others. Though final answers remain elusive, an answer of sorts developed during the late 1930s and came to a head during the early years of the Second World War. As we shall see, many Americans wanted no part of the progressive vision of democratic collectivism and were not shy about using whatever means in their power to make their views known.

REFERENCES

Allling, K. (2005, January 20). Interview with Katharine Alling, stepdaughter of Harold Rugg, conducted by the author.

AHA Committee. (1929). Meeting of the Sub-Committee on Objectives, The American Historical Association Commission on the Social Sciences in the Schools, Krey Papers, as cited by E. A. Winters. (1968). *Harold Rugg and education for social reconstructionism*. Unpublished doctoral dissertation, University of Wisconsin, p. 116.

Akin, W. E. (1977). *Technocracy and the American dream*. Berkeley: University of California Press.

Beard, C. A. (1932). *A charter for the social sciences in the schools*. New York: Charles Scribner's Sons.

Bird, C. (1932). Engineering Our Way Out of Depression Trenches. *Public Ledger*, Rugg Textbook Controversy Scrapbook, Rauner Archives, Dartmouth University.

Bode, B. H. (1950). Boyd H. Bode to John Dewey, November 20, 1950, accession #12359, correspondence, box 23, series 2, John Dewey Papers, Southern Illinois University, Carbondale.

Bowers, C. A. (1969). *The progressive educator and the depression: The radical years*. New York: Random House.

Brooks, V. W. (1915). *America's coming of age*. New York: B. W. Huebsh.

Buckingham, B. R. (1935). *The Rugg course in the classroom*. Boston: Ginn.

Carbone, P. F. (1977). *The social and educational thought of Harold Rugg*. Durham, NC: Duke University Press.

Commission on Social Studies of the American Historical Association. (1934). *Conclusions and recommendations*. New York: Charles Scribner's Sons.

Counts, G. S. (1932a). *Dare the school build a new social order?* New York: John Day.

Counts, G. S. (1932b). Theses on freedom, culture, and social planning and leadership, *National Education Association Proceedings, 70*, 249.

Dennis, L. (1933, May 27). Is capitalism doomed? *Saturday Review of Literature, 9,* 615.

Dewey, J. (1897). Ethical principles underlying education. *National Herbart Society Third Yearbook.* Chicago: University of Chicago Press.

Dewey, J. (1899). *The school and society.* Chicago: University of Chicago Press.

Dewey, J. (1916). *Democracy and education.* New York: Macmillan.

Dewey, J. (1935a). The crucial role of intelligence. *The Social Frontier, 1*(5), 9-10.

Dewey, J. (1935b). The need for orientation. *Forum, 93*(6), 333-335.

Dewey, J. (1937). Education and social change. *The Social Frontier, 3*(26), 235-238.

Dewey, J., & Childs, J. L. (1933a). The social-economic situation and education. In W. H. Kilpatrick (Ed.), *Educational frontier* (pp. 32-72). New York: Appleton-Century.

Dewey, J., & Childs, J. L. (1933b). The underlying philosophy of education. In W. H. Kilpatrick (Ed.), *Educational frontier* (pp. 287-320). New York: Appleton-Century.

Dilling, E. K. (1934). *The red network: A "who's who" and handbook of radicalism for patriots.* Kenilworth, IL: Author.

Eames, M. (1934, February). Creating the "Great Technology": An interview with Harold Rugg. *Independent Woman, 8,* 53-55.

Evers, A. (1987). *Woodstock: History of an American town.* Woodstock, NY: Overlook.

Hook, S. (1933). Review of *The Great Technology,* Sidney Hook papers, Hoover Institution, Stanford University.

Hopkins, C. H. (1940). *The rise of the social gospel in American Protestantism, 1865-1915.* New Haven, CT: Yale University Press.

Kilpatrick, W. H. (n.d.). Oral history interview with William H. Kilpatrick, Oral History Office, Rare Book and Manuscript Library, Butler Library, Columbia University.

Kilpatrick, W. H. (1951). William H. Kilpatrick to Harold Rugg, April 16, 1951. *Harold Rugg: Letters in appreciation of his frontier work.* Unpublished manuscript. New York: Teachers College.

Krug, E. A. (1972). *The shaping of the American high school: Volume 2, 1920-1940.* Madison: University of Wisconsin Press.

Moseley, N. (1936). Content and conduct of teachers' conventions. *Progressive Education, 13,* 337-339.

NEA Committee, Department of Superintendence. (1934). Our social-economic situation and the new education. *Journal of Educational Sociology, 7*(9), 533-544.

Nelson, M. R., & Singleton, H. W. (1977). *FBI surveillance of three progressive educators: Curricular aspects.* Paper presented at the Society for the Study of Curriculum History, Annual Conference.

Ogburn, W. (1922). *Social change with respect to culture and original nature.* New York: B. W. Huebsch.

Phillips, M. (1961). *The seven arts and Harold Rugg.* Unpublished masters thesis, Columbia University.

Price, M. E. (1983). *A thousand year march: The historical vision of Harold Rugg.* Paper presented at the annual meeting of the National Council for the Social Studies, San Francisco, CA.

Raymond, A. (1933). *What is technocracy?* New York: Whittlesey House.

Reed, J. L. (1975). *The newest whore of Babylon: The emergence of technocracy, a study in the mechanization of man.* Boston: Branden Press.

Renney, O. (1934, March). School heads plan pressure on Roosevelt. *Cleveland Press.*

Rudd, A. G., Hicks, H., & Falk, A. T. (Ed.). (1941). *Undermining our republic: Do you know what the children are being taught in our public schools? You'll be surprised.* New York: Guardians of American Education.

Rugg, H. O. (1921, May). Needed changes in the committee procedure of reconstructing the social studies. *Elementary School Journal, 21,* 688-702.

Rugg, H. O. (Ed.). (1923). Problems of contemporary life as the basis for curriculum-making in the social studies. In *The social studies in the elementary and secondary school.* National Society for the Study of Education. Twenty-Second Yearbook, National Society for the Study of Education, Part II (pp. 260-273). Bloomington, IL: Public School Publishing.

Rugg, H. O. (1931). *Culture and education in America.* New York: Harcourt, Brace.

Rugg, H. O. (1932-1933). Social reconstruction through education. *Progressive Education, 9 & 10, 8 & 1*(December and January), 11-18.

Rugg, H. O. (1933). *The great technology: Social chaos and the public mind.* New York: John Day.

Rugg, H. O. (1939). The social studies: What I believe .... In J. A. Michener (Ed.), *The future of the social studies.* Washington, DC: National Council for the Social Studies.

Rugg, H. O. (1941). *That men may understand: An American in the long armistice.* New York: Doubleday, Doran.

Rugg, H. O. (1943). *Now is the moment.* New York: Duell, Sloan and Pearce.

Rugg, H. O. (1949). Harold Rugg to John Dewey on the occasion of Dewey's 90th birthday, October 20, 1949, Accession # 11679, John Dewey Papers, 20/6. In J. Dewey. *Collected Works.* Carbondale, IL: Southern Illinois University.

Rugg, H. O., & Herring, J. W. (1933). *A proposal to establish a national clearing house for social-economic education.* Unpublished proposal. Washington, DC: Progressive Education Association.

Rugg, H. O., & Krueger, M. (1933). *Social reconstruction: Study guide for group and class discussion.* New York: John Day.

Scott, H. (1933). *Introduction to technocracy.* New York: John Day.

Shumaker, R. W. (1941, April). No "new order" for our schools. *American Legion Magazine,* pp. 5-7, 43-46.

Stanley, W. B. (1992). *Curriculum for utopia: Social reconstructionism and critical pedagogy in the postmodern era.* Albany: State University of New York Press.

Technocracy. (1932). Flyer attached to letter from George S. Counts to Sidney Hook, August 22, 1932, "George Counts" folder, box 10, folder 26, correspondence, Sidney Hook Papers, Hoover Institution, Stanford University.

Technocracy, Inc. (2006). http://www.technocracy.org/

Tyack, D., Hansot, E., & Lowe, R. (1985). *Public schools in hard times.* Cambridge, MA: Harvard University Press.

Veblen, T. (1921). *The engineers and the price system.* New York: Viking.

CHAPTER 5

THE GATHERING STORM

During the late 1930s and early 1940s Rugg and his textbook series were engulfed in a crisis brought by an unprecedented level of attack. Textbooks had come under attack before. This was not the first instance, but seemed one more episode in a continuing cycle of criticism and censorship aimed at schools. From the perspective of social studies educators, it turned out to be the most dramatic and pointed controversy ever seen over the issue of curricular control and the question, "Who will determine what the schools teach, and to what end?" (Propaganda Analysis, 1941) On one side were teachers, administrators, and allied organizations who generally favored progressive forms of social studies. On the other were nonschool groups including business organizations and patriotic societies who typically favored a school curriculum dominated by traditional history. At stake was a contest over what form social studies would take and whose version of the American way would be presented to children in schools.

The first of a series of attacks on educators and textbooks took place shortly after the end of the First World War. Beginning with the summer of 1921, Hearst newspapers began attacks against textbooks which included interpretations from the "new historians" in textbooks by David S. Muzzey, Charles Beard and other prominent scholars. Muzzey's high school textbook, *An American History*, was widely used at the time and bore the brunt of the attack. Throughout the early years of the 1920s there were continued intermittent attacks on other authors and textbooks.

This Happened in Ameica: Harold Rugg and the Censure of Social Studies
pp. 143–201
Copyright © 2007 by Information Age Publishing
All rights of reproduction in any form reserved.

However, the logic and focus of the attacks during the 1920s was dramatically different than the rationale for the critiques which engulfed the Rugg books, partially reflecting the changing emphasis of public concern. Muzzey was criticized for portraying the American Revolution in pro-British terms. Indeed, much of the textbook criticism of the 1920s was centered around ethnic xenophobia. By the 1930s, however, the focus of patriotic textbook critics had shifted to economic matters, with intense criticism of anything disparaging of capitalism or that portrayed communism in a favorable light.

Several contextual factors separated the Rugg controversy from those which had occurred previously. The new approach to social studies promoted by progressives and by the National Council for the Social Studies was beginning to make serious inroads on traditional history in schools. During the late 1930s, progressive social studies itself was on trial. Moreover, textbook critics saw themselves as defenders of the American way of life against textbooks that offered critiques of capitalism, which critics held as central to the American way. Business leaders were prone to view schools as gone astray, threatened by a "conspiracy of subversives" and in the hands of left-leaning professors and teachers. Then there was the threat from abroad, with the rise of dictatorships in Europe. By 1940, with the end of the period of phony war, and the fall of Paris and the low countries, the nation was entering a time when fears and concerns were reaching fever pitch. All of these factors combined to spark a textbook controversy of unusual force and intensity.

Attention to social issues and the idea of social reconstruction through education that lay behind it also generated a good deal of opposition from conservative groups who wanted schools to continue to teach in the old ways, to teach, "My country right or wrong." Though the Rugg case was most prominent, he was by no means alone. Opponents emerged to condemn virtually anything critical of American society. By the mid-1930s a broad array of academic freedom issues and cases emerged as a consequence of these trends. If the pages of *The Social Studies* were any indication, academic freedom concerns reached a high point in 1935. The section of the journal titled, "Recent Happenings in the Social Studies," suddenly filled with reports of academic freedom resolutions, conferences on academic freedom, infiltration of PTAs by ultra-patriotic groups, imposition of loyalty oaths, and stories of intellectual lynchings. One of the more famous cases was that of Victor Jewett, a junior high social studies teacher who was singled out for censure in Eureka, California. Jewett was said to have, "criticized the government while extolling the Russian government, belittled great men of American history, received money from Russia for spreading propaganda in the local schools, engaged actively in the lumber strike and made inflammatory addresses at union meetings, and was seen in the company of pickets of the lumber workers union." Despite having taught social studies for five years, Jewett was transferred to teach mathematics, and later suspended from teaching altogether. A sober-minded observer in California noted: "Californians interested in education, justice, and civil liberties ... are witnessing with increasing alarm the growing tide of terror, repression, and violence which is sweeping even the respectable guardians of our most sacred institutions" (Staff, 1935, pp. 482-83).

Hearst newspapers were responsible for many of the academic freedom battles of the times, or at least for fanning the flames. The Hearst syndicate generally reported charges against the schools in the most inflammatory language and in a prominent place in their papers. In 1935, several leaders in American education called on a government committee, the McCormick-Dickstein Committee, to investigate "a campaign of terrorism against teachers in American Colleges, universities, schools, and even private schools." The leaders, including Beard, Counts, Kilpatrick, Bagley, and others based their accusation in part on a ploy by two Hearst reporters who posed as prospective university students at Syracuse and Teachers College in an attempt to secure information regarding "radical" professors (Kappan, 1935, pp. 106-107). The "red scare" campaign was launched partly in response to the Report of the AHA Commission on Social Studies, and news of the publication of the *Social Frontier*, a journal believed to be aimed at bringing the social reconstructionist recommendations of the commission into the school curriculum of the nation.

During the 1930s and 1940s the media was generally in bed with industrialists. It was an era during which the press had to watch what it printed. There was little expose of the National Association of Manufacturers or of native Fascists. The 1935 red-baiting campaign was largely led by the Hearst papers. In their coverage of education, they called "liberal" education, "red" (Seldes, 1938, p. 231). Though the Hearst media empire ranked number one as America's "worst" newspaper, and was called "least fair and reliable" in a survey of public attitudes, a number of other chains were not far behind in their bias and tendency toward sensationalism (Seldes, 1947). Moreover, according to surveys, newspaper and magazine circulation reached a new all-time high by 1941 (Brandenburg, 1941; "Magazine gains," 1941).

In schools, the decade of the 1930s saw the rapid growth of issues-oriented approaches. Developments included the rapid and voluminous sale of the Rugg materials, growing attention to the Problems of Democracy course, increased curricular attention to controversial issues and social problems, plans for the infusion of current topics and issues in discipline-based curricula, and integrated or core curricula that centered on problem-topics or issues. The pages of social studies journals saw a steady growth in articles devoted to various aspects of teaching social problems, relating a variety of successful plans, procedures, and approaches to teaching the modern problems course. Several gave attention to the rationale behind the study of problems, and the problem method of organization. Others indicated serious consideration of difficulties and unresolved issues relating to the course. A few were critical and called for instruction in the social science disciplines in order to avoid superficiality, or a "grab bag" approach. However, the vast majority of articles were supportive, and sought either to win converts or simply to improve practice. By the late 1930s, the number of articles devoted to instruction centered on social problems had grown to the point that it was one of the dominant ongoing themes of social studies scholarship and discourse (Evans, 2004).

CRITICISM AND ATTACKS

Early criticisms of the Rugg social studies materials foreshadowed what would transpire during the late 1930s and early 1940s. One of the earliest attacks occurred during the 1924-1925 period. The second edition of the Social Science Pamphlets was being used in Bayonne, New Jersey, a "Standard Oil Town." One of the pamphlets contained an illustration of a man working for the company and included the caption, "working on a job of this kind reduces your life 20 years." Fearing a reaction, and aware that Standard Oil was paying more than $1 million a year in local taxes, Preston H. Smith, the superintendent, threw the series out of the school.

Then, in April, 1927, the first concerted attack took place, when Otis Caldwell, director of the Lincoln School, received a large packet in the mail from a major corporation, United States Steel, describing the pamphlets as "subversive and un-American." Rugg and associates prepared a defense, and after a 3-hour luncheon with company officials the controversy was resolved (Winters, 1968, pp. 136-37).

As we have seen, Rugg's writings underwent a shift in the early 1930s with more pointed advocacy of social reconstructionism and the goal of moving toward some form of "collectivism." It was primarily these writings and subsequent media coverage of his speaking engagements which attracted the attention of self-appointed censors to Rugg's work. Success and affiliation with unpopular causes combined to make him a target for criticism. Rugg had strongly supported a number of movements that were out of favor with his critics including progressive education, technocracy, and teachers unions. Moreover, his reputation as a "bohemian" gained through association with the Greenwich Village crowd all but invited attack. Finally, Rugg was quite vocal and open in sharing his opinions on the capitalist system.

After Rugg's appearance at a 1933 conference sponsored by the *New York Herald-Tribune* at which Rugg commented favorably on the work of youth groups in Russia, his remarks were reprinted in *The Daily Worker*, newpaper of the Communist Party of America. Despite the fact that this was done without Rugg's knowledge or approval, it was apparently sufficient for Rugg's inclusion in *The Red Network: A Who's Who of Radicalism for Patriots*, published in 1934 by Elizabeth Dilling, a self-described "Super-Expert-Patriot," a crusader against Communism, and a favorite of both patriotic organizations and fundamentalist Christians (Mayer, 1939). The book, which received widespread, at cost distribution to patriotic societies, listed 460 suspected organizations, including the National Education Association (NEA), and it mentioned some 1,300 persons, including John Dewey and many of his progressive colleagues (Dilling, 1934). It is estimated that *The Red Network* ultimately reached over 100,000 readers. Though the listing of Rugg seemed to have little immediate effect, it was referenced frequently in subsequent attacks.

Another incident occurred in 1935 in the Washington, D.C., area which involved the Rugg books. A "red rider" was attached to the 1935 appropriations bill for the District of Columbia stating that no funds could be used to pay the salary of "any person teaching or advocating Communism." The American Legion wanted this interpreted to prevent teachers in the schools from even discussing communism and appealed to the United States Comptroller General, John Raymond McCarl, who ordered all employees of the District public schools to sign an oath to that effect.

Shortly after publication of *The Red Network*, and a few months after Congress had required all Washington, DC, teachers to take a loyalty oath, swearing that they had not "taught or advocated Communism," an attack on the Rugg textbook series occurred in June of 1935. The Federation of Citizens Associations of the District of Columbia, a consortium organized by the American Legion, requested that the local school board remove two of Rugg's books, and one by historian Carl Becker.

Amos A. Fries, a graduate of West Point and former major general who had served under General John "Blackjack" Pershing during World War One and was charged with organizing the Chemical Warfare Service, headed the federation behind the controversy. After the war he had served as chief officer for the Chemical Warfare until his retirement in 1929. Upon retirement, Fries and his wife Elizabeth, devoted their energies to promoting conservative patriotism. In 1935 it was Fries who spearheaded the attempt to "ban the teaching of communism" in Washington, D.C., schools. He organized the Friends of the Public Schools of America, Inc., and he and Elizabeth edited the *Friends of the Public Schools Bulletin*, which continually warned against "subversive influences" in education. Fries once wrote an essay arguing that the communist fights against chemical warfare "because he cannot cope with it" and because "turned loose down a street filled with communists (gas) will make every last one of them helpless and open to capture by a few soldiers with gas masks" (Fries, n.d. a, p. 3). He viewed Rugg and Counts as communists and argued that their brand of "collectivism" was little more than a euphemism for communist rule (Fries, n.d. b, p. 1, 3).

Fries and other critics trained most of their venom on Becker's portrayal of the Russian revolution, but also wanted Rugg's books removed partly because of his allusion to Russian "accomplishments" in public health and recreation. Fries argued before the school board that nothing should be left to discretion when dealing with communism, and that "children should be taught what to think about communism" as a form of "protective teaching" ("Communism foes," 1935). After an investigation, a district-appointed committee declared, on December 18, 1935, that neither of the books in question "taught nor advocated Communism," and the request was denied.

There is little doubt that at least some of the animus toward Rugg was a reflection, if not a creation, of his own actions and bold personality. During 1935 Rugg spoke out against American Legion attempts to censor *Scholastic* magazine. He accused the Legion of "trying to block the scientific study of society," and suggested they would "deport all who disseminate disruptive ideas" ("Patrioteers," 1935). He charged that the Legion's policy was contrary to "the American way of teaching" and dangerous to teacher's freedoms ("Education Policy," 1935). For the balance of the decade, in a series of major speeches, Rugg attacked patriotic societies and business organizations including the Advertising Federation of America, the National Association of Manufacturers, the United States Chamber of Commerce, and even the New Deal itself. His comments and outspoken views critical of the Legion and other groups had the effect of making him the chief target of their attacks.

THE AMERICAN LEGION CAMPAIGN

The sustained campaign against the Rugg books by the American Legion was inaugurated by another former military man, U.S. Army Major Augustin G. Rudd, retired, now general manager of the Newsreel Theaters, New York. Rudd was a resident of Garden City, New York, on Long Island, and father of three school-age children. His interest in the Rugg books came about when, in conversations with his children, Rudd discovered that they were being taught in school that American institutions were but a passing phase of development, and that they would be replaced in the not too distant future by a form of government in which capitalistic ownership of property would disappear. He also found, to his shock, that history, geography, and civics had disappeared as separate subjects and that "a whole new set of concepts and doctrines had been bootlegged into the school curriculum" (Kuhn, 1958, p. 38). He then examined the books and other related works in some detail. When he found that they were being used widely, and that they were popular on a nationwide basis, he decided to take action. In support of his efforts, Rudd later stated that he had "given six months of constant effort and research to unraveling, so that anyone could see, the amazing ramifications and plans of the radical teachers stemming originally from Teachers College in Columbia University, to complete communistic and other subversive teachings in our public schools" (Jones, 1957, p. 9).

Rudd launched his campaign against the Rugg textbook series on January 22, 1938, in an address delivered to the school board in Garden City, New York, titled, "Communism and other Subversive Doctrines in American Public Schools," in which he asked the board to remove the Rugg books (Jones, 1957, pp. 10-11). Following his address, the board decided to replace the Rugg books with other texts.

As a Legionaire, it occurred to Rudd that he might wield greatest influence by making his critique of Rugg and the frontier group available to the National Headquarters of the American Legion for publication and nationwide distribution. In early 1938, Rudd sent a copy of his address before the Garden City School Board to Stephen F. Chadwick, National Commander of the American Legion, and urged the Legion to launch a wider assault on the Rugg books. After a year had passed, and the Legion failed to take official action on his suggestion, Rudd's former commander, Major General J. G. Harbord, United States Army, Retired, wrote a follow-up letter to Chadwick, in February of 1939, in which he urged the Legion to take action on Rudd's request (Harbord, 1939).

Chadwick responded that he would be "most interested" and suggested that the Legion might be able to assist in distributing Rudd's speeches via their mimeographing system and mailing them to all of the Legion's department officers. He also stated that the Legion's Americanism commission would be interested and noted that the Legion had Americanism committees in 11,300 posts nationwide (Chadwick, 1939).

Major Rudd then forwarded copies of his addresses to Commander Chadwick with additional comments detailing the "subversive" nature of the Rugg textbooks. Rudd intimated that he had refrained from circulating his addresses until the Legion "had a chance to consider it." He offered the material to the Legion, "if it will be handled in the comprehensive manner the importance of the subject deserves" and urged that the Legion "bring it home to parents in every state of the Union" (Rudd,

1939a). In a followup letter, sent the next month, Rudd outlined his hope for a national media campaign, led by the Legion's national office, to rid the schools of the Rugg textbooks, and suggested that, "although the direction should be national, the work must largely be done locally." He recommended that each post investigate the situation in its local schools and take the appropriate action. Rudd concluded his letter with the following appeal: "My idea is that the issue is big enough, and time right to give the thing both barrels from the beginning. I think you will be surprised at the support coming to you" (Rudd, 1939b).

Following review of Rudd's speeches and proposal by the national commander and by the Education Committee of the Americanism Division, Rudd was informed, in a letter from H. L. Chaillaux, that the Legion's Americanism Commission "could not place the material in proper form for wide distribution. Such a plan would not be within the province or the practice of our organization." Also, Chaillaux indicated that the Legion could "in no manner adopt the policy of publicizing in book form the objections to the writings of any one individual or group when there may be many others whose views we do not share" (Chaillaux, 1939a).

His plan rebuffed by the Legion's leadership, Rudd decided to take action at the local level that could force the hand of the national leadership. He introduced a resolution at a meeting of the William Bradford Turner Post #265, in his home town of Garden City, again condemning the Rugg social science course but adding his request, "that The Legion make a national investigation of the Rugg social science courses and report the facts of this condition to the American people." The resolution was passed unanimously by his local post, and later by the Nassau County and State of New York branches of the Legion. The resolution then went to the National Headquarters in Indianapolis, Indiana. It was passed by delegates at the National Convention of the Legion in 1939 and National Commander Stephen F. Chadwick ordered that the program of investigation at the local level begin immediately (Jones, 1957, p. 15).

Following this vote, the director of the National Americanism Commission of the Legion, Homer L. Chaillaux, sent a short questionnaire to local posts in the United States which asked the following questions:

Do your schools teach history, geography and civics as separate subjects under their respective names?

Do your schools teach social sciences (sic.) courses, including parts of history, geography and civics?

Do your schools use Harold Rugg's Social Science courses? In which grades?

Name textbooks, if any, in your schools which you consider un-American or subversive. Also the author and publisher (Chaillaux, 1939b).

The Legion posts were instructed to gather this information from their local schools, along with any other information that might be useful, and return it to the National Americanism Commission director. Many posts across the nation began collecting the information and some initiated pressure on local school boards and administrators to eliminate the Rugg textbooks. However, it appeared that the results were somewhat meager due in part to the lack of personnel at the national headquarters needed to follow up the questionnaire. Nonetheless, the first major steps had been taken, and the foundation for a national campaign, waged on multiple fronts against the Rugg textbooks, had been built.

THE CAMPAIGN SPREADS

During 1939 a number of other organizations and individuals became involved in attacks on the Rugg textbooks. Among them were Alfred T. Falk and the Advertising Federation of America, Bertie C. Forbes, publisher of *Forbes* magazine and a new member of the Englewood, New Jersey Board of Education, and Merwin K. Hart, president of the New York State Economic Council. Though the attacks against Rugg and his social studies textbooks appeared to mushroom overnight, in the case of several critics there had been a long build up. Amos Fries had been working at textbook criticism for several years, as had several other committed textbook censors. Also, in each case, the critics of Rugg's textbooks knew of and read each other's work, corresponded occasionally, frequently shared materials and resources, and sometimes sponsored joint meetings.

The Advertising Federation of America, led by Alfred T. Falk, attacked the books for carrying "anti-advertising propaganda," and garnered national media attention. Falk was one of the directors of the Advertising Federation and authored a widely circulated pamphlet titled "Does Advertising Harm or Benefit Consumers?" The pamphlet was distributed in April, 1939, to members of the Advertising Federation and to newspaper editors, accompanied by a letter from Norman R. Rose, president. The letter stated, in part:

> The Advertising federation is fighting this threat. We are campaigning vigorously, nationally and in particular communities, for the expulsion of such books from the public schools.... A new crop of youngsters ... are being taught that advertising, as a whole, is harmful and should perhaps be eliminated.... Whatever the implications about the free enterprise system ... your own interests are being threatened. (Rose, 1939)

The Falk brochure analyzed Rugg's treatment of advertising in a chapter of *Problems of American Culture*. According to Falk, Rugg provided students with a misleading picture of business and taught that advertising was detrimental to consumers interests. Falk refuted Rugg's statement that,"it cannot be denied that advertising has increased the cost of both selling and of buying goods" (Falk, 1939, p. 10). The pamphlet was sent out widely along with the suggestion that those who received it should investigate textbooks in their own communities. Apparently Rugg did not consider Falk's effort to be very effective, as he later wrote, "We did not lose a single school as a result of this" (Rugg papers, n.d., cited in Kay, 1969).

Occurring at almost the same time as the situation was developing in Englewood, the activities of the Advertising Federation were written up in a *Time* magazine article which appeared on July 10, 1939. As reported in the article, at their annual convention in June the Advertising Federation decided to take action:

> This week the Federation urged its 60 affiliated groups to campaign against the use in school of textbooks which carry anti-advertising propaganda. With its message went a pamphlet attacking a text which the Federation considers particularly obnoxious: *An Introduction to the Problems of American Culture* by Professor Harold Rugg of Columbia Teachers College ("Propaganda Purge," 1939).

The Advertising Federation continued its campaign against Rugg into 1940 and simultaneously launched a fundraising effort to finance its crusade. The federation used textbook censorship as a wedge to enlist sustaining members who would make an annual pledge. Funds were used to support attacks on Rugg and to pay for a nationwide program of radio spots aimed at countering antiadvertising propaganda. In April, 1940, President Norman R. Rose sent a letter to large advertisers which began:

> Advertised products are untrustworthy! That is the lesson taught to the children in 4,200 school systems by a social science textbook of Professor Rugg.... Attacking business from every angle, Rugg sneers at the ideas and traditions of American democracy, making a subtle plea for abolition of our free enterprise system and the introduction of a new social order based on the principles of collectivism.... The Advertising Federation has made this its Number One Problem. (Rose, 1940)

The letter concluded with a strong plea for financial contributions in support of its campaign, resulting in a number of letters in response and monetary contributions. One advertising group announced through its local publications that it would "take over the censorship of all textbooks throughout the state," but one or two members of the association said they would resign immediately "if any such thing was done," and the local group tabled its plan (Advertising Groups, 1940). At least one advertiser was moved to write a letter of complaint about Rugg to Columbia University President Nicholas Murray Butler (Meredith, 1939). When queried by Dean William F. Russell of Teachers College regarding the letter, Rugg responded that the letter "does not deserve an answer" and noted that he had received several such letters following the attack on his books by the Advertising Federation of America (Rugg, 1939).

Another Rugg critic, Merwin K. Hart, an insurance executive and president of the New York State Economic Council, also entered the battle over the Rugg books in 1939. Hart addressed a number of conventions and meetings, and charged Rugg with making a "subtle sugar-coated" effort to convert youth to Communism, and with suggesting that capitalism, has been a "failure" and that "socialism should be substituted in its place" (Myers, 1940, p. 18).

Hart, a Harvard educated businessman from Utica, New York, had organized the New York State Economic Council which was dedicated to the twin goals of lowering taxes and reducing national government. Though Hart and his council had a good deal of support and memberships from businessmen throughout the state and region, perhaps his chief supporter was James H. Rand, president of the Remington Rand Company. Other donors to the Economic Council's funds included Lammot Du Pont, president of E. I. Du Pont, and a director of General Motors, A. W. Erickson, board chairman of a large New York advertising agency, Alfred P. Sloan, president of General Motors, and J. H. Alstyne, president of Otis Elevators. Thus, Hart's support was well-heeled and well-connected. In fact, Hart's supporters were among the wealthiest, most powerful families in the nation (Beals, 1941, p. 1). Though Hart denied being a Nazi, Nazi sympathizer, or Fascist, several of his close associates were all of these (Baldwin, 1940). Moreover, he was identified by a prominent journalist and others as a native Fascist (Seldes, 1943).

Hart became aware of the Rugg books after learning of the controversy surrounding them in 1939. Following his own investigation, he linked both Rugg and Rugg's textbooks to the American Historical Association's Commission on Social Studies. Hart read the AHA's *Conclusions and Recommendations* ("Commision," 1934) and concluded that it was "A Marxist document." After learning from a state school administrator that teachers are "very familiar with the book and its contents" and that it would be used in revising the state social studies syllabus, Hart was moved to action. From his own reading of the AHA report, Hart concluded that "Rugg and Counts worked up this report." He viewed *The Great Technology* as an amplification of *Conclusions and Recommendations* and apparently saw Rugg as an "assistant to Counts" in drafting that document. Thus, it appears that Hart's concerns were raised most pointedly by his reading of *Conclusions and Recommendations* which led directly to his attacks on Rugg and the Rugg textbooks (Hart, 1939). Hart reached these conclusions despite the fact that the AHA Commission failed to offer an endorsement for any particular social studies scope and sequence, and seemed, on the whole, to favor discipline-based curricula rather than the kind of fused and issues-oriented approach represented by Rugg.

Also among the most well publicized attacks, Bertie C. Forbes, in his own magazine, attacked the books in a brief article titled "Treacherous Teachings." He charged Rugg with being against private enterprise and urged boards of education to "cast out" the Rugg books (Forbes, 1939). From that point forward, Forbes activities against the Rugg textbooks focused on his attempt to oust them from the schools of Englewood, New Jersey.

A CHANGE OF CLIMATE

By the spring of 1940 the national climate had changed significantly. The Second World War had been underway in Europe for several months, and a number of concerned citizens had begun to publicize critiques of the Rugg textbooks. Among them, Augustin G. Rudd. In an article in the *Garden City News* which appeared on March 7, 1940, Rudd charged:

1. Harold Rugg has for years advocated a "new social order" to be based on collectivism, to replace our traditional American institutions.

2. That to bring about the "new social order" Rugg planned to use the schools to change the "climate of opinion" of our people.

3. That the Social Science courses were to be the main vehicle through which this indoctrination in the schools was to be accomplished.

4. And that Rugg wrote and sold to schools the Social Science books and accessories needed and actually used to accomplish this "purpose" in education (Jones, 1957, p. 22).

Then, Rudd authored an article that appeared in the April, 1940, issue of *Nation's Business*, a widely circulated general interest magazine and chief organ of the U.S. Chamber of Commerce. In "Our 'Reconstructed' Educational System," Rudd posited that the growth of radical youth organizations, such as the American Youth Congress and the Young Communist League, was inspired by an "entire educational system" which had been "reconstructed" with textbooks and courses teaching "that our economic and political institutions are decadent." He blamed the widespread teaching of "'Social science,' an omnibus course practically supplanting specific study of history, geography and U. S. Government." Rudd cited the Rugg textbooks as the major culprit, and argued that Rugg "subtly but surely" implied a need for a state-planned economy and socialism. Rugg, he argued, used "dramatic episodes" to emphasize the worst aspects of our institutions. "Time after time," Rudd wrote, "he uses half-truths, partisan references, and an amazing liberty with historical facts, the net effect of which is to undermine the faith of children in the American way of life. The constantly recurring theme is an effort to sell the child the collectivist theory of society" (Rudd, 1940c, p. 94).

The general thrust of Rudd's article was that Rugg was deliberately attempting to lead the United States to a collectivist society similar to the Soviet Union. An illustration on the first page depicted a bear pointing at a chart for a young child. The chart illustrating a greedy pig refusing to share his wealth with a ragged and pleading homeless man. The bear wore a scholar's mortarboard and held a book with the Soviet hammer and sickle on its cover. A second illustration portrayed Joseph Stalin leading a parade of children away from their little red schoolhouse. Once again, they were carrying books with hammer and sickle on the cover. The cartoon was captioned, "Courses teaching that American economic and political institutions are decadent have been placed in many school systems" (p. 27).

Many of the quotes which Rudd cited were not from Rugg's textbooks at all, but from *The Great Technology* which Rudd referred to as "the key to the entire series of his school textbooks," conveniently ignoring the fact that the textbooks appeared prior to publication of the book he cited. Like most of Rugg's critics, Rudd buttressed his case by lifting quotes out of context from the Rugg textbooks. He concluded the article with the charge that Rugg had "forced into line" many dissenting teachers who were afraid of being labeled "unprogressive" (p. 29). The article was reprinted in the Hearst *Journal-American* in New York City and in other papers in the Hearst chain.

In the spring of 1940, *Liberty Magazine* ran a series of anti-Rugg articles written by George Sokolsky, a self-described "propagandist" and inflammatory columnist who attacked the New Deal and social security, and whose columns were widely read (Sokolsky, 1939). From 1936 to 1938, Sokolsky had served as a mouthpiece for the National Association of Manufacturers and was secretly paid $1,000 a month while writing a column for the *New York Herald Tribune* (Seldes, 1943). At that time, *Liberty Magazine*, which called itself, "a weekly for everybody," was the nation's second most widely read general interest weekly. One Sokolsky article, "Hard-boiled Babes," was typical and captures the tone of the entire series. In this two-page article, illustrated with a picture of George Washington, Sokolsky charged that Rugg's interpretation of history was materialistic and Marxist. To prove his point Sokolsky cited Rugg's treatment of the founding fathers and the creation of the United States Constitution. Sokolsky's opening lines read:

> Children can be taught that life is hard-boiled, materialistic, selfish. Children can be made to believe that nothing moves men but money, that there is a constant and permanent war between the rich and the poor, between the "haves" and the "have-nots" and that nothing in this world matters but that war.
>
> That is the Marxian "economic interpretation of history." It is the precept of Marx's *Communist Manifesto*.
>
> But is it what you want your children taught? (1940, p. 50).

Sokolsky quoted a number of statements from Rugg's work which he declared to be "unpatriotic." These included Rugg's depiction of the Constitutional Convention as "made up chiefly of prominent leaders from the more well-to-do and prosperous classes," and his portrayal of the Constitution as a document that was made difficult to change in an effort to prevent an excess of democracy. To Sokolsky, Rugg was saying, "The Constitution is a rich man's document. To hell with it" (p. 50).

Sokolsky also condemned Rugg for portraying Russia in a favorable light, and wrote:

> And when your child comes home and tells you that Soviet Russia is a heaven on earth and most of the rest of the world, including the United States, is a land of fear—and explains, "Teacher told me. It's in the textbook we read"—what will you say? What can you say? You're not a historian. You're not an economist. But you know that we Americans do not live in fear, and that all Russians do live in fear of purges leading to death. You will know your child is being "indoctrinated" against your every conception of what is right (p. 50).

Like most of Rugg's patriotic critics, Sokolsky provided a skewed critique of the Rugg textbooks by lifting quotes out of context, failing to include passages that balanced Rugg's coverage of controversial topics. Sokolsky's articles appeared in a fashionable, nationally circulated magazine and were written in a popular style. Moreover, reprints were widely distributed by groups opposed to Rugg.

On the Radio. The growing controversy over the Rugg textbooks made it onto the airwaves on a number of occasions. On May 10, 1940, Merwin K. Hart offered the third in a series of radio broadcasts which gave air time to several of Rugg's staunchest critics, presented over several days in that week. The first address was by Major Augustin G. Rudd, who offered his description and critique of the books on Tuesday night, May 7. The second was by Mr. Archibald E. Stevenson who spoke on the background and philosophy of the Rugg books on Wednesday, May 8. Hart's address, on the following Friday, aimed at telling listeners "what the city of Binghamton did about" the Rugg books (Hart, 1940b).

In Hart's radio address he described Rugg's philosophy as one which "would have government bureaucratic control substituted for the liberty of private individuals" (p. 5). He then relayed the story the Binghamton case in which an address by a member of the New York State Economic Council (Hart, 1940b) led to a committee appointed by the school board to investigate charges against the Rugg books, which subsequently resulted in their ouster.

Hart announced that the New York State Economic Council had established a national committee to deal with the situation called the American Parents Committee on Education. The committee had accumulated leaflets, reprints, and copies of materials, prepared a "suggested method of procedure," and offered to assist any citizen who "desires to promote Americanism in his community" (Hart, 1940b). In May, 1940, the American Parents Committee on Education held a meeting under the auspices of the New York State Economic Council, attended by 75 people and drawing coverage from the *New York Times*. During the meeting, Hart, president of the council, urged that use of the Rugg books in the public school system be discontinued, and Columnist George Sokolsky declared that the schools should return to teaching history as a subject instead of the omnibus social science ("Academic Freedom Abused," 1940).

Dewey-Hart Op. Ed. Letters. At about the same time, during early May of 1940, as the intensity of the campaign against the Rugg books grew exponentially, John Dewey entered the fray on Rugg's behalf. Dewey wrote a letter to the editor of the *New York Times* on behalf of the Committee for Cultural Freedom in which he called attention to the dangers inherent in textbook censorship and made specific reference to the removal of the Rugg books from the Binghamton schools. The committee, a watchdog group organized by Dewey in May 1939, aimed to support "the defense of intellectual freedom against the attack of totalitarian forces," and had 96 writers, artists and scholars among its original membership (Martin, 2002). In his letter titled "Investigating Education," Dewey wrote that the problem, "becomes one of determining what is subversive and what is not.... The term 'subversive' may easily become a weapon for the exercise of censorship that is in fact subversive of the best public interest." Dewey went on:

> Increasingly, attempts are being made to invoke such a censorship against some of our foremost textbook authors. Only last month the social science

textbooks of one such writer, Professor Harold Rugg of Teachers College, were branded "subversive" and removed from the public schools of Binghamton, N. Y. at the instigation of the president of the State Economic Council, Inc. By similar action other groups have for years sought to silence Mr. Rugg by forcing his books out of the schools. Nor is Mr. Rugg alone ... Carl L. Becker, David Saville Muzzey, Roy Hatch and the late DeForest Stull were subjected to the same attacks. In the only true sense of the word, the works of these men are not subversive; they are, on the contrary, conducive to unfettered thinking, as opposed to unthinking stereotypes that leave no way out of our dilemmas but resort to violence and arms (Dewey, 1940, May 6).

A few days after Dewey's letter, a response appeared, written by Merwin K. Hart, which charged that the Rugg books aimed to "indoctrinate the pupil with collectivistic ideas and to make school teachers indoctrinators of new social doctrines." Hart suggested that progressive educators and their theories were at least partly to blame for the general increase in school budgets, and charged that Rugg wanted to substitute government control for the free enterprise system. In closing, Hart wrote:

> Dr. Dewey says these textbooks are "conducive to unfettered thinking." This, in my opinion, is untrue. They are, I think, rather part of that program Professor Rugg advocates—namely, to create swiftly a compact body of minority opinion for the scientific reconstruction of our social order." As such, they have no place in American schools. (Hart, 1940a, May 9)

As the multiple campaigns against the Rugg books continued to grow it seemed that an increasing number of Americans were in agreement with Hart's stance. Moreover, there was something to the charge. Though his textbooks were created prior to many of Rugg's bold statements on the reconstruction of the social order, they represented, in Rugg's mind, a strong basic component of the kind of knowledge that needed dissemination if progressives were to create a movement to reconstruct the social order.

Though Dewey publicly backed Rugg in the attempt to censure his school textbooks and materials, and Rugg seemingly worshipped Dewey, it is clear that Dewey never considered Rugg a great thinker. A few years later Dewey mentioned Rugg to Sidney Hook, and wrote, "I can't think that he is intellectually important, though a 'heavyweight' in one sense" (Dewey, 1944).

RUDD AND THE LEGION REJOINED

As the movement against the Rugg textbooks appeared to be gathering steam, Major Augustin G. Rudd seemed to grow impatient with the slow progress of the Legion's activities and addressed a letter to H. L. Chaillaux, the Legion's Americanism director, on May 31, 1940, saying:

> This matter is far more important today than ever before, since it is now the key-stone of national defense ... with prospective soldiers being taught this propaganda of dis-belief we would find our mechanized national defenses superimposed upon a foundation of sand.... This whole issue has developed into a vital part of our national defense ... therefore, it should be the No. 1 activity of The American Legion from here on. (Rudd, 1940)

A short time later Chaillaux replied, saying, "you may be certain that we will be taking positive action to defend our educational system against the fifth column sympathizers" (Chaillaux, 1940a).

Rudd's renewed push for action gained further support that summer when John B. Anderson, secretary of The American Parents Committee on Education, the group which had been created in New York City by Merwin K. Hart and the New York State Economic Council in combination with other patriotic and business groups, submitted a letter to the Legion's Chaillaux on July 9, 1940. In their letter, the American Parents' Committee recommended, first, that the Americanism Commission draft and push through a resolution "covering textbooks which promote Marxian principles," that specifically mentioned the textbooks of Harold Rugg. Second, the letter suggested that the commission "broadcast" the resolution to all of the local posts in order that the Americanism Committees and others interested could "do something about it" (Anderson, 1940a). Following a suggestion by Chaillaux that the resolution must originate from an individual Legion Post, a similar resolution was introduced at a meeting of the William Bradford Turner Post #265 in Garden City, New York, which read:

> Resolved ... that The American Legion emphatically condemns the perversion of our educational system through so-called social science courses, causing negative reaction in the instruction of history, geography, and civics; ... that The American Legion urge its members and affiliated groups to make inquiry and ascertain whether American history, geography, and civics are being well taught and whether subversive or un-American textbooks are being used in our schools. (Jones, 1957, p. 26)

The resolution was subsequently approved at the local, county, and state levels. The Americanism Commission then set to work to launch a determined attack on the Rugg social science textbooks and other similar books aimed at creating a new social order. Once again, the Director of the Americanism Commission mailed a short questionnaire to gather the desired information and spur action. However, this time, in the summer of 1940, the climate had intensified and efforts by local posts to oust the Rugg texts from schools were substantially increased. Of course, such efforts were nothing new to the organization.

The American Legion had a long history of trying to persuade Americans to support its brand of true "Americanism" by distributing pamphlets, suppressing "subversive elements," and supporting textbook criticism. In fact, the American Legion was founded by delegates of American soldiers in March 1919, bankrolled by funds from large corporations, partly in an effort to thwart the spread of Bolshevism (Gellerman, 1938). One of its early leaders had endorsed Fascism, and the organization had a long history of red-baiting, antilabor activity, and efforts to influence the schools (Seldes, 1943).

A WIDENING CONFLICT

By the summer of 1940, controversies over the Rugg textbooks flared far and wide, and the American public was treated to a spectacle that received continuing national media coverage. The attacks centered in the New York metropolitan area and were orchestrated by a relatively small number of people, with many of the specific criticisms being used over and over again. According to an analysis of the attacks by Rugg and his associates at Teachers College, of 240 incidents over 160 were from New York or New Jersey. Only eight other states were represented. Thus, it appeared to Rugg at least, that there was no real popular uprising against the Rugg textbooks, but instead an intense campaign orchestrated by relatively few people. The bulk of the attacks thus far had come from a combine of business writers and publicists, retired military of the American Legion, professional journalists, and a few loose cannons. The flames were fanned by extensive coverage in the Hearst newspaper syndicate. Though the campaign was apparently not very well organized, it was marked by informal cooperation among the attackers who liberally quoted, cited, and reprinted each other's work. Attacks on the Rugg materials were part of a blanket attack on American writers and texts, with Rugg gradually becoming the main target.

At the American Legion offices, the campaign against the Rugg books continued to gather steam, and began to bring tangible results by the summer of 1940. In July, the Legion issued a news bulletin about the success of one of its campaigns to have the books removed by local school boards, this one in Cedar Rapids, Iowa:

> A five-year campaign by Verne Marshall, Legionnaire and editor of the *Cedar Rapids Gazette*, finally met with success when the board of education

voted to remove from the city's public schools all the social science text-books written by Professor Harold O. Rugg of Columbia University. (Marshall) … is an ardent exponent of Americanism. He charged that the Rugg textbooks painted a picture of America in such a light that children would be made dissatisfied and thus prepared for the social change Rugg advocated. (News Bulletin, 1940).

Marshall would later "skyrocket across the country" during 1940 and 1941, announcing "secret information which he had about political affairs." He lasted 29 days on the lecture circuit, suffered a mental break-down, and was commited to a sanitarium (Rugg, 1951). During the next several months more than 30 American Legion Posts reported that they had asked their local school boards to remove the Rugg textbooks from the schools (Jones, 1957, pp. 20-31).

In September of 1940, in their most striking and damaging blow to date, the Legion published an article by Orlen K. Armstrong, a relatively obscure isolationist and Legionnaire from Springfield, Missouri, who was active with Verne Marshall on the No Foreign War Committee of the Legion. Armstrong grew curious about the ideas given credence in schools when his son came home from a class on "democratic living" and asked: "Daddy, was George Washington a big business man?" Following that incident, Armstrong began studying school materials in some detail. His subsequent article was titled, "Treason in the Textbooks," and appeared in the *American Legion Magazine* for September, 1940. This was the official journal of the Legion and was distributed to one million homes. The article was also reprinted in pamphlet form and distributed widely among the media and other organizations. In perhaps its most damning feature, the article was adorned with two dramatic cartoons, graphically described by Rugg himself:

> Two cartoons stretched across two facing pages. In one a leering, bony teacher grins wickedly down at frightened boys and girls. From scrawny hands slime drips down upon four books labeled Constitution, Religion, U. S. Heroes and U. S. History. In the other the same teacher fits black glasses on the eyes of a young boy and girl who are reading books called *The American Way of Life*. A caption reads: "The Frontier Thinkers" are trying to sell our youth the idea that the American way of life has failed." In the article itself a score of authors and books are blacklisted, although nine-tenths of all illustrative references are taken from my writings. (Rugg, 1941, pp. 73-74)

The article contained a bitter denunciation of the writers and teachers of the "new history," and quoted extensively from Rugg's text, *A History of American Government and Culture* and its teacher's guide. Armstrong used these and other books by the "frontier thinkers" to document that the books sought:

- To present a new interpretation of history in order to "debunk" our heroes and cast doubt upon their motives, their patriotism, and their service to mankind.
- To cast aspersions upon our Constitution and our form of government, and shape opinions favorable to replacing them with socialistic control.
- To condemn the American system of private ownership and enterprise, and form opinions favorable to collectivism.
- To mould opinion against traditional religious faiths and ideas of morality, as being part of an outgrown system (Armstrong, 1940, p. 51).

Armstrong also attacked fused courses which consolidate "history, geography, civics and social science," and stated flatly that "these courses form a complete pattern of propaganda for a change in our political, economic, and social order" (pp. 51, 70). Armstrong and the editors went a step further and published a list of 38 "subversive" books and magazines. Once again, Rugg's textbook series was the central target.

The *American Legion Magazine* article created an immediate storm of controversy. Authors, educators, publishers and even some Legionnaires attacked it, and a number of the blacklisted publications received an immediate retraction from the Legion. Rugg's publisher, Ginn and Company sent a letter in late September which threatened legal action:

> I have on my desk a copy of the Armstrong article which appeared in the Legion Magazine. I must say that Dr. Rugg would have entered suit long before this, had it not been for the restraining influence of his publishers, but if retractions do not make an end to such a libelous campaign, we shall have to resort to other means. (Kenerson, 1940)

Chaillaux of the Legion responded, "We in this office cannot control the policy of *The American Legion Magazine* ... but will immediately help correct any damage which has been done" (Chaillaux, 1940b).

The following month the manager of Ginn and Company, H. C. Lucas, wrote to Legion National Commander Milo J. Warner concerning the Armstrong article:

> If the things were true of the Rugg books which are said about them in the article, we would be very much disturbed.... The majority of the statements and quotes from Rugg in this magazine article are twisted by the omission of

Elizabeth K. Dilling, author of *The Red Network* (Special Collections, University of Oregon Libraries)

The Red Network (1934).

General Amos A. Fries (Special Collections, University of Oregon Libraries).

Congressman Martin Dies, Chair of the House Un-American Activities Committee (Hoover Institution Archives).

VOL. 19   MAY, 1960   No. 2

25¢
Year
Two Dollars

Great Citizen -- Great Patriot
(See page 3)

Merwin K. Hart, President, New York State Economic Council (Special Collections, University of Oregon Libraries).

George E. Sokolsky, syndicated columnist (Hoover Institution Archives).

Our machine workers are portrayed as slaves and our
leaders of industry as heartless money-bags

"Heartless Moneybags" (Originally published in *Nations Business*, April 1940.
Reprinted by permission, uschamber.com, October 2006. Copyright 1940, U. S.
Chamber of Commerce.).

Courses teaching that American economic and political institutions are decadent have been placed in many school systems

"Decadent" (Originally published in *Nations Business*, April 1940. Reprinted by permission, uschamber.com, October 2006. Copyright 1940, U. S. Chamber of Commerce.).

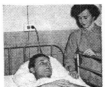

"Battle Over Books," l. to r., Harold O. Rugg, John Dewey, and Major Augustin G. Rudd (*American Legion Magazine*, October, 1958).

"Treason in the Textbooks" (*American Legion Magazine*, September, 1940).

The "Frontier Thinkers" are trying to
sell our youth the idea that the American way of life has failed

"Frontier Thinkers" (*American Legion Magazine*, September, 1940).

"America is *not* a land of opportunity" (*American Legion Magazine*, September, 1940).

Walter S. Steele, publisher, *National Republic* (Hoover Institution Archives).

Dan W. Gilbert, author, "Un-American Textbooks" (Hoover Institution Archives).

"Free Thinker Professor: One Drops a Hook Into Nearly Every School" (*National Republic*, September, 1940).

"Red Schoolhouse" (*National Republic*, February, 1940).

Get Rid of the Pied Piper

"Get Rid of the Pied Piper" (*National Republic*, August, 1940).

Dangerous Bookworm Eats Away

"Bookworm" (*National Republic*, January, 1942).

Teaching Youth Wrong Ideas

"School Library" (*National Republic*, January, 1942).

New York American

Imports From the Bughouse

"Imports from the Bug House" (*National Republic*, March, 1942).

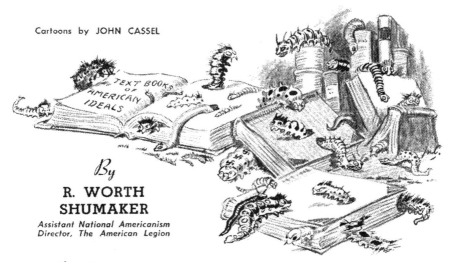

Cartoons by JOHN CASSEL

By

R. WORTH SHUMAKER

Assistant National Americanism Director, The American Legion

NO "New Order"

The philosophy of Counts and Rugg encourages the totalitarian borers-from-within who would destroy our democracy

FOR OUR SCHOOLS

"No New Order" (*American Legion Magazine*, April, 1941).

The vast majority of school teachers are loyal to American ideals. They do not approve of the Rugg and Counts model

"Loyal Teacher" (*American Legion Magazine*, April, 1941).

certain important sentences, words, or parts of sentences in such manner as to make it appear that Rugg makes some statements which he does not make .... (Lucas, 1940)

A number of other publishers responded to the blacklist. Silver Burdett, a textbook publisher, received a letter from James F. Barton, the Legion's director of publications stating that, "The American Legion regrets that *Modern History* by Carl Becker was inadvertently included in the list" (Barton, 1940). Macmillan asked for "a retraction" in the case of one of their books, *America Today*, by Roy H. Nichols, William C. Bagley and Charles A. Beard, and insisted that Beard was a liberal but "in no sense a 'red' or a 'pink'" (Knowlton, 1940).

After receiving additional complaints from editors of a number of the periodicals listed in the blacklist, the National Americanism Commission of the Legion decided that clarifying statements should be issued. Following that decision, retraction letters were sent from the director of publications and from Armstrong himself to editors of several blacklisted publications. The Director of Publications, James F. Barton, sent a letter to the editors retracting the charges of subversion in *The American Observer, The Weekly News Review, The Junior Review,* and *The Civic Leader,* and stated that they were "inadvertently included in the list" and that the Legion finds nothing in them which is "un-American or otherwise objectionable for school use" (Myer, 1940, p. 1). Armstrong's letter of retraction stated: " I sincerely regret that due to an error the publications of your organization were included in the list," and stated that it was, "a result of a misunderstanding" (Myer, 1940, p. 1).

Several Legionnaires responded to the Armstrong article with letters of complaint. One wrote that Armstrong, "wished to wax sensational," and called the article, "drivel" and "a smear article attacking teachers and publishers with intimations and allusions!" (Smith, 1940). Another, from a prominent Legion member in California, described the Legion campaign of repeated attacks as "senseless, inaccurate, unfounded and un-American." He went on to write that the Legion was "now largely discredited," and that unless "the senseless persecution is stopped," the Legion would be "damaged beyond repair" (Getsinger, 1940).

The associate secretary of the NEA wrote that the attack had "no adequate basis in fact." He argued, "It is not 'treason' to teach that American ideals require a fair chance for everyone in terms of economic, social, and educational opportunity," and that it was not treason "to teach that these ideals are not yet fully achieved," and to inspire youth to attain them (Carr, 1940). The NEA, in a research bulletin published a short time after the Legion article appeared, used a recent Gallup survey on education which found that "73 per cent of the people do not believe education is overemphasized today; 85 per cent think education has improved; 72 per cent think that young people should discuss controversial topics; 66 per cent that we are not spending too much for education" (Beals, 1941, p. 10). Another group of educators, the California Association of School Supervisors passed a resolution condemning the attacks as "unfair and groundless" (California Supervisors, 1940).

Armstrong admitted, in the wake of the controversy, that he had not investigated a number of the publications he listed. In fact, it turns out the list had originated with Rudd who wrote, "when I saw the list I was surprised, for it was never intended for publication." Rudd later intimated, "In the many articles I have written on this subject, I have never included a list of the books, knowing full well the risk involved. Apparently it was obtained from my file in your office.." He went on to express his hope that there would be "no unpleasant consequences" (Rudd, 1940b). Yet, as is so often the case, the damage was done. Rugg, who had once boasted that, "the only way to get somewhere in education was to attack someone big," had apparently met his match (Winters, 1968).

In his presidential address to the NCSS membership in November, 1940, Howard R. Anderson countered the charges against social studies and Harold Rugg, and suggested that Armstrong had made "sensational charges without great concern for buttressing them with facts." Rugg read Anderson's speech "with great interest and agreement" and offered his own analysis of the sources of the attack, made by, "Eight hitherto unknown persons of almost no prestige or influence," who were "artificially keeping it alive." The persons included Hart, Forbes, Rudd, E. H. West, Fries, Dilling, Sokolsky, and Armstrong. They were, he charged, gaining success via access to national agencies, chiefly, the Hearst papers, patriotic groups, and business organizations. Rugg went on to suggest that the critics were limiting education by characterizing certain "bad words" as subversive or un-American, essentially labeling them as taboo topics. Rugg wrote that the "Bad Words," which point out deficiencies in American life, "simply cannot be introduced into the school, in any form, without arousing the bitter opposition of certain special-interest groups—persons like ... the Forbes-Hart-Rudd-West combination" (Rugg, 1941, pp. 74-75).

Rugg categorized the Legion's retractions as "halfhearted" and noted accurately, "There was no retraction at all ... of the attack on my books." Rugg was advised by the local chapter of the American Civil Liberties Union (ACLU) and by his publisher that he should sue the American Legion, but demurred, responding that he didn't want the negative publicity a lawsuit would bring because of "something in my past" that he didn't want to come to light. In his book, Rugg described the breadth and organized nature of the Legion campaign quite accurately as well, noting that the Legion had a "special officer in each of hundreds of local communities throughout the country" who disregarded protests and retractions and went into action by bringing up the matter before school boards and superintendents, guided from Legion headquarters.

Rugg believed that this one article did more damage than any other single action in the campaign against his textbooks. It was vividly written and dramatically illustrated, and appeared to spur the officers and members of local American Legion Posts into action. Many school boards held meetings to discuss removal of the Rugg books in the immediate aftermath of the article's appearance (Rugg, 1941, pp. 74-75). In a signal that the Armstrong article was read widely, Rugg received requests from "scores of school boards" that he appear before them and answer the charges against his books. In one day he reportedly received ten such requests by telephone (Rugg Critics, 1940).

Another similar, inflammatory attack on Rugg was launched by the magazine *National Republic*, which published a series of six articles beginning in September, 1940, authored by Dr. Dan W. Gilbert, that portrayed the Rugg series and other textbooks as "un-American," and described them as part of a broader campaign to spread the "Marxian propaganda" of "class hatred" and "class war" (Gilbert, 1940). An editorial in the same issue titled, "Reds in Schools," cited FBI concern about "doctrines wholly un-American" in schools and expressed its hope that textbooks with an "un-American bias" would be "withdrawn." The magazine had "a long history of calling attention to the danger of red penetration" of schools and colleges" ("Reds in Schools," 1940). *National Republic*, established in 1905 as *National Republican*, described itself as "A Magazine of Fundamental Americanism," and devoted its pages to attacking subversive elements of American society and advocating its version of "true Americanism." Owned and published by Walter S. Steele, the magazine's manifest declared that it was "FOR—Fundamental Americanism; Constitutional Representative Government; Constructive National Policies. AGAINST— All Subversive Movements Inimical to American Ideals, Traditions and Institutions" (National Republic, 1940, p. 11). The magazine favored capitalism and Christianity and opposed communists, socialists, atheists and other subversives, sexual promiscuity, racial miscegenation, and "cradle to grave regimentation" by the "exaggerated state." Moreover, its pages were filled with illustrated articles exposing "the enemy" within our gates and threats within the schools and colleges. Though never a major magazine (its circulation was approximately 20,000 at the time it ceased publication in 1960), *National Republic* did have a strong national circulation and was, apparently, quite influential in conservative circles.

Steele, a newspaperman who had worked for the *Marion Chronicle*, the *Muncie Press*, the *Houston Post*, and who also owned *Outdoors Magazine*, was a native Fascist with Nazi sympathies, and was one of the star witnesses questioned by the Dies Committee during the late 1930s in its investigation of subversive groups and un-American activities (Bellant, 1991; Seldes, 1947). After a number of unsuccessful attempts, in the late 1930s congressman Martin Dies convinced the U. S. House of Representatives to establish the Committee on Un-American Activities. Beginning in 1938, the committee began a series of hearings pursuing alleged subversives in government, labor, and other organizations. The committee devoted the bulk of its energy to unearth communist infiltration of American life. Steele testified, in August of 1938, on "un-American" activities in education, claiming to represent 114 patriotic organizations, loosely affiliated in a single national body, the American Coalition which claimed to represent 20,000,000 persons. Though he did not go into detail, Steele made broad general charges, and said that "many professors [were] wound up into the machinery of radicalism in the United States"; some were communists, some were socialists, some were atheists, many were "on the firing line in co-operating movements" (Gellerman, 1972, p. 118).

Another witness before the Dies Committee, Alice Lee Jemison, who testified extensively on radical educators in November, 1938, went into detail and named names. She cited the Progressive Education Association, John Dewey, George S. Counts, Carleton Washburne, Harold Rugg, and many other well known progressives as "radicals" with well known sympathies with "the communist program of Soviet Russia" and attributed many of her charges to *The Red Network* by Mrs. Dilling (Gellerman, 1972, p. 125).

Meanwhile the entire controversy had gathered increasing national attention. According to an article in *Time* magazine, by the end of the spring term in 1940, the Rugg textbooks had been banned from a half-dozen school systems. Critics objected to the Rugg texts, the article reported, "for picturing the U.S. as a land of unequal opportunity, and giving a class conscious account of the framing of the U.S. Constitution." The books were increasingly under attack "in the small town American Legion belt," the article reported, citing two fresh book "burnings" in the towns of Mountain Lakes and Wayne Township, N. J. (Book burnings, 1940).

HAND-TO-HAND COMBAT

Controversies over the books in a number of cities and towns eventually led to school board decisions to either censor the books or to declare that they contained "nothing subversive." The typical pattern was a complaint, followed by appointment of a committee to investigate, then debate and, frequently, public hearings. In a number of well-publicized cases, Rugg appeared in person to defend the textbook series. In several communities concerned citizens and school board members responded to the attackers and pressed for the continued presence of the books.

Legion posts in cities around the nation investigated local schools to determine whether the Rugg textbooks were being used, and then, in many cases, took action as needed. As reported above, the Cedar Rapids, Iowa post, and newspaper editor Verne Marshall had succeeded in removing the books from the schools on July 3, 1940, and, of course, there was Rudd's success in Garden City, New York, in 1938. However, the outcome varied quite a bit from place to place. According to one study, Legion files indicated that with 32 posts reporting (spanning a period from 1939 through 1944), 12 had succeeded in having the books removed from use in the classroom of their local school district. Among these were Cedar Rapids, Iowa, Sunbury, Pennsylvania, Glen Rock, New York, East Cleveland, Ohio, Delta, Colorado, Rochester, New York, San Francisco, California, and Ridgefield, New Jersey. In eleven cases the books were still being used in classrooms and there was no plan to remove them despite the objections. Four posts reported that the Rugg books were not in use in their local schools, and five posts reported that their investigation found nothing subversive or un-American in the Rugg textbooks (Jones, 1957, pp. 53-54).

In several cases, a local post requested more information or ammunition from the Legion headquarters with which to fight the Rugg texts. Correspondence also revealed that in many cases removal of the Rugg textbooks from classrooms caused school districts to incur an expensive loss. After the state of Nevada removed the Rugg books from its state textbook adoption list, one of the members of the state textbook commission wrote, "The discontinuance of the Rugg texts caused the school districts of the state to suffer a considerable expense and I am very anxious to take every precaution now to safeguard against the termination of any adopted text before the expiration of the adoption period" (Corbett, 1943).

In a surprising number of cases, local Legionnaires disagreed with the attack and found nothing wrong with the Rugg books. A committee of the North Canton, Ohio, post read and reviewed four of Rugg's junior high texts and "failed to find any noticeably radical statements or tendencies...." The committee did send a report to the superintendent and school board suggesting that teachers be instructed to guard against "debunking" heroes, "casting aspersions upon the Constitution and our form of government," condemning private enterprise, or "forming of any opinions favorable to collectivism," and "moulding opinions" against traditional religious faith or morality (Committee, 1940).

The Rapid City, South Dakota, post submitted a report on use of the Rugg textbooks in Rapid City schools and stated that after investigating the books one evening with the assistance of the principal, it found:

> These textbooks teach the fundamental principles of all forms of society and government, including Communism. They do not advocate Communism, but point out the bad results of Communism in Russia. They do teach that our Democracy has needed and does need changing. They teach that there are injustices and wrongs practiced in our Democracy which should be stopped; and they teach that our Government should stop these wrongs by making and enforcing regulations ... Every change and regulation which is recommended by these textbooks as being desirable has either already been put into practice, or has been advocated by executive officers of our country.
>
> Therefore ... (we) come to the conclusion that our schools and these textbooks are only teaching what our Government openly advocates. If that is wrong, then the American Legion should have the courage to criticize the Government; but should not pick on our schools for simply following accepted Governmental principles ... The American Legion owes an apology to the schools of the United States. (McDonald, 1941)

Another local committee, the Anti-Subversive Committee of the Fairfield, Connecticut, post reported that it had conscientiously read the textbooks and stated: "it is the collective opinion of this committee that said textbooks do not contain subversive or un-American material as such" (Taylor, 1941). Finally, the superintendent of schools in Fargo, North Dakota, reported, "some of the Rugg books are being used in our schools. We feel that they are serving a useful purpose, and that in the hands of teachers as capable as ours, the cause of Americanism and democracy is not being injured in the least" (Kirk, 1941).

Despite these mixed results and the differences of opinion that surfaced, the legion on the whole appeared to be in general agreement on the undesirability of the Rugg textbooks and continued its campaign to remove them from the schools. The majority of Legionnaires probably agreed with the sentiments of Tom L. Coleman of Ardmore, Oklahoma, who conducted a one-man letter writing campaign, inspired by articles that appeared in the *American Legion* magazine. In a letter addressed to Rugg and Counts and carbon copied to Columbia University President Nicholas Murray Butler, Coleman wrote, "I can't see the use for allowing that particular brand of cootie to exist ... especially the long haired or so called intellectual species" (i.e., Rugg and Counts). Coleman stated his intention to "eliminate you or some of your ilk," and said that he asked the Legion to contact some of the "heavy contributors to Columbia's general fund" to show them that the University seemed to be "harboring 'reds.'" In closing, he wrote, somewhat presciently, "I am going to try and see what can be done.... Maybe the Legion can cripple sales" (Coleman, 1940).

Englewood, New Jersey. In Englewood, despite the best efforts of Berties C. Forbes, Scottish born publisher of *Forbes* magazine, a school board member, and a leading critic of the Rugg textbooks, the effort to remove the books ultimately failed. The Englewood case was especially important partly because it was hotly contested, because it began early in the controversy, because it spawned a good deal of publicity and media coverage that may have influenced a number of other cases, and partly because of its location, just across the Hudson from New York City.

The appointment of Forbes to the Englewood school board in the spring of 1939 marked a turning point. Shortly after taking his seat on the board, Forbes criticism of the Rugg textbooks appeared in his own magazine, and stated:

> I plan to insist that this anti-American educator's textbooks be cast out.... I would not want my own children contaminated by conversion to Communism.... In my humble opinion it is time for members of boards of education all over the continent to inquire more closely into what is being fed our offspring and to consider seriously what action should be taken against teachers who have no use for Americanism. (Forbes, 1939)

Forbes then announced to the board that he was going to launch an investigation of textbooks being used in the schools. His attack on the Rugg textbooks led to a meeting, held on November 20, 1939, in Englewood, to address concerns regarding the Rugg textbooks. The meeting was sponsored by the Parent-Teacher Association in an attempt to resolve the issue. Invitations were extended to both Rugg and his opponents.

Critics who wanted the books removed were spearheaded by a delegation from the Board of Education in nearby Haworth and from its American Legion Post. Earlier in 1939, the Haworth, New Jersey post of the American Legion had requested that the Haworth Board of Education launch an investigation of the social science textbooks being used in the schools and requested it be conducted under the supervision of the Americanism Committee of the Haworth Post. Though this request was denied, the Board did agree to study the textbooks. It was discovered that the Rugg textbooks were being used, but the Board's majority voted to continue their use. On November 13, 1939, the week prior to the Englewood meeting, a minority group of members of the Haworth Board, Legionnaires all, issued a written report titled, "The Rugg Social Science Series of Textbooks," which they forwarded to Legion headquarters in Indianapolis. The report branded the Rugg books "UNAMERICAN," declared that "Rugg's philosophy is opposed to the American way of life," and charged that the books were "part of a subtle and insidious scheme to poi-

son and undermine the faith of our children in the American plan"
(Haworth Committee, 1939).

Rugg was present at the November 20 meeting in Englewood to
defend his work. Assisting Rugg in defense of the textbooks were several
Englewood parents and the Reverend James A. Mitchell of St. Paul's Episcopal Church in Englewood. Forbes, one of the instigators of the attack,
did not attend the meeting, and later claimed that it would serve no
point. Rugg's speech of about 90 minutes on modern education was followed by a "question hour." The chief questioners turned out to be the
delegation from the Haworth American Legion post, which sniped at
Rugg until midnight. The meeting was attended by over 300 people and
must have been lively. It closed with a prolonged chorus of boos for the
Haworth delegation after Mr. George West read a quote from a workbook
which accompanied a Rugg text:

> Is America the land of opportunity for all the people? From a key, Mr .West
> read Dr. Rugg's reply, No not for all people. A statement he contended was
> un-American and the reverse of truth. ("Schoolbook Trial," 1939)

During the meeting, Rugg took the opportunity, in a public forum, to
denounce Forbes as un-American for refusing to meet with him face-to-
face, and for failing to attend the meeting. Though nothing was decided
about the fate of the Rugg books in Englewood schools, Rugg stated that
the meeting had taught him a valuable lesson:

> I learned that the die is cast, that we cannot appease the authoritarians who
> are trying to censor American schools. If we do, freedom of thought and dis-
> cussion in our educational institutions will be made impotent. And I learned
> that night the hate and ruthless determination which motivates the tiny
> minority who would rule our schools. (Rugg, 1941, pp. 28-29)

Also as a result of the meeting, a substantial group of leading citizens
of Englewood were motivated to act in favor of the books. Petitions were
circulated, and Rugg was invited back to speak to citizens. Meanwhile,
Forbes frequently blasted Rugg in his column carried in the Hearst
papers and had petitions circulated to have the books removed from
schools.

In late January of 1940 Rugg appeared before a crowded parish house
at St. Paul's Episcopal Church in Englewood, and explained his beliefs on
the function of schools. He argued that the school should help children
bring order to the "confusion of ideas" that children get from the press,
the radio, and the screen. The school can guide the child's thinking,
Rugg suggested, by telling the truth with the proper attitude:

I cannot tell children all is well when they know this is not so. I cannot lie to them. I believe we should let children see America, first seeing all the good there is in America and then, at the proper ages, letting them see the things that are wrong. ("Rugg Explains," 1940)

During the winter of 1940 it was apparent that the community was deeply divided over the matter; the local papers were filled with charges and counter-charges. The five-member school board was divided as well, with one member who sided with Forbes, Mr. Foote, who had been working behind the scenes for several years to uncover subversive and un-American elements. Another member of the board violently opposed Forbes and supported the texts. Though the issue was frequently discussed at board meetings, no decision was reached, allowing Rugg's supporters to prepare a defense.

Several local citizens who favored retaining the Rugg textbooks organized a Committee of Taxpayers and Parents which sought to win sentiment favoring Rugg's cause. They published and distributed over one-thousand copies of a free pamphlet providing the facts of the case. The pamphlet contained a detailed response to the charges against the books. It was primarily the work of Dr. T. H. P. Sailer, a personal friend of Rugg's (Sailer, 1940).

The battle of Englewood continued throughout 1940. Forbes made one last try to have the books removed, but a motion to retain the books was passed by the school board. When the mayor of Englewood refused to reappoint Forbes to the board in January of 1941, the issue began to die out (Rugg, 1941; Schipper, 1979; Winters, 1968). Forbes' last official act, on January 14, 1941, was to present a motion for the removal of the Rugg books from the school system, but the motion lost when none of the other board members would second it. All but Forbes stated that they found nothing un-American in the books. On learning of Forbes failure to win reappointment, Rugg reportedly declared that it was "a victory for the true American democratic way" ("Rugg Texts Restored," 1941).

Binghamton, New York. In December, 1939, Merwin K. Hart of the New York State Economic Council delivered a "withering blast" against the Rugg textbooks at a meeting of the Binghamton chapter of the Exchange Club. Hart's tirade contained many of the usual charges including that, "Professor Rugg's books are one of the

shrewdest and probably one of the most effective of the Communist Front efforts being made in the United States" (Myers, 1940, p. 17). Hart stated that the Rugg books were "intended to raise questions in the mind of the pupil," and charged the books with making "a subtle sugar-coated effort to convert youth to Communism," and to persuade them that "the American capitalistic system has been a failure and that socialism should be substituted in its place." By April, 1940, the Rugg books were being discussed at a meeting of the Binghamton School Board. In Binghamton the books were used only for reference purposes. And, they had staunch defenders including members of the school board and the superintendent of schools. However, in the Binghamton case, despite substantial support for the Rugg texts, the critics were successful and the books were removed (Boesenberg & Poland, 2001). At one school board meeting, Mrs. Howard R. Swartwood, a member of the Board's Teacher Committee, made the proposal that "a bonfire be made" of the discarded Rugg textbooks. At least two members of the board agreed, but Superintendent Daniel J. Kelly blasted the critics, and stated:

> To my mind the most subversive activity in America today lies in these attacks, and the most dangerous and damnable pressure groups we have consist of those who gang up to start and promote such attacks (Winters, p. 164).

However, in response to the demands of the Board, Superintendent Kelly was forced to remove the books from the schools. On April 3, 1940, he ordered the Rugg books "taken out of circulation and placed on the shelf" ("Kelly Takes," 1940). Edith B. Oagley, director of social sciences for the district, continued her defense of the books, and described them as "harmless" ("Mrs. Oagley," 1940).

The Binghamton controversy, and Kelly's opposition to removal of the Rugg texts, led to publication of an open letter from the American Committee in Defense of Intellectual Freedom (ACDIF) which praised Superintendent Kelly for his opposition to the removal of Rugg's textbooks, and called the Binghamton case evidence of the present "state of panic in which prejudice and hatred are displacing the reason and tolerance essential for the functioning of democratic institutions." The letter went on to suggest that every incident of this sort represented "a challenge to be met vigorously and firmly." Among the signers of the letter were Alfred Harcourt, B. W. Huebsch, Bennett Cerf, W. W. Norton, Lewis Gannett, Van Wyck Brooks, Wesley C. Mitchell, Franz Boas (chair of the Committee) and about 150 others. The Committee had also begun collecting funds to meet growing attacks on the Rugg books ("Publishers Protest," 1940). The Binghamton incident also resulted in the op-ed exchange between John Dewey and Merwin K. Hart discussed previously.

Despite the best efforts of Rugg's defenders, the Rugg textbooks were no longer used in the Binghamton schools. By the summer of 1940, Merwin K. Hart, and probably many other critics of the Rugg series, had come to view the ouster of Rugg's materials as "purchasable" via the application of propaganda literature in the cities and towns where a controversy had been created. As one of Hart's assistants wrote following the decision of Mountain View, New Jersey, to discontinue use of the Rugg books, the decision "nicely demonstrates that ousting the Rugg philosophy is, to use your phrase, purchasable. One—he inquired, Two—we supplied the information, Three—out goes the Rugg books" (Anderson, 1940b).

Philadelphia. Though many of the battles over the Rugg books were fought in small towns, there were also attempts to get the books removed from large city school districts. In Philadelphia the Daughters of Colonial Wars urged removal of the textbooks. Mrs Ellwood J. Turner argued, in a somewhat famous statement that Rugg and his supporters cited frequently:

> the books tried to give the child an unbiased viewpoint instead of teaching him real Americanism. All the old histories taught "my country, right or wrong." That's the point of view we want our children to adopt. We can't afford to teach them to be unbiased and let them make up their own minds ("Book Burnings," 1940).

The question over the Rugg books was resolved in Philadelphia by submitting them to a Special Committee of Three for review. After several months the Committee issued a report supportive of the Rugg books and plainly critical of the "self-appointed censors" who had generated the controversy.

Atlanta. In Atlanta an attempt was launched by local patriotic societies to have the books removed. The initial complaint against the books was filed by Captain Jack Kelly of the Georgia State Police. Kelly was also a member of the American Legion and of the Governor's State Defense Corps. The charges resulted in an open meeting of the state board of education called by the governor to which all participants were invited. Rugg attended the meeting and tried to present his side of the case. He later described the five-hour meeting as having the combined atmosphere of "a Billy Sunday tabernacle of evangelism and political rally" (Rugg, 1941, p. 10). During Rugg's presentation, members of the audience prayed for him and for the country. The opposition commentary at the meeting reached frantic heights. One middle-aged woman, who admitted that she had not read the books, made an impassioned plea:

> Righteousness, good government, good homes, and God—God most of all—Christ is on trial here today. You can't take the youth of our land and give them this awful stuff and have them come out safe and sound for God and righteousness. (Beals, 1941, p. 1)

Captain Kelly of the state police went a step further. Rising from his seat, and pointing a finger directly at Rugg, he said: "There sits the ring master of the Fifth Columnists in America, financed by the Russian government. I want you people to look at him" (Beals, 1941, p. 1). Rugg responded by standing up, smiling, and bowing to the crowd ("Board Delays," 1940).

In Atlanta, as in so many other cases, the board failed to reach a decision at the meeting and a committee was appointed by the governor, to study the texts. However, within a month the committee found that there was nothing subversive in the texts and recommended that they be retained on the state approved list. The board and the governor approved the committee's findings and the matter was dropped.

During the latter part of 1940 and through most of 1941 the Rugg texts became a focal point for school board controversies across the country. Schools banning the texts included Mountain Lakes and Wayne Township in New Jersey, Port Chester, Mount Kisco, and Bronxville in New York. They had previously been banned in Binghamton, Rome, Hornell, and Oneida, New York, Haworth, and Lyndhurst, New Jersey, Cedar Rapids, Iowa, Santa Ana, California, Providence, Rhode Island, Muskogee, Oklahoma, Sterling, Illinois, and Colorado Springs, Colorado (West, 1940).

Book Burnings. Though there may have been many threats to burn the Rugg books, in only one case were the books actually and deliberately burned. In Bradner, Ohio, as in Binghamton and many other school districts, the books were never used as classroom textbooks. In Bradner, the only copies on hand were samples on a shelf in the superintendent's office. It seems that in this case, the struggle over the books in Bradner developed out of an attempt to get rid of the superintendent. At one meeting, the vice president of the board charged that the Rugg books were communistic and quoted several sentences to prove his point. When the board president, also a local minister, refuted the charges, he became the target for attack. During the course of the battle in Bradner a fiery cross was burned on his lawn, a stick of dynamite was exploded, and several threats were made. Finally, in a dramatic finale, during a board meeting the Superintendent ordered the books taken down to the furnace room and burned ("Book Burnings," 1940; Rugg, 1940, p. 26).

Though many of the localized attacks on the Rugg textbooks were good theater, and had attracted a great deal of attention, on the whole, by the end of 1940 they were relatively unsuccessful in removing the books from schools. As we have seen, in many cases the books were retained. Nonetheless, what had begun with a few isolated attacks had mushroomed into a virulent and continuing national campaign to oust the Rugg texts from schools. That spectacle was to have devastating consequences for the Rugg textbooks and dire results for progressive approaches to social studies in schools as we shall see in the next chapter.

REFERENCES

Academic freedom abused. (1940, May 24). *New York Times,* 1940.

Advertising Groups. (1940, September 28). Advertising groups pursuing professor Rugg's books. *Publishers' Weekly,* pp. 1322-1323.

Anderson, J. B. (1940a). John B. Anderson to H. L. Chaillaux, July 9, 1940, Legion dead-letter files (as cited in Jones, 1957, p. 26).

Anderson, J. (1940b). John (Anderson) to Merwin K. Hart, note attached to R. F. Teeling, Board of Education, Mountain View, N. J. to American Parents Committee on Education, August 30, 1940, "Social Science Investigation" folder, box 4, Merwin K. Hart Papers, Special Collections, University of Oregon, Eugene.

Armstrong, O. K. (1940, September). Treason in the textbooks. *American Legion Magazine,* pp. 8-9, 51, 70-72.

Baldwin, R. N. (1940, November 15). Gilt-edged patriots: Presenting the New York State Economic Council and its presiding genius, Merwin K. Hart. *Frontiers of Democracy, 7,* pp. 45-47.

Bellant, R. (1991). *Old Nazis, the new right, and the Republican party.* Boston: South End Press.

Barton, J. F. (1940). James F. Barton to Burr L. Chase, October 2, 1940, Legion dead-letter files (as cited in Jones, 1957, p. 59).

Beals, C. (Ed.). (1941, February 25). Propaganda over the schools. *Propaganda Analysis: A Bulletin to Help the Intelligent Citizen Detect and Analyze Propaganda, 4,* pp. 1-12.

Board delays distribution of textbooks. (1940, September 19). *Atlanta Constitution,* pp. 1-2.

Boesenberg, E., & Poland, K. (2001). Struggle at the frontier of curriculum: The Rugg textbook controversy in Binghamton, New York. *Theory and Research in Social Education, 29*(4), 640-671.

Book burnings. (1940, September 9). *Time,* pp. 64-5.

Brandenburg, G. A. (1941, December 27). Editor and Publisher circulation survey reveals all-time high reached in 1941. *Editor and Publisher,* pp. 3, 12, 16.

California Supervisors. (1940). Report of Resolution by the California Association of School Supervisors at its annual convention in Pasadena, California, October 4, 1940, Legion dead-letter files (as cited in Jones, 1957, p. 71).

Carr, W. G. (1940, November). This is not treason. *The Journal of the National Education Association, 29,* 237.

Chadwick, S. F. (1939). Stephen F. Chadwick to J. G. Harbord, February 14, 1939, Legion dead-letter files (as cited in Jones, 1957, p. 11).

Chaillaux, H. L. (1939a). H. L. Chaillaux to Major Augustin G. Rudd, May 9, 1939, Legion dead-letter files (as cited in Jones, 1957, p. 15).

Chaillaux, H. L. (1939b). H. L. Chaillaux to Major Augustin G. Rudd, May 15, 1939, Legion dead-letter files (as cited in Jones, 1957, pp. 16-17).

Chaillaux, H. L. (1940a). H. L. Chailllaux to Major Augustin G. Rudd, June 22, 1940, Legion dead-letter files (as cited in Jones, 1957, p. 25).

Chaillaux, H. L. (1940b). H. L. Chaillaux to Edward H. Kenerson, October 1, 1940, Legion dead-letter files (as cited in Jones, 1957, p. 58).

Coleman, T. L. (1940). Tom L. Coleman to Professors Rugg and Counts, cc President Nicholas Murray Butler, "Co: 1940-1941" folder, William F. Russell Files, Columbiana Collection, Low Library, Columbia University.

Commission on Social Studies of the American Historical Association. (1934). *Conlcusions and recommendations*. New York: Charles Scribner's Sons.

Committee. (1940). Report of the Special Committee of Members of The American Legion and American Legion Auxiliary of North Canton Post #419, Relating to the Use of Textbooks Written by Harold O. Rugg in the North Canton, Ohio, Public Schools, October 14, 1940 (Cited in Jones, 1957, p. 33).

Communism foes heckle speakers at board meeting. (1935, November 7). *The Evening Star,* p. 1.

Corbett, R. (1943). Roger Corbett to H. L. Chaillaux, November 19, 1943, Legioni dead-letter files (as cited in Jones, 1957, p. 48).

Dewey, J. (1940, May 6,). Investigating education, *New York Times*, p. 16.

Dewey, J. (1944). John Dewey to Sidney Hook, April 25, 1944. Accession #13116, series 1, box 10, Correspondence with Sidney Hook, John Dewey Papers, Southern Illinois University, Carbondale.

Dilling, E. (1934). *The red network: A who's who of radicalism for patriots.* Kenilworth, IL: Author.

Education policy of Legion scored. (1935, November 24). *New York Times*, sec. 2, p. 7.

Evans, R. W. (2004). *The social studies wars: What should we teach the children?* New York: Teachers College Press.

Falk, A. T. (1939). *Does advertising harm or benefit consumers?* New York: Advertising Federation of America.

Forbes, B. C. (1939, August 15). Treacherous teaching. *Forbes*, p. 8.

Fries, A. A. (n.d. a). "Communism and chemical warfare," undated manuscript, folder 13, box 3, Amos A. Fries papers, Ax 234, Special Collections and University Archives, University of Oregon, Eugene.

Fries, A. A. (undated, b). "Collectivism is communism," undated manuscript, folder 10, box 3, Amos A. Fries papers, Ax 234, Special Collections and University Archives, University of Oregon, Eugene.

Gellerman, W. (1938). *The American Legion as educator.* New York: Teachers College, Columbia University.

Gellerman, W. (1972). *Martin dies.* New York: The John Day Company.

Getsinger, J. W. (1940). J. W. Getsinger to Milo J. Warner, November 25, 1940, Legion dead-letter files (as cited in Jones, 1957, p. 62).

Gilbert, D. C. (1940, September). Un-American text books. *National Republic*, pp. 15, 16, 31.

Harbord, J. G. (1939). J. G. Harbord to Stephen F. Chadwick, February 8, 1939. Legion dead-letter files (as cited in Jones, 1957, p. 10-11).

Hart, M. K. (1939) Handwritten note attached to Council Letter 66, October 15, 1939, "Social Science Investigation" folder, box 4, Merwin K. Hart Papers, Special Collections and University Archives, University of Oregon, Eugene.

Hart, M. K. (1940a, May 9). Dr. Dewey's stand disputed. *New York Times*, p. 22.

Hart, M. K. (1940b). Press release: Address of Merwin K. Hart, President of the New York State Economic Council, May 10, 1940, WIBX Radio, Utica, New

York, Merwin K. Hart Papers, box 4, "Social Science Investigation" folder, Special Collection and University Archives, University of Oregon.

Haworth Committee. (1939). "The Rugg Social Science Series of Textbooks," A Minority Report from the Committee Appointed by the Haworth, New Jersey, Board of Education, November 13, 1939 (Cited in Jones, 1957, p. 29-31).

Institute for Propaganda Analysis. (1941, February 25). Propaganda over the schools. *Propaganda analysis: A bulletin to help the intelligent citizen detect and analyze propaganda*, *4*, pp. 1-12.

Jones, O. E. (1957). *Activities of the American Legion in textbook analysis and criticism 1938-1951*. Unpublished doctoral dissertation, University of Oklahoma, Norman.

Kappan. (1935, January). Report published in *Phi Delta Kappan, 17*, 106-107.

Kelly takes six Rugg books "out of circulation." (1940, April 4). *Binghamton Press*. "Rugg, Harold" folder, subject file, box 74, Myers G. Lowman Papers, Hoover Institution, Stanford University.

Kenerson, E. H. (1940). E. H. Kenerson to H. L. Chaillaux, September 28, 1940, Legion dead-letter files (as cited in Jones, 1957, p. 58).

Kirk, H. H. (1941). H. H. Kirk to R. Worth Shumaker, December 16, 1941, Legion dead-letter files (as cited in Jones, 1957, p. 43).

Knowlton, H. L. (1940). H. L. Knowlton, Editor-in-Chief, Macmillan Company, to H. L. Chaillaux, October 4, 1940, Legion dead-letter files (as cited in Jones, 1957, p. 60).

Kuhn, I. C. (1958, October). Battle over books. *American Legion Magazine*, pp. 20-21, 37-40.

Lucas, H. C. (1940). H. C. Lucas to Milo J. Warner, October 29, 1940, Legion dead-letter files (as cited in Jones, 1957, p. 60).

Magazine gains. (1941, December 27). *Editor and Publisher*, p. 31.

Martin, J. (2002). *The education of John Dewey*. New York: Columbia University Press.

Mayer, M. S. (1939, July). Mrs. Dilling: Lady of the red network. *American Mercury*, *47*, 293-299.

McDonald, W. (1941). Walter McDonald to Milo J. Warner, June 17, 1941, Legion dead-letter files (as cited in Jones, 1957, p. 39).

Meredith, E. T. (1939). E. T. Meredith, Jr. to President Nicholas Murray Butler, June 9, 1939, "Harold Rugg" folder, box 58, William F. Russell Papers, Gottesman Libraries, Teachers College, Columbia University.

Mrs. Oagley continues defense of Rugg social science books. (1940, April). *Binghamton Press*. "Rugg, Harold" folder, subject file, box 74, Myers G. Lowman Papers, Hoover Institution, Stanford University.

Myer, W. E. (1940, September 30). The American Legion and civic education service. *The Civic Leader, 8*, p. 1.

Myers, A. F. (1940, October). Attacks on the Rugg books. *Frontiers of Democracy*, *7*, pp. 17-22.

National Republic. (1940, October). Masthead. *National Republic*.

News Bulletin. (1940). National Publicity Division, The American Legion, Indianapolis, Indiana, July 3, 1940 (as cited in Jones, 1957, p. 31).

Mrs. Oagley continues defense of Rugg social science books. (1940, April 4). *Binghamton Press*.

'Patrioteers' are scored. (1935, July 31). *New York Times*, p. 20.

Propaganda purge. (1939, July 10). *Time*, p. 42.

Publishers protest removal of Rugg textbooks. (1940, June 22). *The Publishers' Weekly*, p. 2345.

Reds in schools [Editorial]. (1940). *National Republic*, *28*, p. 12.

Rose, N. S. (1939). Norman S. Rose, President, Advertising Federation of America, letter to major advertisers, 1939, Rugg Textbook Controversy Scrapbook, Rauner Archive, Dartmouth College Library, Hanover, New Hampshire.

Rose, N. S. (1940). Norman S. Rose to Richard B. Carter, President, The Carter's Ink Company, April 1, 1940, Rugg Textbook Controversy Scrapbook, Rauner Archive, Dartmouth College Library, Hanover, New Hampshire.

Rudd, A. G. (1939a). Major Augustin G. Rudd to Stephen F. Chadwick, February 18, 1939, Legion dead-letter files (as cited in Jones, 1957, p. 12).

Rudd, A. G. (1939b). Major Augustin G. Rudd to Stephen F. Chadwick, March 6, 1939, Legion dead-letter files (as cited in Jones, 1957, p. 13).

Rudd, A. G. (1940a). Major Augustin G. Rudd to H. L. Chaillaux, May 31, 1940, Legion dead-letter files (as cited in Jones, 1957, pp. 24-25)

Rudd, A. G. (1940b). Augustin G. Rudd to Homer L. Chaillaux, September 20, 1940, Legion dead-letter files (as cited in Jones, 1957, p. 61).

Rudd, A. G. (1940c, April). Our "reconstructed" educational system. *Nation's Business*, pp. 27-8, 93-4.

Rugg critics lose ground. (1940, October 12). *Publishers' Weekly*, pp. 1492-1493.

Rugg explains his views in talk here. (1940. February). *Englewood Press*, February 1, 1940, sec. 2, p. 1, "Social Science Investigation" folder, box 4, Merwin K. Hart Papers, Special Collections, University of Oregon, Eugene.

Rugg papers. (various dates). Papers of Harold O. Rugg at Rugg's home as viewed by George Allan Kay. Cited in Kay, G. A. (1969). *Harold Rugg: Educational pioneer and social reconstructionist*. Unpublished doctoral dissertation, State University of New York, Buffalo.

Rugg, H. O. (1939). H. O. Rugg to William F. Russell, July 11, 1939, "Harold Rugg" folder, box 58, William F. Russell Papers, Gottesman Libraries, Teachers College, Columbia University.

Rugg, H. O. (1940). "Confidential Analysis of the Current (1939-1940) Attacks on the Rugg Social Science Series, Prepared by Harold Rugg in May-June 1940," "Harold Rugg" folder, box 58, William F. Russell Papers, Gottesman Libraries, Teachers College, Columbia University.

Rugg, H. O. (1941). *That men may understand: An American in the long armistice*. New York: Doubleday, Doran.

Rugg, H. O. (1951). Text of Rugg Speech from May 19, 1951. Taped excerpts made in Rugg's study, October 9, 1965 by George Kay. In the possession of the author.

Rugg textbooks restored in Englewood. (1941, January 25). *Publishers' Weekly*, 1941, p. 434.

Sailer, T. H. P. (1940). *Statements regarding the use of the Rugg series of social science texts in the Englewood school system*. Englewood, NJ: Committee of Parents and Taxpayers.

Schipper, M. C. (1979). *The Rugg textbook controversy: A study in the relationship between popular political thinking and educational materials*. Unpublished doctoral dissertation, New York University.

Schoolbook 'trial' staged in Jersey. (1939, November 21). *New York Times*, p. 25.

Seldes, G. (1938). *Lords of the press*. New York: Julian Messner.

Seldes, G. (1943). *Facts and fascism*. New York: In Fact.

Seldes, G. (1947). *One thousand Americans*. New York: Boni & Gaer.

Smith, D. R. (1940). David R. Smith to Boyd B. Sutler, September 25, 1940, Legion dead-letter files (as cited in Jones, 1957, p. 63).

Sokolsky, G. E. (1939). *The American way of life*. New York: Farrar & Rinehart.

Sokolsky, G. E. (1940). "Hard-boiled babes," *Liberty Magazine*, March 16, 1940, pp. 49-50.

Staff. (1935). Recent happenings in social studies. *The Social Studies*, 26, 482-483.

Taylor, T. J. (1941). Talbot J. Taylor, Chairman, Anti-Subversive Committee, Anthony S. Stumpp, Commander, George Alfred Smith Post #74, Fairfield, Connecticut, July 7, 1941, Legion dead-letter files (as cited in Jones, 1957, p. 41).

West, E. H. (1940). E. H. West to Mrs. William Sherman Walker on Guardians of Education letterhead, July 26, 1940, "Rugg, Harold" folder, subject file, box 74, Myers G. Lowman Papers, Hoover Institution, Stanford University.

Winters, E. A. (1968). *Harold Rugg and education for social reconstruction*. Unpublished doctoral dissertation, University of Wisconsin, Madison.

CHAPTER 6

THE STORM UNLEASHED

The next major development in the Rugg story raised the stakes considerably as it involved the activities of the National Association of Manufacturers (NAM), a mainstream business organization with considerable resources and many of the biggest names in American business among its members. National Council for the Social Studies (NCSS) and the NAM had a relationship that went back at least to May of 1940, when H. W. Prentis, president of the NAM wrote to NCSS offering to provide conference speakers to address "Fundamentals of the American Way." These fundamentals included, "Opportunity, Freedom of Religion and Speech, Representative Democracy, and Private Enterprise." Furthermore, he wrote, "Behind these watchwords is a story—a dramatic and inspiring message which, in the best interests of our country, cannot be told and retold too often" (Prentis, 1940). Evidently, the NAM believed that social studies teachers needed a strong reminder.

The National Association of Manufacturers, the nation's largest and most influential trade association, was founded in 1895 in Cincinnati, Ohio, with the avowed aims of promoting trade and commerce and championing the interests of business. The eighty founding members of the organization were a who's who of American business power. In its earliest years, the NAM campaigned against the rights of labor and opposed limits on child labor. In the 1910s the Garrett Committee found documentary evidence that the NAM had bribed members of Congress. "Colonel" Martin M. Mulhall, a secret lobbyist of the NAM, confessed the criminal

This Happened in Ameica: Harold Rugg and the Censure of Social Studies
pp. 203–252
Copyright © 2007 by Information Age Publishing
All rights of reproduction in any form reserved.

activities of the NAM in a series of articles he published in the *New York World* and *St. Louis Post-Dispatch*. Congress could not ignore the disclosures and launched a 4-month inquiry through which the NAM was totally discredited.

During the 1930s, concerns over many of President Roosevelt's New Deal programs and proposals led the organization to launch a public relations campaign "for the dissemination of sound American doctrines to the public." Subsequently, the NAM's National Industrial Information Committee spent more than $15 million over 13 years to promote its views and concerns (National Association of Manufacturers, 2006).

According to a 1930s investigation by the U. S. Senate Committee on Education and Labor, better known as the LaFollette Committee, the NAM was founded primarily in an effort to fight labor. After the 1932 election of Franklin D. Roosevelt, the NAM, which had been led by smaller industrialists, was taken over by large industrialists, the "brass hats" of corporate America, who reorganized the NAM, developed a plan with the goal of "business salvation," and created a program of united action by corporate interests, opposing the New Deal and flooding the country with biased propaganda. It was during this time that the NAM popularized use of the term "free enterprise" as a replacement for "capitalism," adopting the term at its 1932 national convention. According to one investigator, the term was coined by Adolph Hitler in *Mein Kampf* (1925), a book in which he proclaimed his economic policy of "freie unternehmungen" or "free enterprise." So, it was a Nazi term long before the NAM popularized it (Seldes, 1968, p. 112-113).

During the course of the 1930s, the NAM engaged in secret activities, using money in a corrupt manner to defeat labor, using "poison gas and machine guns" at their plants, hiring "spies, thugs, stool pigeons and other racketeers" to enforce their will, and creating a "network of propaganda" (Senate Committee, 1939). Moreover, according to a Senate report commissioned under the auspices of the Monopoly Investigation, the nation's economic system was largely controlled by a few (13) ruling families, headed by the du Pont, Mellon, and Rockefeller groups (Temporary National Economic Committee, 1940). Virtually all of these ruling families or their corporations were members of the NAM. Moreover, the findings of the Monopoly Investigation were suppressed, reported in the press in only the most general terms. The *New York Times*, for example, omitted the names of the organizations investigated, such as the NAM, from its story and did not divulge the most important findings of the O'Mahoney Committee, which conducted the investigation. The Committee's report was a damning indictment that portrayed big business, of which the NAM was the epitome, as the chief enemy of the general welfare of citizens, and identified the press as its main weapon (Seldes, 1968).

According to George Seldes, a noted independent journalist and editor of the newsletter, *In fact*, the NAM was "the center of American Fascism" and was engineering a great campaign through newspapers, magazines, and "a propaganda program in high schools and colleges" against the New Deal, labor, and social security (Seldes, 1943, pp. 80, 100). At the time of the Rugg textbook controversy, the NAM was "the peak association of big business ... (and) ... the most powerful private organization in the country." It served as the spokesman and "chief propagandist" for big business. It was a dominant power in the media and aimed its resources at "manufacturing public opinion" (Seldes, 1947, pp. 43, 61). The U.S. Chamber of Commerce, which had published the Rudd article, "Our Reconstructed Education System," in April, 1940, was a subsidiary of the NAM created in 1913, and served similar interests (Seldes, 1947).

The NAM had a long history of conducting propaganda campaigns, and had, almost from its beginnings, engaged in activities designed to influence the schools. With reorganization in 1933, the NAM established its Public Relations Committee, directed by James P. Selvage, and funded its expanded mission through the newly formed National Industrial Information Committee. The NAM conducted its propaganda campaign through newspaper and billboard advertising, stressing such themes as "The American Way" and "Harmony," through radio programming, newsreels, and direct mail. It circulated "You and Industry," a series of pamphlets which explained the operation of the business system. One which was titled, "The American Way," recited a catechism of American political principles, and argued against "bureaucratic control" of the citizenry and government regulation of industry. It also presented misleading and erroneous figures and graphs showing wide distribution of ownership of the economic system (R. J. Forbes, 1947).

The NAM viewed the New Deal as a regime which threatened the free enterprise system. NAM leadership was especially concerned about textbooks which purported to give students a "realistic" view of American life. It urged its members to scrutinize textbooks and to remove objectionable literature from schools. So, NAM involvement in textbook criticism was a logical extension of its long-term goal of public education aimed at telling the story of business, limiting the efforts of organized labor, and turning public opinion against "collectivism."

THE NAM CONTROVERSY

On December 11, 1940, the *New York Times* reported that the National Association of Manufacturers announced it would initiate a survey of textbooks then in use in the schools to see if it could find evidence of subversive teaching. The activities of the NAM received extensive coverage from George Sokolsky in the Hearst papers and were featured prominently in the *New York Times*. Ralph Robey, an assistant professor of banking at Columbia University, a columnist for *Newsweek*, and a well-known critic of the New Deal, was hired by the NAM to prepare a series of abstracts of some 800 currently used social studies textbooks to show the author's attitudes toward government and business. The *Times* reported that the congress of the NAM annually consolidated the opinions of 8,000 members employing some 2 million workers, and that it spent $1,600,000 a year on staff work and public information. The study was undertaken, it said, so that its members might move against any textbooks that are found prejudicial to our form of government, our society or to the system of free enterprise. As a well-known critic of the "socialism of the New Deal," Robey was far from an unbiased reporter. Nonetheless, the association pointed out that he was hired merely to develop abstracts, and that the reader could then judge the merits of the books ("N.A.M Will Survey," 1940).

Announcement of the NAM study was met by a good deal of concern and controversy and drew reactions from a number of social studies educators. Tyler Kepner, a teacher in Brookline, Massachusetts, and a member of the Commission on History a few years earlier, wrote to the Academic Freedom Committee of NCSS and suggested that the NAM "study" was "quite a different thing from the attack recently emanating from a well-organized minority group." Assuming "that more of this business is yet to come," he asked whether the council had in mind any "specific action" to offset the attacks. "How long," he wrote, "do leaders in social education propose to let Mr. Rugg carry the burden practically alone?" (Kepner, 1940). Howard Wilson responded that he agreed with Kepner's assessment of the NAM project, calling it "both ridiculous and dangerous." He was, however, "a little disturbed by Kepner's question about Rugg, and wrote, "Generally speaking, Rugg has enjoyed carrying his burden alone, I think. He has said and done a good many things that I, for example, could not support him on. However, on this one issue of freedom of speech and writing I agree wholeheartedly that we must support him." How to do so, "without at the same time supporting some of his educational positions which are not acceptable, is a difficult matter to decide." Wilson also mentioned that faculty at Harvard had recently appointed a committee to consider ways and means to defend "educational interests," and that NCSS would do something to help (Wilson, 1940). By late December, one prominent NCSS insider, Edgar Dawson, described the developing controversy over the textbooks as, "National Council for the Social Studies vs. 'United States of America or the civilized world ... which I am more interested in, that in any other movement I know of" (Dawson, 1940).

The Harvard committee, on January 2, 1941, issued a statement warning of the dangers in the process of abstracting textbooks, and urging that the National Association of Manufacturers join with other groups in support of a broad study of education. "The first and most obvious danger," they wrote, "is that the abstracting of the textbooks may be done with bias.... The second is the grave possibility of misuse of the abstracts which are produced." Their statement received a reassuring reply from the NAM, who claimed to be in complete accord with the group of Harvard professors in their view of education. The NAM response went on to say that it had received many requests for information regarding the "growing volume of criticism" of what is being taught in our schools, and undertook the study with the intent of providing information to their members. Their intent, the statement read, was "merely to determine the facts—to determine whether there is any basis ... for the growing apprehension about school textbooks." The response indicated that the NAM and Professor Robey would "refrain from interpretation," but would let readers make up their own minds (National Association of Manufacturers, 1941, pp. 2-3).

Despite such reassurances, not everyone was satisfied that the NAM acted with such a benign intent. In his editor's column in *Social Education*, Erling M. Hunt wrote that there was still "cause for concern" because of other disturbing factors in the situation. Moreover, he wrote that H. W. Prentis, Jr., president of the NAM for 1940, had made vigorous and repeated declarations repudiating the development of political and social democracy during the past 150 years. Hunt described the repeated "investigation of textbooks" by various groups over the past quarter century as "unfortunate and ineffectual." Specifically, he charged, "The implication that teachers, administrators, textbook authors, and publishers are delinquent in their patriotic duty ... is unjust and misleading," and that "focusing of attention on individual statements" rather than the school program as a whole obscures the main issues rather than helping the situation (Hunt, 1941b, pp. 88-89). Hunt was right about H. W. Prentis, Jr. He was a pro-Fascist, antilabor, and anti-Democracy business leader who had been named as a leading native Fascist by U.S. Attorney General Robert H. Jackson in 1940. He was later named a leading American Fascist by the dean of the House of Representatives, Adolph Sabath, and was an associate of Merwin K. Hart's in propaganda work (Seldes, 1943; Seldes, 1947). His views on education were equally conservative as he was "a staunch advocate of mental drill and discipline as the means of developing the ability to think accurately and persistently" (Armstrong Cork, 1961, p. 40).

The Story Breaks. On Saturday, February 22, 1941, a headline at the top of the front page of the *New York Times* read:

UN-AMERICAN TONE
SEEN IN TEXTBOOKS
ON SOCIAL SCIENCES

————

Survey of 600 Used in Schools
Finds a Distorted Emphasis
on Defects of Democracy

————

ONLY A FEW CALLED RED

————

Tendency Chiefly is to 'Tear
Down,' Dr. Robey Holds—
Propaganda Study Decried

The article reported:

A "'substantial portion'" of the social science textbooks now used in the high schools of this country tend to criticize our form of government and hold in derision or contempt the system of private enterprise, Dr. Ralph Robey, assistant professor of banking at Columbia University, said yesterday in summarizing his personal conclusions from abstracting the textbooks for the National Association of Manufacturers.... There is a notable tendency, he said, for books to play down what has been accomplished in this country and to stress the defects of our democracy. Only a few of the textbooks are actually subversive in content and follow the Communist party line, according to the study. On the whole, the books do not bow to any "line" as such, but tend to create discontent and unrest by their approach and treatment of government and business questions, the educator found.

The article went on to describe the sponsorship of the study, and pointed out the NAM's statement that "no position would be taken" by the organization, that it would be purely an objective study designed to give members a first-hand view of the books. Next, the article reported:

During the last year or so a controversy over subversive textbooks has disturbed the educational world. The social science textbooks by Dr. Harold Rugg of Teachers College have come in for a particularly severe attack. Several school systems have banned his books from the classroom, charging them with being too critical of our existing form of government. In one or two communities they were publicly burned. (Fine, 1941, p. 1)

All of this, including the reference to Rugg, appeared on the front page. Excerpts from the abstracts, printed on page six, were included from texts labeled economics, government, history, social problems, and social studies. Of the seven abstracts published in the *Times*, two were from Rugg books, one was from a book by Leon C. Marshall, an advocate of a social process approach, and another was a problems text titled "Society and Its Problems." The abstracts provided selected and provocative quotations from the texts, segments in which textbook authors critically described or raised questions about the functioning of government, the distribution of wealth and incidence of poverty, or the interplay of power and wealth. The quotations were provided without any sense of the remainder of each text, much of which would be found utterly innocuous. Yet, the selected evidence cited did suggest, quite strongly, that many textbooks were raising difficult questions about the real functioning of American institutions (Evans, 2004). Behind the headline, "Un-American Tone …," was a multiyear history of investigation by the Dies Committee gathering evidence and testimonials on "un-American activities" in American social and cultural institutions, and growing tensions and fears in the buildup to the United States entry into World War II.

"Protests, corrections, and replies" to Dr. Robey's findings came quickly. The *Times* earlier editions on February 22 had cast Dr. Robey's statements as part of his report, while later editions, as cited above, identified his remarks as "his personal conclusions." Robey later confirmed that the remarks were his personal opinion, and that the National Association of Manufacturers had not authorized his statements or the release of excerpts from the "abstracts." Nonetheless, the story led to a flurry of communications, clarifications, and statements of concern and other developments (Hunt, 1941a).

On the day of the story, Wilbur Murra, executive secretary of NCSS, wired a telegram to Walter D. Fuller, President of the NAM for 1941, stating that the Board of Directors "instructs me to express its deep concern about generalized statement on textbooks made by Ralph Robey in New York Times for Saturday, February 22. Please wire collect whether National Association of Manufacturers repudiates or endorses statement" (1941b). On February 24, Mr. Fuller replied, "Dr. Robey's opinion entirely personal. The National Association of Manufacturers neither endorses nor repudiates it because such endorsement or repudiation would infer that our organization has an opinion of its own." The wire went on to restate the NAM's official position that it did not have an opinion but merely wished to "epitomize the attitude expressed" in the textbooks under study (Fuller, 1941).

Fuller, who had been a member of the NAM's National Industrial Information Committee which funded its propaganda campaigns, was one of the "brass hat" clique who reorganized the NAM in 1933, president of Curtis Publishing Company, publisher of the *Saturday Evening Post*, and the person most responsible for the *Post*'s pro-Fascist attitude. In the 1920s the Post had run articles praising Mussolini and had more recently published two native-Nazi articles, titled "The Case Against the Jew," and "Will Labor Lose the War?" (Seldes, 1943, p. 96). It was Fuller who also gave the *Post*, the *Ladies Home Journal* and other Curtis publications a probusiness and industry slant. A noted orator, during the 1930s his main theme had been decreasing the rate of taxation on corporations. He was, apparently, rewarded for his stance when the NAM elected him its president for 1941.

NAM Backpedals. On the same day that Fuller wired his reply to Murra, February 24, the NAM issued a press release which included a letter sent to all NAM members declaring that Dr. Robey's criticisms represented his "personal opinion only," and insisting that the abstracts themselves were "completely unprejudiced." The letter also included several "considerations" printed at the beginning of each abstract, suggesting that textbooks should not be condemned for explaining unpopular political or economic philosophies "provided they are not advocated." And that they should treat "favorable aspects" of our institutions but "should not be required to ignore unfavorable aspects or important dissents" (Hunt, 1941a).

The date of the Robey story and release of initial findings of the N.A.M. survey coincided with the convention of the Progressive Education Association in Philadelphia and allowed press coverage of educators initial responses to the survey. In the closing session of the conference, Rugg defended "modern histories" in a roundtable held before 2,500 persons. Rugg was, in turn, criticized for his textbooks by Merwin K. Hart of the New York State Economic Council, and Alfred T. Falk of the Advertising Federation of America. Others participating in the roundtable and defending Rugg's position included George S. Counts, representing the American Federation of Teachers, Roger Baldwin of the American Civil Liberties Union, Kenneth M. Gould, editor of Scholastic, and Colston E. Warne of the Consumers Union.

Rugg quoted at some length from a speech that Hart had given earlier at Princeton, which he claimed marked Hart and his associates for what they really were: "These men are not friendly enemies; they are enemies, enemies of our children. Mr. Hart speaks as a representative of business, I as a representative of the American people." He then read from Hart's speech:

> Democracy is the rallying cry under which the American system is being prepared for despotism. If you find any organization containing the word democracy in its name it is probably directly or indirectly affiliated with the Communist Party. (MacDonald, 1941, p. 47)

Rugg accused Hart and others of attempting to destroy the American system and claimed that he and his supporters were the true defenders of the American way. Hart responded by pointing out that Rugg was one who "would play down the accomplishments of America and praise the accomplishments of Russia." The discussion appears to have then become a personal battle between Rugg and Hart.

Hart blasted Rugg for interjecting personalities into the argument and stated:

> I reject the socialist viewpoint contained in Doctor Rugg's books because among other things, it leaves out … one of the most vital factors. That factor is human nature. People do their best work when they are free. Under the socialist conditions as it seems to me the Rugg books stand for, the moment anybody gets ahead in business he becomes subject to more and more regulation, control and dictation by government bureaucrats. (MacDonald, 1941, p. 47)

The meeting drew to a close with charges of "liar" tossed back and forth.

In addition to the confrontation in Philadelphia, the CBS radio network, in its program "The People's Platform," broadcast a lively discussion held in Atlantic City, New Jersey, also on February 22, 1941, the eve of the National Education Associations annual meeting, titled, "Subversion in the Textbooks." In the roundtable discussion, charges and counter-charges were made. The most prominent critics to appear were Merwin K. Hart, conservative leader of the New York Economic Council who had instigated a number of local battles, and Orlen K. Armstrong, author of the *American Legion Magazine* article, "Treason in the Textbooks" which had appeared the previous September.

Armstrong was quoted as follows:

> I believe that starting around 1932 or 1933 there was a definite effort on the part of some textbook writers to write materials that would tend to depreciate our American ideals and institutions. There was a studied effort to teach that our government was founded by men who were particularly loyal to our classes. I think that when you destroy the faith in the fine work done by our founding fathers you do irreparable harm to the boys and girls of this country. (Textbook Writers, 1941, p. 47)

Other participants in the roundtable discussion at Atlantic City were Lyman Bryson of Teachers College, Hobart M. Corning, superintendent of schools, Omaha, Nebraska, and Dr. Howard E. Wilson, assistant professor of education, Harvard University. Armstrong and Hart attacked the spread of "subversive" material in textbooks, while Corning and Wilson took the opposite view, arguing that the problem was greatly exaggerated and challenging Hart and Armstrong to provide "documentary evidence" (Textbook Writers, 1941, p. 47).

The controversy was also addressed at the annual meeting of school-book publishers which happened to be in session in Philadelphia at the same time. The NAM survey was roundly criticized by the chair and speakers from the floor of the meeting. Several speakers questioned the honesty of the critics making the charges against the textbooks. After debating the issue for some time the group released a statement to the press:

> It is the consensus of this group that the charges made by those representa-tives of the N.A.M. cannot be substantiated by truth, that we believe that there are few, if any, of the texts used in the schools deliberately or otherwise written to break down the American plan of life. ("Publisher Fight," 1941)

Meanwhile, statements condemning the "recent attacks upon text-books" were issued by a number of organizations. The National Council for the Social Studies charged that the attacks were "unjust and mislead-ing," and that they brought discredit upon the entire school system. Press accounts of the meeting of the Progressive Education Association, which coincided with the *Times* story, included quotes from Rugg and from the authors of one of the other textbooks, vigorously defending their texts, attacking the critics, charging that the excerpts selected were unfair, and defending their books against the charge of un-Americanism. In addition, a committee of ten social scientists chaired by Wesley C. Mitchell, profes-sor of economics at Columbia University, was appointed by the American Committee for Democracy and Intellectual Freedom (ACDIF) to examine the textbooks charged with being subversive.

The wide coverage of the controversy, and of the response of school leaders, apparently had an immediate effect. On February 25, 1941, the National Association of Manufacturers issued a six-page statement that distanced itself from Professor Robey's charges. They also pointed out that he had violated their agreement not to make a premature release of findings and that the report was made without the permission of the Man-ufacturer's Association (Hunt, 1941a). Despite this statement from the NAM, the charges carried in the *New York Times* of February 22 triggered a series of investigations in school systems throughout the nation.

Editorials appeared in many newspapers and took positions on both sides in the controversy, though many were critical of the NAM and Robey. The *New York Herald-Tribune* gave some support to the criticism and suggested that "conflicting theories" were unsuitable for schools, given the possibility of bias and oversimplification, and the immaturity of youth. The *New York Post* was critical of both the NAM and Robey, and suggested that the Association's attempt to "disassociate itself" from Robey's comments would be a "hard trick" and calling the response from educators and publishers, along with the NAM backtracking, "a fine show of democracy," countering a threat to free speech. It stated that supporters of the NAM study of school books were the same influences that oppose most reform efforts. The *Des Moines Register* characterized the NAM study as a "witch-hunt; the *St. Louis Post-Dispatch* argued that there was "more real hope" in the criticisms contained in the texts "than in all the platitudinous whitewash in the world"; and, the *St. Louis Star-Times* defended "intellectual freedom and the spirit of inquiry" as the "essence of education in a democracy." For his part, Erling M. Hunt, editor of *Social Education*, expressed a skeptical attitude toward the manufacturers' failure to "disavow" Robey's comments. Hunt concluded that the entire enterprise created "confusion, suspicion, and embarrassment for teachers and administrators ... who stand in devotion to American government and the bases of our economic system" (1941a, pp. 291-292). Commentary on the NAM survey continued in the press through the month of March, and it was still a major topic of conversation at educational meetings.

On April 3, the NAM released a belated statement attempting to further distance itself from the entire controversy and offering to "cooperate with teachers at any time" to assure proper use of the abstracts. The NAM also sent a long letter to 38,000 social science teachers and 10,000 school officials in which Mr. Fuller asserted the NAM's confidence in American teachers and expressed regret that "distorted" impressions of the project had been given such wide currency. He also asserted that from the beginning, the NAM "believed that the issue of subversiveness in textbooks was being immensely exaggerated" (Hunt, 1941c). Later, in September, 1941, the NAM explored the idea of an exhibit at the annual meeting of the NCSS, but confessed a "hesitation ... born of a very strong feeling that it might be misinterpreted. "We do not wish to create the impression that we are seeking to promote, advertise or urge the use of NAM literature" (Abbott, 1941). Wilbur Murra, executive secretary replied, "You are right in anticipating that teachers might misunderstand your motives" (Murra, 1941a).

The NAM abstracts and subsequent communications were shaped and influenced, in part, by members of the publicity office, administration and office staff of the NAM. The organization had a long history of interest and concern regarding the general portrayal of American business in schools and textbooks, prior to involvement in the textbook controversy. The organization's general hope was that schools, teachers and materials would inculcate patriotism by a focus on "the historical and spiritual foundations of the American system of government, free enterprise and religious liberty." Teachers should not "ignore the defects" of our form of government, but they should point out that "the advantages and strengths of our republican system far outweigh its defects and weaknesses." Similarly, they did not mean that teachers should "deny the existence of defects in the operation of private enterprise," but that "free enterprise should be advocated for what it is—namely, an essential element in the preservation of representative democracy and religious freedom" (Committee on Educational Cooperation, 1939, pp. 3-5).

By April, 1940, the NAM, had clearly outlined a set of possible activities for "educational cooperation" aimed at stimulating better understanding of the business point-of-view. Industrial leaders, meeting on April 22 at the Waldorf-Astoria in New York, engaged in discussion of textbook bias as part of a larger meeting and made plans for what was called the Mobilization for Understanding of Private Enterprise (NAM Educational Cooperation Meeting, 1940). By late summer, 1940, concerns over schoolbooks had evolved through preliminary investigation and discussion into a plan to develop textbook abstracts. The campaign was aimed at improving understanding via individual conferences between local business leaders and school administrators, who would be armed with greater knowledge of the textbooks as facilitated by the textbook abstracts. The abstracts were ostensibly prepared in an effort to provide unbiased information regarding the texts, so that interested persons could decide whether to read or further investigate any particular book.

Internal memoranda from the files of the NAM suggest that many in the organization's offices were rather squeamish about the entire enterprise, and that it was considered a "ticklish subject." Because of the nation's tradition of academic freedom, and previous business association miscues which had led to negative publicity, many staff members believed that it could result in a less than positive outcome for business and the NAM. The organization dismissed the notion of issuing a "black list" or a "white list," despite the fact that it was suggested by H. W. Prentis, then President of the NAM (Harrison, 1940). One advisor within the organization even suggested that it was "a mistake to get involved in the textbook question, even if we are doing it in an entirely proper fashion, and that inevitably, the criticism we will receive will do more harm than any good that can result" (Harrison, 1941a). In the aftermath of the Robey story, the executive assistant most involved with the abstracts project, C. E. Harrison, wrote, "I think we have learned enough to gather that few of the books present any clear-cut case of 'advocating collectivism.' There are many, however, which take pretty one-sided viewpoints on controversial issues … it may inculcate a cynicism in the mind of the student which makes him susceptible to the glittering advertisements for collectivism which he may encounter outside the schools" (Harrison, 1941b).

Representatives of the opposing sides in the NAM conflict met on Town Meeting of the Air, broadcast by the National Broadcasting Company on May 1, 1941. The presenters included Hamilton Hicks, a judge and Legionnaire and contributor to the *American Legion Magazine*, Ralph W. Robey, Erling M. Hunt, and James Marshall, president of the New York City Board of Education. The May, 1941, issue of *American Legion Magazine* had carried an article written by Hicks critiquing Rugg, titled, "Ours to Reason Why." The article contained charges similar in tone to what had appeared earlier in the Armstrong article, but carried a striking comparison:

> The professors who use the classroom for dissemination of political propaganda ... understand the average parent's prejudice against such conduct. They proceed, therefore, with as much secrecy as possible.... Dr. Harold O. Rugg ... admits that he is a propagandist. While (seeking) to destroy American traditions and bring about a new, collectivist social order, Rugg flatly committed himself in favor of totalitarianism.
>
> Like Hitler, Rugg gathers like minded followers by stating his aims clearly in a 'Mein Kampf' and disarmed the public by stoutly denying the implications of that book, while carrying them out to the letter. (Hicks, 1941, p. 5).

On the Town Meeting of the Air on May 1, 1941, Hicks and Robey repeated their published accusations against the Rugg textbooks. In response, Erling Hunt, during his initial statement, described the schools, and particularly the social studies, as a "battleground" for special interest groups, and noted:

> often the appeals, and the types of pressure used, are undemocratic and misleading. Sentences and paragraphs have been, and are being torn from textbooks and twisted or interpreted into meanings that were never intended. Efforts have been, and are being, made to discredit textbooks by discrediting their authors. Minority groups, whose membership, financial support, and actual aims are sometimes concealed under patriotic names, appeal at times to religion, "good citizenship," and "Americanism," and at times to fears of communism, fascism, and "radicalism." In statements careless of facts and in the use of evidence, they have attempted, and are attempting, to break down confidence in public education ... after weighting the charges and studying the textbooks, I am convinced that the sensational charges rest on garbled data and on misrepresentations. Our textbooks are *not* dangerous. But irresponsible attacks on public education at a time when that indispensable source and support of democracy needs to be strong rather than weak, can be very dangerous indeed (Applause). (Town Meeting, 1941, pp. 8-11)

Later in the program, Hunt correctly pointed out that Rugg's textbooks were written in the 1920s, and that they were "all out in the first editions before *The Great Technology* ever was thought of." He then called it "a very interesting dodge" for the textbook critics to talk about *The Great Technology* instead of the textbooks (p. 24).

Mr. Marshall's comments were equally effective:

> The attack on textbooks has become an epidemic.... Evidently these critics want our children to believe that everything is hunky-dory with our country—that big business handles itself like the corner grocer it has gradually been replacing, and that unemployment is all a mistake.... Are we to tell them a fairy tale about our economic well-being? I think that the people who are afraid to have our children face the truth in these matters have themselves a sense of insecurity.... It is the psychology of the dictator who does not permit criticism for fear that it will indicate weakness in him. And yet we know that to point out the shortcomings in capitalist economics need not imply the abolition of private property and the slavery of state capitalism or state socialism.... (Textbook critics) are the very people who have lobbied against all social legislation and all government control of business for the last twenty years.... Teachers will watch their step. They will be afraid to step on the toes of the local chamber of commerce.... Therefore, these pressure groups, which attack school textbooks and the social studies, become, in fact, terror groups in their relation to the schools. (Town Meeting, 1941, pp. 16-17).

From that point, the meeting quickly devolved into name-calling and an exchange of charges and accusations.

THE STRUGGLE CONTINUES

The battle over the books continued through the spring of 1941 in a number of other venues. The American Economic Foundation of Cleveland, Ohio, sponsored a radio forum broadcast on the Mutual Broadcasting Network in New York City titled, "Wake Up, America!" which featured a debate between Rugg and Dr. Ruth Alexander, a noted economist, writer and lecturer, on the evening of April 28, 1941. The debate was officially centered on the topic, "Does Capitalism Offer Youth a Fair Opportunity?" though a good portion of the discussion was devoted to the Rugg textbook controversy. It seems that in the course of the program, and in an effort to prove his support for private enterprise and training of "leaders," Rugg made a statement implying to his opponents that he had received Rockefeller funding to support development of his social science textbooks. The statement, from a transcript, reads as follows:

> Leadership, we want leadership. Why have I been in private schools, why was I financed by the Rockefeller people for nine years in the Lincoln

School teaching their children and the children of their young people who were to be the leaders of today? (Wake Up America, 1941)

Rugg's statement was challenged by B. C. Forbes and Ruth Alexander, who, in the days following the broadcast, communicated their objections to John D. Rockefeller, Jr. (Alexander, 1941; B. C. Forbes, 1941). Though the issue was, apparently, never publicly aired, Rugg was, in truth, "financed by the Rockefeller people" only indirectly. He was employed by the Lincoln School during his early years at Teachers College, years which coincided with development of the pamphlets and textbook series. His employment as both school psychologist and professor furnished him access to the Lincoln School and time to develop the social science materials, though there was never any specific connection. In the series of letters exchanged following the program, Abraham Flexner, an officer of the General Education Board who had taken a leading role in development of the Lincoln School wrote of Rugg, "He has no more right to mention you or the 'Rockefeller people' as financing him than he has to mention me." Flexner castigated Rugg's comment as "shameful," describing him as a "clever but thoroughly superficial person in so far as the social sciences are concerned" (Flexner, 1941). Rugg's veracity on this and other points was subsequently challenged by patriotic critics (Rudd, Hicks, & Falk, 1941).

The Legion Marches On. The American Legion campaign to remove the Rugg books continued into 1941 and beyond. As we have seen, publication of the Armstrong article, "Treason in the Textbooks," produced a storm of controversy, a partial retraction from the Legion, and inspired countless discussions in cities and towns across the nation. The Legion's offices received a mix of feedback, largely supportive of the attack on Rugg, but frequently asking for clarification or additional evidence. After considering the suggestions, the Legion took a new tack. One prominent Legionnaire, past vice commander of the Michigan department, questioned the Legion about the Armstrong article, and wrote:

Are the materials and textbooks listed in the September issue "Treasonable' in content? If you say they are, can we be assured of the backing of the National Organization of The American Legion in having them thrown out of the schools? In other words, if we put out our neck on material appearing in the official magazine, are we certain that we shall have competent and intelligent support from the home office? (Johnson, 1940a)

A follow-up letter from the same Legionnaire went on to suggest that the Legion consider employment of a man with "a comprehensive background of American history and the social sciences ... a man of integrity, sincere and fearless … (with) … intelligence enough to handle such problems with tact and diplomacy" (Johnson, 1940b).

The response from the Legion's director of publications read:

> the national Executive Committee at its meeting here yesterday authorized the employment of a man with an educational background to handle contacts between The American Legion and educational institutions, and to make a thorough study of the entire textbook situation. (Barton, 1940)

Legion Commander Milo J. Warner informed Ginn and Company, Rugg's publisher, of the Legion's intent, and on December 16, 1941, the Legion issued a special news release announcing that Warner had appointed R. Worth Shumaker, superintendent of Upshur County Schools in West Virginia, to serve as Assistant Director of the National Americanism Commission, "to specialize in the study of Legion activities in the field of education" and bring "expert knowledge" to the campaign against "un-American" school textbooks (News Bullletin, 1940). Shumaker had a long history of service in administrative posts and appeared to be well suited to the position.

In the spring of 1941, under Shumaker's direction, and while the controversy over the NAM abstracts was still raging, the Legion published a series of articles and pamphlets designed to put an end to the entire matter by supplying additional leverage to local Legionnaires. There was the article by Hamilton Hicks, discussed earlier, which appeared in May, 1941. One month earlier, in April, 1941, the *American Legion Magazine* published an article authored by Shumaker titled, "No 'NEW ORDER' for Our Schools." The article contained an analysis of the work of the "Frontier Thinkers" attempts to "capture control of American education" and accused Counts and Rugg of "attempting to build a new social order of a collectivist type" through their various publications and school textbooks. Like the Armstrong article, Shumaker's commentary was accompanied by a dramatic illustration on the first page which showed termites, worms, and vermin eating holes in "Textbooks of American Ideals." One of the worms was wearing wire rimmed glasses and swastikas on a chubby face and body, and was strongly reminiscent of Rugg himself. A caption read: "The philosophy of Counts and Rugg encourages the totalitarian borers-from-within who would destroy our democracy" (Shumaker, 1941, p. 5). The article included evidence of Counts exploits in the Soviet Union, and an account of Rugg's statements at the PEA convention in Cleveland on March 2, 1934, discussed earlier, that described the 3-year "New American" campaign to be financed by $50,000 per year which would aim to obtain the support of all intelligent liberals in the country and organize a group of 14,000,000 people to push President Roosevelt "to the left"

(Shumaker, 1941, p. 44). The article also contained numerous quotes from *The Great Technology* and Rugg's textbooks, and argued, "Throughout Dr. Rugg's publications one inevitably gets the impression that he is constantly and subtly driving towards a socialistic state which can be grafted on American democracy" (p. 45). Though its conclusions were similar, when compared to the Armstrong article, Shumaker's article, and the pamphlets which followed, seemed quite scholarly and less sensationalistic. In a few cases, Shumaker acknowledged revisions in the textbooks. Still, the most damaging passages were drawn from Rugg's speeches and theoretical writing, not from his school materials.

A number of Rugg's other critics began circulating a report of the Cleveland meeting in 1934 and citing Rugg's statement that efforts would be made:

> to organize 14,000,000 persons into a "pressure group" to force more radical changes in the economic system within three months. He said funds were forthcoming, but would refuse to reveal the source. He outlined the plan—to include a "central planning agency," probably in New York—to tie together thousands of groups of citizens who believe that the capitalist system should come to an end. (Rudd et al., 1941, p. 38)

In a confidential memorandum prepared for his superiors at Teachers College, Rugg denied the claims that many of his critics were making regarding his statements at the Cleveland meeting in 1934, charging, "they lie straight out ... I have never said or implied that our adult education plans were "to tie together thousands of groups of citizens who believe that the capitalist system should come to an end." Rugg branded the allegations, "unmitigated falsehood," and wrote, "Every statement ascribed to me and my motives is by the implication that somebody 'is said to have said,' etc; all was obtained from newspaper reporters' accounts, oral hearsay accounts, and the like" (Rugg, 1940, pp. 16-19). One report on the Cleveland conference, written by the editor-in-chief of the U.S. Office of Education who attended the session at which Rugg spoke, concluded that the convention as a whole was "distinctly pink." He reported that discussion at the symposium chaired by Rugg, "produced agreement that we must move toward a socialized, cooperative society" and called for "organizing local groups into a party which would in an election take over the government, which would take over nearly everything?" However, the author cast Goodwin Watson, rather than Rugg, as the source of the most radical statements (Boutwell, 1934, p. 298).

On April 18, 1941, another news bulletin was issued by the American Legion, this one announcing publication of a series of four pamphlets describing the philosophy and textbooks of Harold Rugg. The pamphlets prepared by Shumaker were titled, *Rugg Philosophy Analyzed*. The first vol-

220 R. W. EVANS

ume was devoted to *Basic Excerpts from The Great Technology.* In the preface to the pamphlet Shumaker explained, "The Great Technology is not a textbook but in order to understand Dr. Rugg's philosophy, it should be the first book read. It explains the doctrines and methods which he plans to introduce into the schools." The pamphlet then illustrated, through a series of paragraph length excerpts, the Rugg philosophy as explained in his book. On the second page of the pamphlet Shumaker summarized Rugg's "Axioms for the Great Technology" then provided quotes from Rugg supporting each axiom. Though Rugg would have worded the summary differently, it reflected the essence of Rugg's ideas, transposed into stark and troubling, even inflammatory language. Shumaker's summary appeared scholarly and thoughtful, even listing page number for quotes, but gave Rugg's work a rather extreme spin through Shumaker's paraphrasing and subheadings. It ignored Rugg's debt to technocracy. More damaging, it suggested that the axioms contained in *The Great Technology* formed the basis for Rugg's social science textbooks, and that many of the axioms, "subtly or otherwise, carry over into his textbooks" (p. 3).

This suggestion was at the heart of the charges against Rugg. There was little doubt that many of Rugg's ideas for social reconstruction were more advanced than many other thinkers of the day, though in 1933, in the depths of the depression, he had many compatriots. However, to assert that Rugg's textbooks contained propaganda for his advanced social ideas was to put the cart before the horse. As we have seen, Rugg's social ideas were still in the embryonic stage as his pamphlet and textbook series was taking shape. Given more than half-a-century distance, the charge that the axioms contained in *The Great Technology* were advocated, even subtly, in the textbooks appears a major stretch and suggests either a cursory and biased reading or a conscious propaganda campaign.

The second pamphlet developed by Shumaker was titled, *The Complete Rugg Philosophy—Its Transfer to the Textbooks.* This pamphlet contained an abstract and an analysis of Rugg's educational and social philosophy. It reiterated the charge that "the philosophy" of Rugg's adult books was "identical" with that portrayed in the textbooks. The introduction stated:

The basic concept on which the books are constructed is "change."

The basic objective is "reconstruction."

The books are built on "scientific design."

The author considers America a "depressed society."

The "content-core" of the Rugg social and education program was contributed by "frontier thinkers."

New Allegiances are sought.

The "new society" will be collectivistic.

The author is friendly to many Socialist and Communist ideas and principles.

History and geography are sacrificed for political, social and economic discussion inserted for the purpose of promoting the "reconstruction" objective (National Americanism Commission, 1941b, p. 1).

The third volume in the series by Shumaker, titled, *Textbook Abstracts*, consisted of brief analyses of the Rugg junior high series and contained many quotes from the textbooks. The introduction stated:

The textbooks seek social reconstruction. This "reconstruction" objective is based on social, economic, political and educational changes. The books are depressing rather than stimulating and there are few statements purposely designed to stimulate self-reliance, control, initiative, integrity or intellectual honesty. The books are conspicuous for their omissions and inaccuracies.... . The Rugg textbooks do not make any direct statements to the effect that we should overthrow the American government. Dr. Rugg creates his effects by implication and inference and by destructive methods rather than openly subversive statements. Dr. Rugg has very little respect for those things which Americans of an older generation held were sound and worthy of preservation. Pupils who are taught Rugg's depressing American picture during the child's tender formative years will feel that America is not worth defending.

America cannot have Socialism or Collectivism, no matter how it is disguised, and the American form of government, and the American way of life, at one and the same time" (National Americanism Committee, 1941c, p. 1).

This charge, that the Rugg textbooks sought social reconstruction, was largely an extrapolation read into the Rugg social science series from his other books and speeches. Though the textbooks were forward looking, they were never as forthright as Rugg's stated philosophy in other venues. The fourth volume in the series, *Rugg Philosophy Further Analyzed*, contained a reprint of an article by Major Augustin G. Rudd titled, "Education for 'New Social Order,'" which first appeared in *National Republic* magazine (National Americanism Committee, 1941d; Rudd, 1942).

Approximately 100,000 copies of the four Shumaker pamphlets, *Rugg Philsophy Analyzed*, were distributed nationwide. Many of the pamphlets undoubtedly reached school administrators and board of education members. In an address to the Twenty-Fourth Annual Convention of the American Legion in Kansas City, Missouri, on September 19-21, 1942, Shumaker reported:

The effort of the American Legion to eliminate all un-American teachings from the schools of the nation has been a real success.... The Rugg books are being dropped quietly and without fanfare. Literature and other aids are mailed out from national headquarters daily, and unheralded but decisive eliminations are continuously reported from the field. This quiet, effective process of elimination has proved highly satisfactory. In fact, radical advocates of the use of the Rugg books have frankly and publicly admitted that the books are being "quietly removed from the schools" and the "national sale of the series has dropped markedly." (Shumaker, 1942)

The Legion campaign against the Rugg textbooks had apparently done its job. Following the highly publicized Armstrong article, and the subsequent partial retraction, the Legion this time around had done its homework. Through the presence of R. Worth Shumaker, it provided the kind of depth and apparent scholarly support that could win the day in many towns and cities.

Most Legionnaires probably shared the sentiments of Mr. Eugene C. Pomeroy, an official in the Veterans of Foreign Wars, a competing patriotic organization, who wrote to Shumaker, "Your analysis of the Rugg books is complete and I think it is the most valuable contribution that any organization in our country has made to date for Americanizing our grade and junior high schools" (Pomeroy, 1948). Others likely held a view similar to that of one Legionnaire who wrote to Nicholas Murray Butler, "Have you fired those Communists yet? As it stands now Columbia is a very active cell" (Coleman, 1941).

However, not all Legionnaires supported the continuing campaign against Rugg. Albion Roy King, a Legionnaire and professor at Cornell College in Mount Vernon, Iowa, wrote to Shumaker, complaining of his "negative approach to the whole problem," and suggested that the pamphlets would contribute to "a further deepening of the suspicion ... that the Legion is just another pressure group with no important suggestions of a positive sort." King described the attack as "short-sighted." He went on:

What ... is education for if not to produce certain changes in our democracy.... An educational philosophy which merely strengthens the determination of students to preserve the status quo and to do absolutely nothing about poverty or industrial plutocracy or political chicanery ... seems to me to be the last thing in the world that Legionnaires want to hold ... . I beg of you to lay off the negative stuff at once and proceed to outline a program of constructive social education. (King, 1941).

Despite the objections of Professor King and a few other fair-minded Legionnaires, the American Legion sustained its attacks on Rugg and continued to bring pressure on local school boards and state textbook adoption committees in the states where they existed. In Nevada, the State Textbook Commission removed the Rugg books from the state textbook adoption list after receiving objections from the Legion (Corbett, 1943). The Legion sponsored a similar campaign in New Hampshire.

THE DEFENSE

The defense against the attacks on the Rugg textbooks was mounted on several fronts. Although they received much less publicity than Rugg's critics, there was an extensive and well-organized defense of Rugg mounted by many of his colleagues teaching at universities, and it was initiated almost from the beginning of the attacks. Committees were organized in his defense at Columbia University and at Harvard. Other groups who sprang to his defense included The American Civil Liberties Union, The National Council for the Social Studies, The Progressive Education Association, The Association of Textbook Publishers, The Committee for Cultural Freedom, and his publisher, Ginn and Company.

Perhaps the most active of these committees was the American Committee for Democracy and Intellectual Freedom (ACDIF), previously organized by many of Rugg's colleagues at Columbia University and led by anthropologist Franz Boaz, who served as national chair. This Committee's main efforts in the textbook controversy were made through use of open letters sent to the individual school people involved in local struggles to remove the Rugg textbooks. The open letters were then often published in other venues. The letters carried an impressive list of at least 150 people, many of them the very "frontier thinkers" that Rugg frequently cited as the basis for his work.

The ACDIF was made up of academics and civil libertarians who had engaged in the battle for academic freedom from earlier in the 1930s. They encouraged a "democratic approach to textbook selection" but held that only professional educators were fully qualified to select textbooks (Zimmerman, 2002, p. 72). As we have seen, in its response to the NAM textbook investigation, the ACDIF appointed a Committee on Textbook Censorship chaired by economist Wesley C. Mitchell and composed of 10 "outstanding" social scientists who, in an effort to "combat the censorship threat inherent in the textbook investigation" were each asked to examine one of the textbooks involved, "test the accuracy of the NAM abstract," and prepare a brief analysis of the book. A press release announcing the effort stated that the committee was "apprehensive of the use which may be made of the NAM abstracts" (ACDIF Press Release, 1941).

Later, the committee wrote another open letter, this time addressed to Vierling Kersey, superintendent of the Los Angeles schools, denouncing Kersey's arguments for removing the Rugg books from the city's schools, and "dissenting vigorously" from his interpretation that development of

Ralph T. Robey, author of NAM textbook abstracts (Courtesy of Hagley Museum and Library).

H. W. Prentis, Jr., President, 1940, National Association of Manufacturers (Courtesy of Hagley Museum and Library).

Walter D. Fuller, President, 1941, National Association of Manufacturers (Courtesy of Hagley Museum and Library).

"Death to Organized Labor" (*Facts and Fascism*, 1943).

Franz Boas, Chairman, American Committee for Democracy and Intellectual Freedom (American Philosophical Society).

John Dewey, 1859-1952 (Morris Library, Southern Illinois University, Carbondale).

"That Men May Understand," 1941 (Columbia University Archives).

" 'Tis education forms the common mind.
Just as the twig is bent, the tree's inclined."
ALEXANDER POPE, *Essay on Man* (1600 A. D.)

—Courtesy N. Y. Journal-American

THE SLIP SHEET

"The Slip Sheet" (Guardians of American Education, 1941).

YOUR CHILD is their TARGET

How a small but well organized minority is attempting to manipulate our
public schools to condition our children for what they call "a new social order."

By IRENE CORBALLY KUHN

"Your Child is Their Target" (*American Legion Magazine*, June, 1952).

Progressive Education Increases Delinquency (Dartmouth College Library)

"constructive" attitudes "in any way justifies elimination of criticism of the way our society is functioning." This was the first major city to oust the Rugg textbooks, and the letter denounced Kersey's action as "a grave threat to educational freedom ... in our country as a whole" (Mitchell, 1941).

Ginn and Company, which had a major investment in the Rugg materials and stood to lose the lion's share of the junior high social studies textbook market, seems to have carried on its own independent campaign in Rugg's defense. The Rugg series was Ginn's best seller and they defended it vigorously, frequently publishing Rugg's statements and other favorable materials contained in media reports. Two representatives of the company later reported that the Rugg series was one of the company's all-time best sellers, that they felt a debt to Rugg for keeping the company "in the black" during the depression years, and so, went all out to defend him against attackers (Winters, 1968, p. 185). One memo circulated by Ginn and Company at the height of the controversy was addressed, "To those who love the TRUTH," and read:

> Today once again social-science teaching is under fire. Inspired by various motives, over-zealous patriots and the spokesmen of certain pressure groups are hurling at the textbooks of Dr. Harold Rugg a miscellany of charges – that the author is a communist, that he is seeking to overthrow American institutions and the American way of life....
>
> Dr. Rugg is one of America's most distinguished educators. He has asserted and re-asserted time and again his faith in America, in democracy, and the American way ... he believes that "true Americanism means the courage to face realities, not the criminal negligence of ignoring them."
>
> Because we felt that his books in their emphasis on reasoning from the facts, on clear thinking, and on tolerant understanding represented a forward step in American education, we published them. Time has not changed our opinion.
>
> Ginn and Company
(Ginn, undated memo).

Rugg's friends and associates on the journal *Frontiers of Democracy* were also active in his defense. The board of editors of the journal commissioned a series of articles covering the controversy which appeared in succeeding issues. Though clearly supportive of Rugg, they also gave his opponents a chance to express their views in the journal, while, at the same time, tearing them apart in their editorial columns. In the December, 1940 issue, Merwin K. Hart published an article titled, "Let's Discuss This on its Merits," which contained Hart's response to a story in the previous issue titled, "Gilt-Edged Patriot: Merwin K. Hart" written by Roger Baldwin of the ACLU, and accompanied by editorials from Jesse Newlon and Frederick Redefer which contained bitter denunciations of Hart and his attacks on the Rugg texts (Baldwin, 1940; Hart, 1940).

A range of other concerned professional organizations also rose to Rugg's defense. Organizations of high school social studies teachers in New York City and state were active on Rugg's behalf. In several instances, Rugg was provided the opportunity to address the organization and express his views, and the attendant publicity gave added support to his defense.

The Academic Freedom Committee of NCSS played a supportive role as well. It issued a statement supporting academic freedom, and later prepared "a packet of reading matter on freedom of teaching in the social studies area," which included a 66-page booklet on fending off attacks on textbooks (Curti, 1941). Historians also came to Rugg's defense. The Council of the American Historical Association asked Professor A.M. Schlesinger to draft a statement regarding controversial issues in textbooks. The statement, which was then approved by the Council, gave strong support for the inclusion of controversial questions in "the historical account," and for encouraging a "spirit of inquiry" in young people. However, the statement also read that the textbook writer has "an obligation to give both sides" and made no mention of current issues (American Historical Association, 1941). Many textbook writers, including Rugg, had, in Schlesinger's view, failed to follow the edict to "give both sides," and many historians were less than fond of the focus on social problems and social issues in schools. So, the statement of support from the AHA was not as strongly worded as it might have been.

In addition to the organized efforts on his behalf, the first line of defense was offered by administrators at Columbia University and Teachers College. During the late 1930s and early 1940s the president of the University, Nicholas Murray Butler, and William F. Russell, dean of Teachers College received what was described by the provost as "a good many inquiries by telephone and by mail" (Fackenthal, 1940). In the majority of cases, the letters and inquiries were instigated by the multiple campaigns conducted by Rugg's opponents. A few of the inquiries came from university alumni. Archival materials suggest that Rugg's administrators did an admirable job of deflecting criticism. When responses were sent, Rugg's administrators defended their controversial professor. In reply to an inquiry regarding one of the earliest attacks, Dean Russell responded to the concerns of a school board president, "Professor Rugg is not a Communist, has never been a Communist, and has no connection whatever with any red net-work. He is a scholar.... I would not hesitate to recommend his books for study by my own children" (Russell, 1938). In response to another letter from an alum, President Butler stated that the charges against Rugg and his colleagues "have absolutely no basis in fact" (Butler, 1940).

Rugg himself was undoubtedly the chief advocate for the defense of social studies, and the Rugg textbooks, against the attackers. Rugg gave an able defense of his work, and attempted to meet every attack directly, appearing in person "whenever and wherever possible." It seemed that Rugg enjoyed face to face confrontations with his attackers, and it was said by people who knew him well that Rugg "lived for an argument," often playing the role of 'devils advocate' to stir up controversy, provoking opponents into making rash statements which he would tear apart with cold and sarcastic responses (Winters, 1968, p. 186).

Rugg's confrontations with his accusers followed a familiar pattern. First, he would be accused of being a Communist because he wrote for *The Daily Worker* (he did not) and because he was included in *The Red Network* (he was). Then he would be criticized over his plan for a socialistic society in *The Great Technology*. Then the accusers would turn to the textbooks themselves. Confronting a similar situation again and again, the critique and Rugg's responses became somewhat routine. When pressed, critic after critic would admit they had not read the books.

Under siege on every side, Rugg was urged frequently by publishers to tell his side of the story. In the confidential memorandum that he submitted to the administration at Teachers College, Rugg had drafted an analysis of his own view of the controversy as of June, 1940 (Rugg, 1940). Not long after that, he accepted an offer from Doubleday to produce a semiautobiographical work that would tell the story of the books, how they came to be written, and offer Rugg's side in the controversy. *That Men May Understand* was published in April, 1941, and received generally favorable reviews. A writer for *The New York Times Book Review* scoffed at the idea of Rugg being a communist, and described his generation of educational reformers as having "imbibed the antique liquor of utopianism which was always turning New England heads" (Shuster, 1941). A review published in *The Saturday Review* called the book "significant" because it so clearly revealed a great "struggle between social ideals" (Gotesky, 1941). A reviewer in *The New Republic* praised the book and described Rugg as a thoughtful educator who "knew his business" (Dexter, 1941). *The Nation* compared Rugg to St. Paul carrying the gospel, and Teachers College to the early church. *Publishers Weekly* endorsed the book and joined Rugg in attacking his critics:

The harm which 1940 did to American education cannot be recalled. Mrs. Elizabeth Dilling, Bertie C. Forbes, Merwin K. Hart, may know little about American history but they did know how to work on the prejudices of the American people....

No writer is above criticism ... but no one can read the story of how the anti-Rugg campaign of 1940 was conducted and still feel that it was conducted by citizens intent on elevating the instruction in the schools. (Melcher, 1941, p. 1533)

Though Rugg's account of the crisis was well received, it was probably ignored by the majority of readers due to the rising level of American involvement in World War II.

After a little more time had passed, heated discourse on the controversy largely subsided, yet discussion of the general pattern of attacks continued in the professional literature. One article, written by a school superintendent, argued that many of the attacks were part of a deliberate effort to undermine "public confidence in the schools so that school appropriations may be reduced" (Dannelly, 1941). Another author provided a larger historical context for the attacks and suggested that they were part of a broader "War on Social Studies." The real animus of the critics, he wrote, "is against the whole modern conception of the social studies as a realistic approach to life." In opposition to the critics, he argued that young people have "the right to know what the world is all about and to learn what can be done about it" (Gould, 1941). Later still, one social studies professor wrote that "controversial issues ought to be taught," but he cautioned that treatment of issues must be "intelligible" to students; that it must be "rational," appealing primarily to reason rather than emotions; that it should be used in conjunction with the "historical method," a critical examination of sources; that it must be "fair to both sides and all viewpoints;" and that presentation must be clear and complete (Haefner, 1942). There is little doubt that this more "balanced" approach was the new order of the day.

By December, 1941, when the United States entered World War II, the media campaign against the Rugg textbooks was nearing its conclusion. As the months went on, and news of the war effort dominated the newspapers, patriotic organizations continued their campaign against the books and received occasional publicity ("Dusting of Bridges," 1942).

Rugg believed that of all the organizations and persons campaigning against his books, the most effective campaign was the local action by American Legion posts (Rugg, 1956). A look at the decline in sales figures for his junior high text series suggests that sales dropped only slightly during 1940, but dropped precipitously in 1941. A list of sales figures, prepared by Rugg himself from royalty statements, reflects total annual sales of the junior high series. Sales for 1939 totaled 177,000 volumes, an increase from each of the previous years. Sales for 1940 declined slightly, to 152,000. However, sales for 1941 dropped to 40,000 volumes, and for 1942 to only 23,000 volumes, a fraction of the previous high (Rugg,

1943). By 1945 sales had declined even further, and in 1950, Ginn and company destroyed the plates and allowed the books to go out of print (Ginn & Company, 1950).

Though the local campaigns by American Legion Posts undoubtedly contributed the greatest organized effort to eradicate Rugg's dominance over the junior high social studies textbook market, the NAM textbook investigation and the attendant media publicity in the Hearst Press, the *New York Times*, and other media sources combined with the changing national climate brought a precipitous decline and, ultimately, the disappearance of the Rugg texts from schools.

In what was probably the last instance of an actual ban on Rugg's work, the school board in Carver, Massachusetts, voted to discontinue use of the Rugg textbooks in December, 1952, after using the texts for a decade. The action was taken, reportedly, after a complaint by a parent to the school committee who found that *America's March Toward Democracy* was "subversive and Communist-inclined." Asked about the incident, Rugg reportedly replied that he hadn't realized that any of his books were still in use ("School Bars Textbook," 1952).

During the summer of 1943, after the campaign against the Rugg books had done its damage and largely died out, the education editor of the *New York Times*, who was working on a story about the campaign and its results, wrote to Shumaker and asked how many schools had eliminated the Rugg books as a result of the Legion campaign. The editor was informed that:

> While we are wholly convinced that the number of schools from which the Rugg textbooks have been removed reaches, and greatly exceeds, the 1,500 mark, this office is not in a position to present objective evidence.... Our knowledge on the removal of the books is not cumulative and a great deal of it has been obtained from confidential sources. (Shumaker, 1943)

Rugg's own assessment of the fall was even more dramatic. According to journalist George Seldes, when the NAM had issued its abstracts, and distributed them with the help of the House Un-American Activities Committee, the American Legion, and others, Rugg's books were in use in some 4,200 school districts. "Within a year or so, Dr. Rugg informed me, his books had been banned in 4,000 of them" (Seldes, 1968, p. 113).

In the 1950s, Rugg recalled the entire episode during a speech to the New York Geriatric Society in Cold Spring. Rugg addressed the role of various persons involved in the textbook controversy, after being asked about the influence of "reactionary groups":

They are sort of the symbols and the mouthpieces of minority movements which do hold back (social progress). It's their leadership, it's not the rank and file of the men themselves, most of them aren't interested in it.... Take the American Legion ... or ... take the Sons of the American Revolution. I can give you some wonderful stories about the Sons of the American Revolution, and the Daughters. They tried to put my books out of the schools. They never made a dent ... in the whole period.

The American Legion, they succeeded in three years time. They had machinery to do it. They had numbers and power and they had a clever gang at the top. In the background of it all is the education of enough of the people so they can't be swept off their feet, either by the prestige of one man or ... the patriotic organizations ... some of which are really diabolical things.

Take this man, Hart. Merwin K. Hart. Merwin K. Hart's Economic Council is a mean and vicious thing and I've had to deal with it for 15, 20 years. There's no doubt about that man's purposes and the people behind it. The same thing was true for various little councils, which sprang up in the depression years, and they were also Fascist organizations of the worst kind. They were minority groups ... when they got the great mass groups such as the American Legion to work concertedly on a program with them. And, they had a lot of money of course, millions each year that come in. (Rugg, 1956)

DISCUSSION

The story of the Rugg textbook controversy raises several important issues. First, what was behind the textbook critics' animus toward Rugg? What would motivate such a sustained, expensive and determined campaign? Criticism of the Rugg social studies textbooks and program materialized from the concerns of several individuals and groups who held a competing definition of "the American way" and a vision of America's future quite different from the one advanced by Harold Rugg and other "frontier thinkers." The American Legion's critics and their campaign against Rugg perhaps best exemplifies this. Rudd, Marshall, West, Fries, Shumaker, Chaillaux, Armstrong and other Legionnaires had a sincere belief in a traditional and conservative version of the American way, one that lionized America's founders and heroes, one that perpetuated and celebrated the cultural mythology of the nation they loved and had fought for. Similarly, for many businessmen, Rugg's version of Americanism represented the conspiracy of subversives attempting to redirect and reform American life, partially at the expense of the businessmen's success.

From its inception, the American Legion was devoted to promotion of "100% Americanism" and established the National Americanism Commission of the American Legion to create and maintain a continuous education program aimed at combating "all anti-American tendencies, activities and propaganda" and fostering "the teaching of Americanism in all schools." The Legion was devoted from the start to "nationalism and patriotism." By 1936, the most important focus of its Americanism program, according to Homer L. Chaillaux, director of the National Americanism Commission, was, "TO FIGHT COMMUNIST AND RADICAL PACIFIST PROPAGANDA BY GIVING THE CITIZENS OF YOUR COMMUNITY TRUE FACTS CONCERNING THESE TWO DANGEROUS UN-AMERICAN AND UN-PATRIOTIC ACTIVITIES" (Chaillaux, 1935).

Moreover, the Legion had long aimed its programs at eliminating "subversive elements" and crushing "radicalism" and "disloyalty" in the schools. For the most fervent Legionnaires, this meant that individuals were not allowed to hold opposing views on fundamental principles, and that explosive words could be used as weapons to condemn opponents. The plans, policies and programs of the American Legion were in strong accord with those promoted by conservative business, banking, and military interests. In fact, the leadership of the Legion was controlled, from the time of its founding, by business interests, many of whom had endorsed Fascism (Seldes, 1943). Perhaps most importantly, by the late 1930s the Legion was one of the most powerful pressure groups in American society. Its educational programs sought to preserve institutions that supported the status quo, to turn the American people's attention away from class conflict, and to discredit as "unpatriotic" or "un-American" doctrines of social change aimed at helping to remedy the nation's economic dilemmas (Gellerman, 1938).

To the Legion and other critics Rugg epitomized the threat of subversion in schools and the community partly because his textbooks were innovative and successful in reaching their target audience, and partly because he was the most prominent of the "progressive" textbook writers. Kenneth Gould, editor of *Scholastic*, and a Rugg supporter, wrote a perceptive analysis in the article titled, "The War on the Social Studies," mentioned earlier. In that article, he explained the critics focus on Rugg in the following passage:

> In a riot the most conspicuous heads are bound to be hit ... a little elementary analysis reveals that the attack on certain textbooks is merely a smokescreen for a deeper-lying, more insidious philosophy of obscurantism ... if there were no Rugg, they would have to invent him. The elimination of one man's books ... would only be a convenient entering wedge—a foreshadowing of the complete blackout. This is a war of attrition, in which the whole fabric of the social sciences, the application of intelligence to the study and solution of contemporary problems, the hard-won educational and social

gains of modern thought, the concept of public, tax supported education for all the children ... the questing mind of free men itself, are the stakes of conquest. (Gould, 1941, p. 87)

The "sticking point" he continued, was the ominous-sounding phrase, "social studies":

> The real animus of the critics, it should now be clear, is against the whole modern conception of the social studies as a realistic approach to life. What they really want eliminated is every vestige of controversial matter—every issue that touches the springs of control in the delicately balanced political, social, and economic world of today—every idea or questions that might arouse dissension, class consciousness, or a critical attitude toward the distribution of privilege, the power of authority, or the mores of habitual conformity. (p. 90)

As demonstrated earlier, the Rugg textbooks were pedagogically advanced, and delivered a modernist, even avant-garde approach to social studies in a creative and interesting way, or as one critic put it, with a "smooth pedagogic smile." And, it was true that in the hands of a competent teacher, they raised troubling questions in the minds of students that went to the heart of many fundamental American institutions: questions about power, about the role of government in business and the economy, about wealth and poverty, and about the way the nation treated all of its people. Though similar questions had been raised by social critics persistently for some time, they seldom made it into the school curriculum. Rugg was perceived as dangerous and subversive for precisely that reason. His books, and the questions they raised, had made it into the schools and were exerting growing influence.

It is important to keep in mind that the context of the depression, the advent of the New Deal, the rise of totalitarianism in various forms, and the general tensions generated by all of these factors were instrumental in the focus of critics on social and economic issues in "subversive" textbooks. Capitalism, as the quintessentially American economic form, was under attack along a wide front, and its future was seriously in doubt. Rugg's critics appeared at a moment in time in which many Americans resonated to the strong insistence of patriotic groups on preserving the American economic system against any form of "collectivism." It was a time during which those campaigning against the modern school found it convenient to identify the American form of government and the American "way of life" with laissez-faire capitalism under the control of private enterprise. During the 1930s, the share of the nation's wealth held by the top 1% had declined, from its peak of 44.2% in 1929, to 33.3% in 1933 and 36.4% in 1939, partly as a result of the stock market crash, but also due to progressive income tax rates which took some money from the rich to help provide government services (Wolff, 1996). For the wealthy, and other apologists for laissez-faire capitalism, attacking school textbooks was a logical extension of fighting against the New Deal.

Moreover, the forces supporting educational reaction were well-entrenched, highly organized, and quite powerful. Several of Rugg's critics exemplified and frequently expressed the ideological and cultural fundamentalism that lay behind their attacks. As we have seen, the American Legion had a long history of promoting their fundamentalist view of "Americanism" which stressed a rather extreme faith in traditional American institutions, as if they should remain constant and unchanging, and their fear of any perceived threats to the status quo (Gellerman, 1938). An equally strong example of reactionary thought, the *National Republic* magazine, reads as a primer on cultural fundamentalism, supporting traditional American institutions including constitutional representative government, laissez-faire capitalism, Christianity, and traditional education, and opposing any movements "Inimical to American Ideals, Traditions and Institutions." Among these "inimical" movements were socialism, communism, atheism, subversion, and "Ruggism" or any other form of nontraditional social studies (*National Republic*, 1940).

The hearings and investigations conducted by the Dies Committee beginning in 1938 were rooted in a similar form of cultural fundamentalism. In the first report of the Committee to Investigate Un-American Activities, submitted to Congress on January 3, 1939, Dies and the committee defined "Americanism" as a "philosophy of government based upon the belief in God as the Supreme Ruler of the Universe." Dies version of Americanism held that "the fundamental rights of man are derived from God," and listed "inalienable rights" drawn from the Declaration of Independence and Constitution of the United States. However, the definitions he developed were skewed to reflect his own likes and dislikes and aimed generally to support the status quo. Notably, his definition of Americanism explicitly endorsed "the protection of property rights," and minimized the right to protest or advocate change (Gellerman, 1972, pp. 140-144).

Dies also defined his un-American opponents as any "organization or individual" who advocates "class, religious, or racial hatred," or who "believes in or advocates a system of political, economic, or social regimentation based upon a planned economy." Thus, socialism, communism, fascism, and Nazism were viewed as "forms of dictatorship which deny the divine origin" of fundamental rights. Communists, he stipulated, were successful because "they bore from within" in "churches, schools, youth organizations" and other venues, carrying out the instructions of the Communist International and Moscow, continually exerting "subtle and indirect influence," and trying to overthrow the American system through "Trojan Horse" tactics (Gellerman, 1972, pp. 144-145).

Many supporters believed that Dies investigation was a necessary public service to save the republic from subversion. On the other hand, opponents believed that Dies had crossed the line between patriotic investigation and persecution, and refused to condone the singling out of any minority because its views were unpopular. As one critic of the Dies Committee wrote, "What is un-American? 'Why,' said the professor, 'anything I don't agree with'" (Cadden, 1939, p. 46). As another commentator put it, the committee sought to achieve these ends by "applying the epithets 'communist' and 'communism' to every person and every principle which it hopes to discredit" (Anderson, 1938, p. 198).

Nonetheless, supporters of the ongoing quest to root out un-American activities believed that their concerns were warranted, and prompted not by a "misguided patriotism but by logical confidence in the American form of government and its future." They believed that "a loss of confidence in America" was a serious thing, and that Americans had "the right to defend ourselves against our enemies, by eliminating them from the public schools!" (Kelty, 1935, pp. 735-736).

In the mind of Dies, Rugg was, if not a Communist, at the very least a "fellow traveler" who served the purposes of the Communist party through his program of textbooks and other writings and through his activities in "front" organizations. Moreover, in the fundamentalist mind, Rugg was among those associated with what Dies might have termed "every crack-pot scheme to undermine our system of free enterprise and private initiative" (Gellerman, 1972, pp. 140-146). The existence, hearings, and reports of the Dies Committee, and the media attention it attracted, testify to the prevalence of a strong strain of fundamentalist inspired hysteria in the United States of the late 1930s. This was a key part of the social context of the times during which the Rugg textbook controversy was spawned.

The roots of cultural fundamentalism may also have links to religious fundamentalism, which is often a religion of rage, and usually a religion "rooted in deep fear" (Armstrong, 2000, p. 216). The fundamentalist critics did not see the complete Harold Rugg, but focused only on the most controversial aspects of his work, projecting their deepest hopes and fears onto Rugg as a convenient target. Through this lens and filter, he was perceived as a serious threat to the fundamentalist's cherished values. Thus, part of the core inspiration for the attacks on the Rugg textbooks may be found in the nexus of religious and cultural fundamentalism and its expression of fears against anything the most extreme of the faithful, whether religious or secular, considered inconsistent with a fervent belief in their preferred religious, cultural and political traditions. For the true fundamentalist, there is one clearly defined and comforting version of truth. The fundamentalist holds tight to certainty. The fundamentalist's certainty in his or her faith and accompanying cultural and political beliefs allows the dismissal or even the annihilation of anyone who disagrees. These insights regarding the nature of cultural fundamentalism may help us understand the ferocity and sustainability of the attacks on Rugg.

In the propaganda from business and patriotic groups that engulfed the Rugg textbooks, fear and anxiety were operating and played upon by publicists for the fundamentalist's cause, at a time of stress in the nation and the world. Fears were behind attacks on Rugg, along with a long-standing desire by many conservative groups to reduce the tax support and funding of education. As one publication put it at the time:

> In the propagandas over this issue ... the psychological factor of Anxiety is operating. First, there are those who fear that excessive school taxation will reduce their incomes; there are those who fear that modern education will teach children to be too critical of religion, nation, and economic system. These fears are communicated to others. Thus, fear arouses fear. Anxiety breeds anxiety. In times of stress such as the present there is the desire common to most persons to escape present fears by the process of Regression. They would go back to more stable, happier days, to the old-time religion, the free enterprise of their fathers, and to simple common schools which taught only "fundamentals." That the simple school is less expensive makes it doubly attractive. (Beals, 1941, p. 12)

Moreover, while many of Rugg's critics might be characterized as cultural fundamentalists, others were openly Fascist. Fascism may be defined as a "centralized autocratic government headed by a dictatorial leader, severe economic and social regimentation, and forcible suppression of opposition" (Webster's, 1987, p. 450). It may also be defined as a dictatorship from the extreme right in which government is run by "a small group of large industrialists and financial lords" (Heywood Broun, quoted by Seldes, 1943, p. 278). The latter definition is probably most applicable to the native Fascist elements in the textbook battles. Behind those who were leading the attacks on Rugg was a large contingent of business leaders who either quietly supported the campaign, or were complicit in its finance.

As we have seen, during the early 1930s the NAM had reorganized and was now controlled by the largest national industries. Behind the NAM attack on Rugg were the Nation's leading business and industrial corporations, ranging from General Motors and U.S. Steel to American Telephone and Telegraph (AT&T) and Campbell Soup (Senate Committee, 1939). A few persons of inordinate wealth led the nation's economic system and constituted the vanguard of the nation's most powerful pressure group (Temporary National Economic Committee, 1940). Most often, they acted to ensure their own profits and position, and not on behalf of the general welfare. In this instance, they supported removal of Rugg's textbooks.

Second, aside from the question of its origins, and its focus primarily on Rugg, the textbook controversy also raised troubling questions about academic freedom, about the role and influence of textbook criticism, and about the supposed "neutrality" of education on social questions. To be sure, schools and school textbooks had never been neutral. Since the founding of the American common school they had advanced a traditional love of country, support for American institutions, and a conservative patriotism (Elson, 1964). One of the questions raised by the Rugg textbooks was whether schools and textbooks should raise difficult fundamental questions about American structures and institutions? It was clear that many of the critics did not want alternative or critical ideas presented or discussed in schools. The controversy also raised difficult questions about the fine line between balanced discussion of issues and social criticism, about the relationship between a textbook author's personal point-of-view and the portrayal of issues and institutions, past and present, contained in texts. Indoctrination of some sort was inevitable, especially in the early grades. But how far should it go, and what were its limits?

Third, the Rugg textbook controversy brought the social studies wars over curricular issues to the forefront. Critics and patrioteers were not only critical of "subversive" doctrines and ideas being brought into the schools, but were unified in their condemnation of the new approach to social studies represented by the Rugg program and textbooks. Instead of an integrated, "omnibus" social studies that opened the door to the social sciences and allowed space in the curriculum for some discussion of critical questions, they wanted a return to traditional history and all that it implied. They wanted history taught in a traditional manner and centered on developing an appreciation for the American past and a deep love and respect for American institutions. For many cultural fundamentalists, this meant imposition through schools of a rather limiting and backward looking version of Americanism aimed at perpetuating the existing order. And, as we have seen, for many of the business leaders behind the controversy, the aims ranged from enhancing their positions of power to the possible creation of a Fascist state.

Fourth, the Rugg textbook controversy raised questions of curricular hegemony, questions about who should control the curriculum. Was the curriculum the sovereign province of teachers, administrators, curriculum supervisors, professors of education, textbook authors and other "experts"? Was it something to be decided by parents, taxpayers, and the

American public? Or, would it ultimately be controlled, or at least framed or hemmed in, by the most persistent, vocal, organized and well-financed critics? To what extent would it be limited by clouds of suspicion, hearsay and innuendo? This question in particular, the question of who controls the curriculum, was deeply related to the broad progressive challenge to give experts increased control in a variety of areas of American life, while at the same time giving the average citizen leverage and access in both political and cultural institutions.

Finally, and perhaps most importantly, in trying to understand both the dimensions and import of the Rugg controversy, it is of paramount importance to keep in mind the context of late 1930s America. In the early and middle parts of the decade, in the depths of the depression, American capitalism was coming under fire and was seriously questioned like never before. Rugg's books exemplified that questioning stance and time. By the late 1930s and early 1940s, and increasingly so as the United States became more involved in the wars in Europe and in Asia, the context for questioning American institutions, and capitalism in particular, shifted dramatically. What had been permitted during the heights of the nation's economic misery was suddenly out-of-place in a world in which survival itself was in question. Hyper-patriotic Americans and business interests who supported laissez-faire economic policies and strong leadership or even a dictatorship of the business elite became more concerned about the threat of subversion, from outside or within. The Rugg textbooks were a convenient sacrificial lamb.

CONCLUSION

As it turned out, February 22, 1941, the date of the Robey story, was a watershed in the war on social studies and the attacks on Harold Rugg. Up to that point tension built while the movement for integrated social studies and a focus on issues and problems with a meliorist or reconstructionist purpose gathered steam. After the Robey article, the tide had turned. The struggle over the Rugg textbooks continued in many communities. In a many cases the attempt to censor the texts was successful. In others, they were retained for some time, then quietly dropped when it came time for the adoption of new books. By the middle of the decade, the Rugg textbook series and program had virtually disappeared. Social studies in general, it seemed, was on the defensive. The possibility of a critical, reflective social studies was seriously in doubt, and attacks on progressive educators continued to mount throughout the decade.

Progressives would have both proponents and defenders, but criticism of progressive education seemed a rising tide that no seawall could restrain. The attacks on the Rugg textbooks, and the war against social studies of which it was a part, were pieces of a much larger pattern, one which would continue for some time to come (Evans, 2004). For Rugg, though he presented a strong public defense and never admitted it in a public forum or in writing, the controversy appeared to be fun while the outcome was still in doubt, but was, ultimately, devastating to both his career and persona once the returns were in and it was clear that his books would no longer be welcome in the classrooms of American schools.

REFERENCES

Abbott, H. E. (1941, September 16). Letter to Wilbur Murra, Executive Secretary, NCSS. File 1, Box 45, Series 4C, Executive Director Correspondence with Organizations, NCSS Archive.

Armstrong Cork. (1961). H. W. Prentis, Jr., 1884-1959. Lancaster, PA: Armstrong Cork Company.

ACDIF Press Release. (1941). "A committee of ten outstanding social scientists ..." Sunday, February 23, American Committee for Democracy and Intellectual Freedom, New York. Franz Boas Professional Papers, B61p, sub collection 2, box A-Bend, ACDIF folder, American Philosophical Society, Philadelphia.

Alexander, R. (1941). Dr. Ruth Alexander to John D. Rockefeller, Jr., May 15, 1941, box 8, folder 45, Civic Interests Series, Record Group 2, Rockefeller Family Archives, Rockefeller Archive Center, Sleepy Hollow, NY.

American Historical Association. (1941). Freedom of textbooks. *Social Education*, 5, 487-488.

Anderson, P. Y. (1938, August 27). Fascism hits Washington, *The Nation*, 147, pp. 198-199.

Armstrong, K. (2000). *The battle for god*. New York: Ballantine Books.

Baldwin, R. (1940). Gilt edged patriot: Merwin K. Hart. *Frontiers of Democracy*, 7(56), 45-47.

Barton, J. F. (1940). James F. Barton, director of publications, The American Legion, to H. O. Johnson, November 22, 1940, Legion dead-letter files (as cited in Jones, 1957, p. 86).

Beals, C. (Ed.). (1941, February 25). Propaganda over the schools. *Propaganda Analysis: A Bulletin to Help the Intelligent Citizen Detect and Analyze Propaganda, 4*, pp. 1-12.

Boutwell, W. D. (1934). The Cleveland meeting. *School and Society, 39*, 296-304.

Butler, N. M. (1940). Nicholas Murray Butler to Hamilton H. Howry, Esq., Baltimore, MD, "Hon. 1940-1941" folder, William F. Russell files, Columbiana Collection, Low Library, Columbia University.

Cadden, J. (1939). Answer by Joseph Cadden in, What's YOUR opinion? What shall we do about un-American activities? *Current History, 51*, December 1939, p. 46.

Chaillaux, H. L. (1935). *Americanism ... A call to action*. Indianapolis, IN: The American Legion.

Coleman, T. L. (1941). Tom L. Coleman, Ardmore, Oklahoma, postcard to Nicholas Murray Butler, June 10, 1941, "Co: 1940-1941" folder, William F. Russell files, Columbiana Collection, Low Library, Columbia University.

Committee on Educational Cooperation. (1939). Official draft of a memorandum of industry's recommendations for the improvement of American educational methods in the preparing of students for citizendhsip in a republic. June 28, 1939. Accession # 1411, "Robey Textbook Survey" folder, box 847, series 111, National Industrial Information Committee, Subject Files, NAM Papers, Hagley Museum and Library, Wilmington, Delaware.

Corbett, R. (1943). Roger Corbett to H. L. Chaillaux, November 19, 1943 (as cited in Jones, 1957, p. 48).

Curti, M. (1941, October 14). Merle Curti to Wilbur Murra. File 1, Box 2, Series 7, Committee Records, Academic Freedom Correspondence, NCSS Archive.

Dannelly, C. M. (1941). Facing a major threat. *The School Executive, 60*, 32.

Dawson, E. B. (1940, December 22). Edgar Dawson postcard to Wilbur Murra. "Textbook Controversy" folder, box 5, series 4B, NCSS Archive, Gottesman Libraries, Teachers College, Columbia University.

Dexter, B. (1941, July 14). Review of *That Men May Understand*, *New Republic*, 105, p. 61.

Elson, R. M. (1964). *Guardians of tradition: American schoolbooks of the 19th century.* Lincoln: University of Nebraska Press.

Evans, R. W. (2004). *The social studies wars: What should we teach the children?* New York: Teachers College Press.

Fackenthal, F. D. (1940). Frank D. Fackenthal (provost) to W. F. Russell (dean), "General Correspondence" files, "Ro, 1939-1940," William F. Russell papers, Columbiana Collection, Low Library, Columbia University.

Fine, B. (1941, February, 22). Un-American tone seen in textbooks on social sciences. *New York Times*, pp. 1, 6.

Flexner, A. B. (1941). Abraham B. Flexner to John D. Rockefeller, June 12, 1941, box 8, folder 45, Civic Interests Series, Record Group 2, Rockefeller Family Archives, Rockefeller Archive Center, Sleepy Hollow, NY.

Forbes, B. C. (1941). Bertie C. Forbes to John D. Rockefeller, Jr., May 5, 1941, box 8, folder 45, Civic Interests Series, Record Group 2, Rockefeller Family Archives, Rockefeller Archive Center, Sleepy Hollow, NY.

Forbes, R. J. (1947). *The National Association of Manufacturers and the public schools.* Unpublished masters thesis, Claremont Colleges, Claremont, CA.

Fuller, W. D. (1941, February 24). Telegram to Wilbur Murra. File 1, Box 2, Series 7, Committee Records, Academic Freedom Correspondence, NCSS Archive.

Gellerman, W. (1938). *The American Legion as educator.* New York: Teachers College, Columbia University.

Gellerman, W. (1972). *Martin Dies.* New York: The John Day Company.

Ginn. (undated memo). "To those who love the TRUTH." Memo circulated by Ginn and Company during the Rugg textbook controversy, Rugg Textbook Controversy Scrapbook, Rauner Archive, Dartmouth College.

Ginn & Company. (1950). Ginn & Company to Harold O. Rugg, January 3, 1950. On tape made by George Kay transcribing documents in Rugg's study at his home in Woodstock, New York, October 9, 1965. Tape in possession of the author.

Gotesky, R. (1941, June 7). Testament of an independent. *The Saturday Review of Literature, 24*, p. 14.

Gould, K. M. (1941, Autumn). The war on social studies. *Common Ground*, 83-91.

Haefner, J. H. (1942). The historical approach to controversial issues. *Social Education, 6*, 267-269.

Hart, M. K. (1940). Let's discuss this on its merits. *Frontiers of Democracy, 7*(57), 82-87.

Harrison, C. E. (1940). C. E. Harrison, inter-office memo. to W. B. Weisenburger, July 25, 1940, Accession # 1411, "Robey Textbook Survey" folder, box 847, series 111, National Industrial Information Committee, Subject Files, NAM Papers, Hagley Museum and Library, Wilmington, Delaware.

Harrison, C. E. (1941a, January 10). C. E. Harrison to H. W. Prentis, Jr., January 10, 1941, and attached inter-office memo., C. E. Harrison to W. B. Weisenburger, January 10, 1941, Accession # 1411, "Robey Textbook Survey" folder, box 847, series 111, National Industrial Information Committee, Subject Files, NAM Papers, Hagley Museum and Library, Wilmington, Delaware.

Harrison, C. E. (1941b, March 19). C. E. Harrison to H. W. Prentis, March 19, 1941, Accession # 1411, "Robey Textbook Survey" folder, box 847, series 111, National Industrial Information Committee, Subject Files, NAM Papers, Hagley Museum and Library, Wilmington, Delaware.

Hicks, H. (1941). Ours to reason why. *American Legion Magazine, 16*, May, 1941, pp.

Hunt, E. M. (1941a). Dr. Robey versus the NAM? *Social Education, 5*, 288-292.

Hunt, E. M. (1941b). The manufacturers and the textbooks. *Social Education, 5*, 88-89.

Hunt, E. M. (1941c). The NAM restates its policy. *Social Education, 5*, 328.

Johnson, H. O. (1940a). H. O. Johnson to James F. Barton, Director of Publications, The American Legion, New York, New York, November 15, 1940, Legion dead-letter files (as cited in Jones, 1957, p. 85).

Johnson, H. O. (1940b). H. O. Johnson to James F. Barton, director of publications, The American Legion, New York, New York, November 25, 1940, Legion dead-letter files (as cited in Jones, 1957, p. 86).

Kelty, W. (1935, June 1). Is it "misguided patriotism"? *School and Society, 41*, pp. 735-736.

Kepner, T. (1940, December 12). Letter to Messrs. Anderson, Hunt, Murra, Rugg, Wesley. File 1, Box 2, Series 7, Committee Records, Academic Freedom Correspondence, NCSS Archive, Gottesman Libraries, Teachers College, Columbia University.

King, A. R. (1941, April 30). Albion Roy King to R. Worth Shumaker, Legion dead-letter files (as cited in Jones, 1957, p. 93).

MacDonald, W. A. (1941, February 23). Dr. Rugg defends modern histories. *New York Times*, pp. 42, 47.

Melcher, F. G. (1941, April 12). Editorial: Rugg deserves freedom of education. *Publishers Weekly*, p. 1533.

Mitchell, W. C. (1941). Wesley C. Mitchell to Dear Colleague, May 6, 1941, ACDIF, folder 5, Boas papers, American Philosophical Society, Philadelphia.

Murra, W. (1941a, September 17). Reply to H. E. Abbott. File 1, box 45, series 4C, Executive Director correspondence with organizations, National Council for the Social Studies Archives, Gottesman Libraries, Teachers College, Columbia University.

Murra, W. (1941b, February 22). Telegram to Walter D. Fuller, NAM, sent from Atlantic City, file 1, box 2, series 7, Committee Records, Academic Freedom Correspondence, NCSS Archive.

N. A. M. will survey school textbooks. (1940, December 11). *New York Times*, p. 29.

National Association of Manufacturer Educational Cooperation Meeting. (1940). Suggested local activities to stimulate better understanding between industrialists and educators. Monday, April 22, Waldorf-Astoria, New York City, Accession # 1411, "Robey Textbook Survey" folder, box 847, series 111, National Industrial Information Committee, Subject Files, NAM Papers, Hagley Museum and Library, Wilmington, Delaware.

National Association of Manufacturers. (1941, January). Statement by NAM. *Educational Cooperation Bulletin*, pp. 2-3.

National Association of Manufacturers. (2006). http://www.nam.org/about us/

National Americanism Commission. (1941a). *Rugg philosophy analyzed, volume 1: Basic excerpts from The Great Technology*. Indianapolis, IN: The American Legion.

National Americanism Commission. (1941b). *Rugg philosophy analyzed, volume 2: The complete Rugg philosophy—Its transfer to the textbooks*. Indianapolis, IN: The American Legion.

National Americanism Commission. (1941c). *Rugg philosophy analyzed, volume 3: Textbook abstracts*. Indianapolis, IN: The American Legion.

National Americanism Commission. (1941d). *Rugg philosophy further analyzed, volume 4*. Indianapolis, IN: The American Legion.

News Bulletin. (1940). National Publicity Division, The American Legion, Indianapolis, Indiana, December 16, 1940.

National Republic. (1940, October). *National Republic: A Magazine of Fundamental Americanism*, p. 11.

Pomeroy, E. C. (1948). Eugene C. Pomeroy to R. Worth Shumaker, April 24, 1948, Legion dead-letter files (as cited in Jones, 1957, p. 94).

Prentis, H. W., Jr. (1940, May 8). Letter to Howard Wilson, File 1, Box 45, Series 4C, Director's Correspondence with Organizations, NCSS Archives, Gottesman Libraries, Teachers College, Columbia University.

Publishers fight textbook charges. (1941, February 24). *New York Times*, p. 1, 10.

Rudd, A. G. (1942). Education for "new social order," *National Republic*, May, pp. 5-6, 20, 30, and June, pp. 21-22, 32.

Rudd, A. G., Hicks, H., & Falk, A. T. Ed. (1941). *Undermining our republic: Do you know what the children are being taught in our public schools? You'll be surprised*. New York: Guardians of American Education.

Rugg, H. O. (1940). "Confidential Analysis of the Current (1939-1940) Attacks on the Rugg Social Science Series, Prepared by Harold Rugg in May-June 1940,"

"Harold Rugg" folder, box 58, William F. Russell Papers, Gottesman Libraries, Teachers College, Columbia University.

Rugg, H. O. (1941). *That men may understand: An American in the long armistice*. New York: Doubleday/Doran.

Rugg, H. O. (1943). List of junior high school textbook sales prepared by Harold O. Rugg from royalty statements. Rugg papers as described in tape prepared by George Allen Kay during visit to the Rugg home, Woodstock, New York, October, 1965. As cited in G. A. Kay. (1969). *Harold Rugg: Educational pioneer and social reconstructionist*. Unpublished doctoral dissertation, State University of New York, Buffalo, p. 170.

Rugg, H. O. (1956). Cold Spring Tapes. Rugg speaking to New York Geriatric Society, Cold Spring, N.Y., June 15, 1956. Tape in possession of the author.

Russell, W. F. (1938). William F. Russell to Mr. J. H. Florea, Mount Morris, Illinois, December 16, 1938, "Harold Rugg" folder, box 58, William F. Russell Papers, Milbank Library, Teachers College, Columbia University.

"School Bars Textbook." (1952). "School Bars Textbook." *New York Times*, December 3, 1952.

Senate Committee. (1939). *Violations of free speech and rights of labor*. Senate Committee on Education and Labor, 76th Congress, 1st Session, Report No. 6, Part 6. Washington, DC: United States Government Printing Office.

Seldes, G. (1943). *Facts and fascism*. New York: In Fact.

Seldes, G. (1947). *One thousand Americans*. New York: Boni & Gaer.

Seldes, G. (1968). *Never tire of protesting*. New York: Lyle Stuart, Inc.

Shumaker, R. W. (1941, April). No "new order" for our schools. *The American Legion Magazine*, 1941, pp. 5-7, 43, 44-46.

Shumaker, R. W. (1942). R. Worth Shumaker address, Proceedings of the Twenty Fourth Annual Convention of the American Legion, Kansas City, Missouri, September 19 21, 1942, p. 8.

Shumaker, R. W. (1943). R. Worth Shumaker to John E. Thomas, August 4, 1943, Legion dead-letter files (as cited in Jones, 1957, p. 82).

Shuster, G. M. (1941, April 27,). Review of *That Men May Understand*, *New York Times Book Review*, Section VI, p. 5.

Temorary National Economic Committee. (1940). *Monograph No. 29: The distribution of ownership in the 200 largest nonfinancial corporations*. Investigation of Concentration of Economic Power, 76th Congress, 3rd Session. United States: Government Printing Office.

"Textbook writers reply to attack; 'Censor' fight on." (1941, February 23). *New York Times*, pp. 1, 47.

Town Meeting. (1941, May 5). Are our schoolbooks dangerous? *Town Meeting: Bulletin of America's Town Meeting of the Air*, 6.

Wake Up America. (1941, April 28). Does capitalism offer youth a fair opportunity? "Wake Up America" Radio Forum Broadcast, Mutual Network, New York.

Webster's. (1987). *Webster's Ninth New Collegiate Dictionary*. Springfield, MA: Merriam-Webster.

Wilson, H. E. (1940, December 20). Response to Kepner. File 1, Box 2, Series 7, Committee Records, Academic Freedom Correspondence, NCSS Archive.

Winters, E. A. (1968). *Harold Rugg and education for social reconstruction.* Unpublished doctoral dissertation, University of Wisconsin, Madison.

Wolff, E. N. (1996). *Top heavy: The increasing inequality of wealth in America and what can be done about it.* New York: The New Press.

Zimmerman, J. (2002). *Whose America?: Culture wars in the public schools.* Cambridge, MA: Harvard University Press.

CHAPTER 7

OLD DOC RUGG

THE AFTERMATH

By the fall of 1942 it was clear that Rugg's struggle to maintain a presence for his textbooks in the schools was over, and that his efforts had largely failed. Even in the schools which had decided to keep the Rugg program, it would only be used until money was available to purchase the next set of books. The impact of the textbook controversy on Rugg's fortunes as a scholar and as a leader among progressive educators was enormous. As late as 1939, it seemed that everything he touched in his professional life turned to gold. His school materials quite literally created a small personal fortune. After the fall of the Rugg textbooks, Rugg's leadership in social studies and his visions of a large personal fortune were finished.

The impact of all of this on him must have been immense, though he never admitted it publicly. Rugg's friends and colleagues have expressed somewhat contradictory opinions about how all of this affected him (Nelson, 1975). Two younger colleagues, Paul Hanna and R. Freeman Butts believed that the fight left Rugg feeling embittered. Butts remarked in an interview that "Harold became much more embittered after the American Legion thing" (Butts, 1974). However, one close personal friend of Rugg's, Frederick L. Redefer, who lived an hour's drive from Woodstock, and visited frequently until Rugg's death, thought that Rugg still wanted recognition, and said "Rugg's ego was so enormous that even after 1942, he felt he could sell new books and come back" (Redefer, 1974). One

This Happened in Ameica: Harold Rugg and the Censure of Social Studies
pp. 253–291

former student, who returned to Teachers College after the war, described Rugg as being "somewhat withdrawn" while another described him as "disillusioned" by his friends and colleagues failure to support him during the controversy (Winters, 1968, p. 192). Rugg himself later expressed disappointment over the same phenomena (Davis, 2006). Though most of his close friends and colleagues publicly supported Rugg's defense, at least one anonymous colleague communicated his disdain for Rugg to Dean Russell (Confidential, n.d.). Another friend of Rugg's, Alf Evers, a writer who lived in Woodstock and saw him frequently during Rugg's later years, supports the theory that the controversy affected him deeply, and stated in a recent interview, "He felt very keenly that rejection," but that Rugg "took it well." "It was all very fresh in his mind. Rugg said he 'lived through it.' He didn't seem embittered," though "he did feel that he hadn't been treated very well ... and he never went back to social studies" (Evers, 2003).

Another friend, Florence Cramer, wife of painter Konrad Cramer, noted in her journal, a party at the Rugg home that the couple attended on Saturday, June 7, 1941. The party was given in honor of Waldo Frank, whom she talked with for a while. She described Frank as "an unusually simple man and sincere person with a quiet kingly manner that was disarming." She noted that the Rugg's "son Harald is handsome—a blond four year old—he was playing with a toy bow and arrow when we arrived," and that "the Rugg's looked well—Harold seems happier than last year and Louise said her school (she was Director of the Walt Whitman School) has done well" (Cramer, 1941).

Family members recall a somewhat more severe impact on Rugg's persona. Rugg's nephew, who visited Rugg in Woodstock with Earle and his family a few times during those years thought that the episode "dealt a severe blow to Harold" (J. E. Rugg, 2003). Katharine Alling, Rugg's stepdaughter who knew Rugg from the early 1940s and lived with him much of the time from 1947 until her marriage to Norman Alling in 1957 stated that he was deeply hurt by the controversy and seemed at times, "rather bitter about it ... He had a very nice income from the textbooks, and he lost that. He believed that he was viciously and unjustly attacked." Whenever the topic came up in later years there would be an "edge in his voice" (Alling, 2005).

Though Rugg suffered some financial hardship when his texts were withdrawn from the market, he was able to retain ownership of his country estate in Woodstock, and maintain an apartment in Manhattan. While a significant downsizing in his visions of personal fortune was apparent, and must have been a difficult blow given his affinities, the loss of audience and of his position of leadership in the school curriculum surely must have been even more devastating. Still a prominent figure, and more famous than ever because of the attacks on his work, his influence over the public schools was greatly weakened.

Some years later, Rugg was interviewed for a story on progressive education that appeared in *Colliers Magazine*. Asked where he stood ideologically, Rugg replied, "I am a New Dealer, but they [people who have taken exception to school textbooks he has written] object to me." He went on, "They don't call me Communist anymore though, because I've threatened to sue." From the 1930s and for the remainder of his life, Rugg was suspected by conservatives and admired by liberals. Always, he remained a controversial progressive educator (Whitman, 1954, p. 36).

Several close colleagues and former students later remarked on his gallantry and perseverance in standing up for his beliefs regardless of the costs. One in particular captured Rugg's outward approach to the controversy when he wrote that Rugg was "setting a precedent for writers. Pull no punches—hold your ground!" Moreover, he went on, Rugg was widely admired for standing up to the attacks. "Liberals and forward-looking men the country over have always identified themselves with you as an honest, courageous educator" (Fox, 1951).

Years later, when asked about the impact of the textbook controversy on his work, Rugg responded:

> I'm doing now what I should have been doing 20 years ago.... I was very much, my work was very much interfered with about the beginning of World War Two by the various reactionary groups in the country who destroyed my earlier work in the social sciences. The American Legion, for example.
>
> I gave four or five years of my life to that, which I ought not to have had to do ... Even though I hadn't retired from Teachers College, I more or less withdrew from all sorts of things. It took another four or five years to get going.
>
> See, I gave twenty years to the work in the social sciences, and I'd say that was ten years more than I should have given. I ought to have done my work at Lincoln, and put the stuff together once and then quit, but I couldn't. I was a slave to the books. I had so many of them, you see. And it was a treadmill, until they got me off. After a while I recognized, that's a good thing, probably, because I was free, I was really free. (H. O. Rugg, 1957a)

Though he was able to regroup and continued his writing and professional activities, in some important ways Rugg was never the same. His marriage of some 13 years to Louise Krueger came to an end in 1943. Louise Kruger Rugg was not only his wife but also his partner in writing the elementary school texts and the mother of his son, Harald, born in 1936. Young Harald would have been about 7 years old at the time of the divorce. Simply from the timing of the divorce one suspects that this change in his personal life, occurring in the wake of the textbook controversy, was somehow related to his emotional state. Moreover, unlike his previous divorce and remarriage, this time he would spend several years as a single divorcé, as if those years were needed to help him through his most difficult passage.

If nothing else, despite the many charges and claims made by Rugg's detractors, the Rugg Social Science series was an expression of a grand vision in the progressive tradition, that social studies education in schools could prepare students for social life with an honest and comprehensive look at social realities of the past and present and imbue them with a desire to make the world a better place. That vision was shattered. Rugg's leadership in social studies had ended. Though he referred to, and critiqued his attackers in some of his later works (1943a; 1952b), and even joked about the controversy in a letter to his brother Earle in later years (1958), he never attempted another textbook series for public school use, nor did he write any new materials on the social studies curriculum. Instead he turned the page of life to a new chapter and turned his attention to new topics of interest. However, he never gave up his either his progressive ideals or his social reconstructionist beliefs and continued to uphold them in his writing and professional involvements to the end.

That Rugg remained true to his beliefs is a testimony to his make-up. The textbook controversy and attacks on the social frontier group had at least two immediate effects. First, the attacks led many of Rugg's colleagues to back down. Counts and Childs were motivated by the attacks to state, in unequivocal terms, their commitment to American ideals. They no longer believed that education had a revolutionary role to perform or that schools should serve on the forefront of social change (Childs, 1950; Counts, 1945). Second, the broad hysteria over subversion in schools and textbooks "fused together in the conservative mind progressive education and the ideology of the radical educationists" (Bowers, 1970, p. 49). From that point forward, many conservatives would begin to regard the entire frontier group as part of a Marxist conspiracy to undermine national security. The result was a continuing drumbeat of conservative zealots, throughout the 1950s and beyond, imbued with the mission of extinguishing progressive education in the schools.

Though progressive education writ large was not quite dead, it was clearly under siege. That the siege would be lifted temporarily during and immediately after World War II is understandable, in hindsight, given the enormous focus on the war effort. The Rugg controversy was perhaps the first major battle in what I have described as the war on social studies, and it signaled the beginning of the end for progressive education. Though it would take another decade for the looming deluge of attacks on progressive education to begin in earnest, the general trend had shifted, a line had been crossed. In hindsight, it is apparent that the attacks on Rugg marked an important turning point in the nation's educational history.

TEACHER AND SCHOLAR

Rugg continued working on a variety of projects after the climax of the textbook controversy. In the year immediately following, Rugg shifted his scholarly attention to planning for the peace and for global interdependence even as the war continued to rage. Merwin K. Hart, Rugg's old nemesis from the textbook controversy and a proponent of isolationism in the years prior to the war, was again at odds with Rugg and saw no need for world interdependence, declaring, "we should think about peace only after the war" (1942).

Rugg's concern for the peace and his continued hope for a reconstructed world order led him to write *Now is the Moment* (1943a). In this volume he urged development of interdependent global planning and argued that the alternative would be a Fascist future. Rugg continued to make the case for social and educational reconstuction. In one of the book's central passages Rugg wrote:

> It is my thesis that this is our moment. That by taking thought now ... focusing our total energies at the fulcrum and lifting together ... we can move the social world. Now is the moment to lift the social system up from the low rut of Exploitation onto the High Road toward the Great Tradition. (1943, p. 1)

Rugg argued that in the coming decades, up through the 1960s, we would make crucial decisions which would "determine the kind of society that industrialized peoples around the globe will live in for generations to come" (1943, p. 1). The final chapter of the volume consisted of four open letters directed to President Roosevelt, Commissioner of Education John Studebaker, Rugg's colleagues in education, and to superintendents of the nation's schools expressing his vision and plans for the "battle for consent." The letters reiterated Rugg's hope for a new society, spawned by "a million study-discussion clubs" and "a senior high school curricula made over to incorporate this same study of winning the peace" (p. 239). Rugg restated the vision expressed in *The Great Technology* that we would cultivate a sizable and vocal minority of citizens who understand the problems of the society and of the peace and would make themselves heard in reconstructing the social order. It is clear in this book, that Rugg held fast to his vision of social reconstruction through education:

> This really is our moment to make dreams come true. Long have we looked toward a millennial day when the American citizenry would become intelli-

gent and alert, when understanding and tolerance would be abroad in the land. The dawn of that New Day is now on the horizon and it seems possible for us to usher it in to throw fuller light on our problems. (p. 240)

The concluding pages of the book expressed Rugg's hopes for the future in very clear terms. He cited 10 ideas and issues that "if grasped by the Ten Million, would win the peace." Among these were global disarmament, an end to "imperial exploitation of the weak by the strong," global interdependence, full employment, and economic abundance (p. 244). The book ended with a poetic vision that nicely summed up Rugg's social reconstructionism:

Tomorrow is Today ... that
The mammoth glacier of social trend
    Taking movement down the Valley of History
    can be diverted by man
Into pathways toward Tomorrow. (p. 245)

In a sense, the book was another answer to his critics. It signaled that Rugg would not be bowed, that he would continue his quest for a progressive and worthy society, and that he still believed the progressive vision was worth fighting for.

Professional Involvements. Over the years Rugg had nurtured many professional involvements and was an active member and leader in a wide variety of educational organizations. One of those longstanding professional involvements was with the Progressive Education Association (PEA) and especially, the Social Frontier group. As younger members of both groups were drawn into military service Rugg took on an increasingly active role. In 1939, the PEA had taken over publication of *The Social Frontier*, but had renamed it *Frontiers of Democracy* partly in an effort to remove the journal's "radical tint," but also to make the journal more amenable to the general membership. The membership of the PEA had for years been struggling over competing visions of progressive education, especially the child-centered version versus social reconstructionism. Financial support and subscribership for the journal was at low ebb, and the journal was in debt. Rugg served on the journal's editorial board, and in May, 1943, agreed to serve as editor in a last ditch effort to keep the publication alive. As if to exemplify the rift in the PEA, the first issue of the journal under Rugg's editorship, published in October, 1943, carried a statement by Vinal Tibbetts, PEA president, stating that the journal's new policy would be to "report rather than editorialize." In the same issue, Rugg expressed his opinion clearly and directly: "Frontiers will not be neutral—on every issue it will take sides—every month it will point a direction." Shortly thereafter, the board of directors voted unanimously, without Rugg present, to discontinue publication. Far from a sudden decision, some members of the board had long resented Rugg's attempts to move the organization into a position more supportive of social reconstructionism.

The action of the board hurt Rugg deeply and he struck back in the final issue of the journal, arguing that the decision was not merely economic, but was rooted in fear: "It was," he wrote, "the fear of the officers that *Frontiers* would endanger the new program they were making for the Association, and in addition would endanger their own personal security." He also accused that association of being "too old—too tired" to lead in a time of crisis (Rugg, 1943b). Last minute efforts to keep *Frontiers* alive were unsuccessful and with the December, 1943 issue, the journal ceased publication.

Rugg continued to serve on the board of directors of the PEA, though the organization was in severe financial difficulty by the wars end. During the war and after, the organization lost much of its social reconstructionist wing and never really recovered. In Rugg's view it had failed to adapt to the changing times. After the war the social reconstructionists attempted to formulate a new social action philosophy for the organization based on a proposal from Theodore Brameld at the 1947 PEA conference. Rugg made a stirring speech in support of the proposal, and it was adopted by the membership. However, the new direction was short lived, a victim of the changing times, and the PEA was disbanded a few years later.

Rugg had also been heavily involved in the international affiliate of the PEA, the New Education Fellowship (NEF), beginning in 1927, and gradually undertook leadership of the international education movement in the United States. For many years he attended NEF conferences and had assumed a position of leadership. He continued this involvement throughout the decades following the textbook controversy. In the 1950s he also became an active member of the Philosophy of Education Society.

Writing Projects. In the years following the textbook crisis and after publication of *Now is the Moment*, Rugg worked on a broad interpretation of American education based on his years of teaching foundations of education. The book was written primarily as a textbook for his course and similar courses throughout the country. It not only helped replace some of the income from his textbook series, but gave him, once again, a position of recognized leadership. It was his most scholarly effort to date, and provided a synthesis of his mature social and educational thought.

While it was true that *Foundations for American Education* (1947) was presaged by some of Rugg's previous work from the 1930s, especially *Culture and Education in America* (1931) and *American Life and the School Curriculum* (1936) the volume offered a broad new synthesis. Rugg presented what he termed the four foundations of education which included a new biopsychology, a new sociology, a new esthetics, and a new ethics. Much of the book was devoted to tracing the historical development of each of these foundational areas, and the final portion emphasized the school curriculum. The volume revisited many of Rugg's main themes, critiquing the subject centered curriculum and curriculum by committee, much as he had in the 1920s.

After a detailed look at the foundations of American society and schooling, and examination in some detail of various approaches to curriculum design, Rugg posited his view that the curriculum must include areas that were neglected prior to that time. These included socially and personally useful work, sex, love, and home life, and psychological problems such as inferiority and the intimate problems of personal living. Moreover, in keeping with the general thrust of his previous work, he argued that study of the insistent controversial issues of the social system must be central to the curriculum. Among these were property and the struggle for power, racial conflict, and control of public opinion. Other vital areas, especially so for realization of social reconstruction, were the need for an education-centered community, building a high esthetic life, and creating a workable democratic idea. Though much of this was reminiscent of his earlier work, he went beyond his previous proposals and recommended a broad fields approach, centered around three main categories: the sciences, the arts of expression, and the techniques of life. Although Rugg did not detail a complete program for the schools, what he did propose was a "broad core program" that would draw on subject fields as needed. To reach fruition, the program would require development of an "artist teacher." Though it was not entirely new, this book summed up Rugg's thinking on the social world and the curriculum and offered a revised and challenging description of Rugg's vision for the future. The book received generally favorable reviews in education journals, and was later called Rugg's "magnum opus" by historian Lawrence Cremin (Cremin, 1960).

A New Marriage. Harold Rugg met Elizabeth May Howe (then Elizabeth Page) in 1941 while she was attending classes at Teachers College and working on a masters degree during a sabbatical from her duties at The Brearley School, on the east side of Manhattan, where she served as headmistress of the lower school. Rugg was an "enthralling lecturer" and Elizabeth was very taken with him. His ideas on education meshed with her own. Her husband, a career Army officer, was stationed in Washington, DC, at the time. Though they were 18 years apart in age, Rugg was attracted to Elizabeth immediately, and she to him. During the next 4 years, Elizabeth worked as the headmistress of the lower school of Milton Academy in Milton, Massachusetts, within a few miles of her parents home in Cambridge. After they were married on September 9, 1947, Elizabeth and her daughter Katharine, then about 14 years old, went to live with Harold at his apartment at 263 West 11th Street in Greenwich Village, near Bleeker Street. The following year, the family would travel to the Rugg home in Woodstock almost every weekend.

Harold would remain married to Elizabeth for the remainder of his life. Having failed twice in previous marriages, Rugg was wary at first, but this marriage proved to be a happy one. According to Katharine, Harold and Elizabeth were "profoundly happy" together. Their partnership was built on a number of similarities. Not only did they share similar views on education, their core beliefs and origins were also compatible in important ways. Elizabeth had roots in a distinguished family of Concord, Massachusetts, transcendentalists, and many of her ancestors were educators, Unitarians, and abolitionists. While Elizabeth and Katharine were members of a Unitarian congregation, Harold would attend only occasionally. Though he never joined the Unitarian church, Harold's beliefs, and the Rugg family's possible links to Congregationalism, might have been a good fit with Unitarianism, especially in terms of the independent and nonconformist side of his persona.

The Rugg's apartment building in Greenwich Village was home to famous literary figures. Thomas Wolf had lived there at one time, and Norman Cousins, editor of *The Saturday Review*, lived downstairs. The apartment could have easily been the setting for the opera, "La Boheme." It was a walk-up flat on the top floor of the building and had a large living room, a bedroom and nook bedroom, and was decorated throughout with modern art. It also had a large studio, with floor to ceiling bookcases and a glass ceiling through which the snow fluttered in. Harold had huge classes at the time, 400 students in one, and students and colleagues often came to the apartment to visit. Among those who visited the apartment with some regularity were Kenneth Benne, Carlton Washburne, Fred Redefer, Bunny Smith, Lauren Zillacus, and David Bailey of Vermont's Country School. During time in Manhattan, the Rugg's were friends with many musicians and dancers including Martha Graham, Hanya Holm and Doris Humphrey, and frequently attended recitals (Alling, 2005).

At the time of his marriage to Elizabeth, Harold was still seeing his son, Harald. During the first year of the new marriage, Harald visited the Rugg home in Woodstock on at least two weekends. He was about 11 years of age. His step-sister recalls a nice young fellow who was fond of spitting and throwing rocks. Following that year, Harold did not see his son frequently, if at all. He did see him again some seven years later, when Harald was about 18. Yet, he was very fond of Harald and wanted to see him more regularly. Katherine Alling recalls sensing some resentment in Harold that his former wife, Louise Kruger, kept the boy from him. Moreover, there was an edge in Harold's voice whenever Louise or the textbook controversy entered the conversation. Apparently, there was very little contact.

Though his relationship with his new stepdaughters, Katharine, and her older sister Betsy, who was away at college, may have been difficult at times (both were teenagers during the first years of Rugg's marriage to Elizabeth), he quickly won the heart of at least one of them, and probably both. Katharine remembers Harold as a marvelous and caring stepfather, always considerate of her needs and interests. She describes him as "acutely perceptive with another's best interests at heart." He was "very forgiving of a difficult step-daughter ... and very encouraging of intellectual pursuits."

In 1953, on the occasion of Elizabeth's 50th birthday, the Rugg's planned a festive party at their home in Woodstock, inviting local artists and many good friends. Katharine, a student at Sarah Lawrence College at the time, wanted to be there, but had no transportation to Woodstock. One of her friends had an acquaintance with a car, a male student at another college, who agreed to drive the small group up to Woodstock for the weekend. Upon meeting the young man who drove them to Woodstock, Norman Alling, and after having only a brief conversation with him, Harold said, from across the room, "Elizabeth, I believe that is the man Katharine should marry" (Alling, 2005). Norman Alling would later become Katharine's husband.

On the occasion of Harold's 70th birthday in January, 1956, Katharine honored her stepfather with a letter stating:

> You have all the things that matter most, and have them in good store; better than having them, you give them too.... But I cannot let the day pass without reminding us both of the love I send you dayly [sic], nor without thanking you, on this most special day for the volumes of special days that you have given me. I thank you most for sharing yourself ...
>   Yours with the deepest affection ever ...
>
> Kina (Katharine) (Page, 1956).

After the triumphs, trials and tribulations of his long career, and the joys and difficulties of two previous marriages, Harold Rugg had found domestic happiness and a stable, supportive and happy family life. He had the love and support of his wife Elizabeth, his two step-daughters and his son Harald. In his professional life he had become one of the leading authorities on the social and philosophical foundations of education. He had also found absorbing scholarly projects which engaged his tireless and continuing efforts, and he had many friends and supporters in Woodstock, New York City, and throughout the nation and world. Moreover, he was still considered a lion of the left and was an inspiration to many teachers and educators, despite the fact that attacks on progressive education continued and his schoolbooks were no longer in vogue.

Writing Projects. Rugg's subsequent writing projects detailed his visions for both teachers and teacher education. In 1950, Rugg, with coauthor Marian Brooks of City College of New York, published, *The Teacher in School and Society.* The volume was part of the New-World Education series with Rugg, Brameld, B. Othaniel Smith, and Lawrence E. Cole as educational consultants, and marked Rugg's first publication to fully address teacher education. Though he had expressed interest in the proper education of teachers as early as 1920, as he focused most of his attention on writing the social science pamphlets and textbooks, he seemed to assume that teacher education was at least adequate. However, Rugg later acknowledged, in conversations with his brother Earle, that he had mistakenly assumed that teachers could both understand and properly teach his social studies materials, in essence assuming that they were so good as to be "teacher proof." The reason the social studies pamphlets didn't work was, according to Earle, "teachers didn't know how to teach 'em ... they were then taught ... to teach history with a little of civics, economics, and sociology. They did not understand how to teach social studies" (E. U. Rugg, 1965).

While his materials were pedagogically innovative, they required a teacher well versed in an interactive teaching style in order to do them justice. Rugg did give some attention to teaching in the Teachers Guides that accompanied each of his textbooks, and he had devoted a chapter of *Culture and Education in America* (1931) to the need for a revamped teacher education. However, it was in *The Teacher in School and Society* (Rugg & Brooks, 1950), and 2 years later in *The Teacher of Teachers* (1952b), that Rugg gave sustained attention to the problems of teacher education. In the latter book, he argued that to further democracy in society, and to prevent or derail Fascist trends, "new pubic minds must be created" and in that effort the teacher educator must be a leader (H. O. Rugg, 1952b, p. 11). He recommended a turn to the creative man, who had "found the conceptual keys to the problems of our times." On the whole, Rugg was advocating a program of teacher education similar to the graduate program at Teachers College with its strong foundational emphasis. A constantly recurring theme of the book was the need for "artist teachers" who would use the schools as an agency for social reform, or as Rugg put it, "the creative reconstruction of American life" (p. 247). Thus, for Rugg, the primary task of teacher educators was to help further the aim of reform by helping teachers understand the need for social reconstruction, and how that might be advanced by their work in the schools. He was, in each of these works, true to his vision and philosophy.

Teaching. Though Rugg loved to teach, and had a reputation as an excellent speaker, he was, according to most assessments, never a great discussion teacher, and seldom created the kind of issues-oriented discussion in his own classes that he recommended for the schools. Of course many of his classes were large lecture sections. Perhaps most vexing, Rugg struggled with a speech impediment, a serious stutter, which especially bothered him when he read aloud. He would sometimes get tripped up, and found the experience humiliating. Mostly, he lectured, and he was a bit long-winded. Despite the speech impediment, his lectures sometimes evoked spontaneous applause, stemming from "genuine admiration for the man's incisive mind" (Fisher, 1961). Several former students described his teaching in glowing terms, citing the "honesty and contagious enthusiasm of the lecturer," his "communicative classroom personality," or his skills as an "enthralling lecturer" (Teachers College, 1951). Another former student noted that he had a strong reputation, and that on arrival at Teachers College he was greeted with a "avalanche of advice to 'take a course with Rugg.'" In at least a few classes, "the students analyzed the ideas of Rugg," and Rugg in turn, "critically analyzed the ideas of his students ... (and) together, they laid the groundwork for a thoughtful, probing, and constructive analysis of American society and education" (Cremin, 1951).

But frequently, with his busy writing and travel schedule, he gave only a little attention to his courses. Though conscientious in class attendance, he was known for frequently discussing his current scholarly interests rather than course materials. Most students, no doubt, enjoyed this as an interesting, entertaining, and enlightening detour. Perhaps it reflected his true interests. One family member stated that Rugg thought of teaching as an imposition because it took him away from his writing (J. E. Rugg, 2005). Nonetheless, many former students and colleagues commented on the brilliance of Rugg's "scintillating" mind and his range of knowledge. Rugg often "displayed a grasp of the whole problem at issue," and insisted upon "a broad humane knowledge on the part of educators, in contrast to the pedantic, pedestrian, and mechanical approach," characteristic of so many teachers. Perhaps even more important, he "courageously supplied a social vision which was acutely needed" in what is sometimes described as "the timid profession" (DeBoer, 1951).

Over the course of his career at Teachers College Rugg taught a variety of courses. Initially, he taught a seminar in educational psychology with E. L. Thorndike and others. Then, beginning in his second year at Teachers College, he taught courses in the scientific reconstruction of the school subjects. He added a curriculum seminar and a course in social psychology in 1928. Also, during the late 1920s, Rugg entered into the collaborative, new, team taught foundations of education course, 200F, in which he frequently shared the podium with Kilpatrick, Dewey, Newlon, Counts, Childs and other Teachers College luminaries. Rugg continued to teach the course until his retirement. In 1935 he began teaching a course titled "Arts in Education and Life," reflecting his fascination with creativity and the arts. His concerns over postwar planning were reflected in a course titled "Education and the Problem of Peace" which he taught for two years in the immediate post-war period (Nelson, 1975).

Rugg's persona has also been the subject of a good deal of comment and conjecture. He had a reputation among the media as a "mild mannered" professor. And, to some friends and colleagues, he seemed to be always in a hurry. During the years devoted to writing the pamphlets and textbooks that was likely the case. He was very hard working, driven by his background in puritan New England and his own inferiority complex. As Rugg later recalled:

> I have, for much of my life, been rebelling against myself, or feeling that I wasn't measuring up to what I was capable of doing. I had a puritanical streak there that would drive me to do things whether I wanted to do them or not.... My former wife said, one of the things I remember about you, from the very beginning, was your impatience.... You were always so impatient to make things go the way you wanted them to go.... I was a driver (H. O. Rugg, 1956a).

According to his stepdaughter, who knew him well, Rugg was anything but the personification of a mild professor. His reputation as "mild mannered" may have been a reflection of his politeness, as he was polite to a fault. He was also energetic and forceful, a very bold man who conveyed great strength, even in the way he walked across a room. He did have an ego, but that was well founded as he had accomplished a great deal. Rugg felt that he had risen way beyond his origins, and it was true. He was known all over the world. He was very sure he was right in his ideas, and he asserted those ideas in a remarkably fearless and forceful manner. He was also very personable, friendly and sociable. Yet, he had the self-confidence necessary to sustain a man whose ideas were ahead of their time.

Rugg's persona did undergo at least superficial change in his later years. From early in his career until at least the mid-1940s, Rugg dressed like a businessman: three piece suits, rather shiny neckties, wing-tip shoes. Over time, and while married to Elizabeth, his preferred style of dress altered significantly. His clothing became more muted and he came to prefer gray or khaki slacks, a tweed jacket, a woven wool or cotton tie, and simple dress shoes with a brass buckle on the side. Increasingly, his clothing seemed to "fit" the man he had become. He also grew a small white goatee at the suggestion of his stepdaughter, Katharine. The family all agreed that it suited him well (Alling, 2005).

During Harold's last years on the faculty at Teachers College, the family would spend most weekends in Woodstock, and they developed something of a routine. On a typical Friday, Harold would purchase an enormous slab of beef. Then he and Elizabeth would pick up Katharine at her school and drive to Woodstock. Once they had arrived, Harold would build a vast fire in the large hearth and lay the meat into the fire, suspended in a mesh frame, along with a few potatoes and other vegetables. The beef would gurgle while it cooked, and when it was done the family would enjoy a great feast, eating before the fireplace. Harold Rugg was a bold and vigorous man with a great thirst for life (Alling, 2005).

A NEW RUGG CONTROVERSY

In Retirement. Rugg retired from teaching classes at Teachers College following the spring semester, 1951, at the age of 65, after spending 31 years on the faculty. On the afternoon and evening of May 4, his colleagues held a symposium and dinner in his honor at the New Lincoln School on West 110th Street in Manhattan. At the dinner, which was held to coincide with the AEF Spring Conference, "Frontiers in Culture and Education," several friends and colleagues gave brief statements honoring Rugg's service. Among the speakers were William H. Kilpatrick, R. Freeman Butts, Frederick L. Redefer, and Carleton Washburne. Norman Cousins, editor of the *Saturday Review of Literature*, and a friend and neighbor of Rugg's, and Rugg himself gave major addresses. Goodwin Watson of Teachers College served as toastmaster (Nelson, 1975; Retirement Dinner, 1951).

The theme for the dinner meeting was, "The New Education: Its Tasks and Opportunities." It was sponsored by the New York City members of the American Educational Fellowship and by the department of social and philosophical foundations at Teachers College (News Release, 1951). In his address, Rugg declared that "a critical study of the curves of social change" convinced him that there would not be a third world war prior to 1975. On education, Rugg stated that in the past educational philosophers and psychologists had been too preoccupied with the "thinking" aspect of education. He believed that more attention should be given to "feeling" and to the development of the whole child.

At the symposium which preceded the dinner, also held in Professor Rugg's honor and chaired by Theodore Brameld, Ashley Montagu, Professor of anthropology at Rutgers University, said that "human nature" was not inherited, that man was "educable," and that educators world wide should, "decide the kind of human nature man should have" ("Rugg, Whose Texts Drew," 1951). Later, after the retirement dinner,

Rugg was presented a memory book of testimonials, consisting of more than 185 letters and telegrams from numerous contacts and admirers, including many colleagues and former students his life had touched. They included professors, school administrators, teachers, publishers, neighbors, NEF members, and friends and colleagues from all over the world. Only a few of the accolades came from colleagues outside of schools of education, and those were from a limited number of sociologists and anthropologists, most notable among them, Gordon Allport of Harvard. None of the letters were from historians (Teachers College, 1951).

As professor emeritus, Rugg's professional life was far from over, but shifted to a new phase. His days were busy and fulfilling, spent mostly in writing, speaking, and traveling. He accepted a Fulbright Fellowship to travel and teach at the Institute of Higher Education in Cairo, Egypt, during the 1951-1952 academic year. He wrote to R. Freeman Butts, "We are living in a retired Cook River Steamer tied up at Gezia Island in the Nile. It's wonderful" (Rugg, 1952a). Rooms on the steamer were tiny, but the Captain gave Harold an additional small cabin with a desk. While teaching at the Institute of Higher Education, Harold, Elizabeth, and Katharine traveled through the middle east. Typical of Harold, he was happy to have Katharine along. In late January of 1952, the Rugg family was confined to their boat for a time due to the overthrow of the king and subsequent declaration of martial law. While confined to their quarters, the family members entertained each other by sharing punch lines from "old New Yorker" jokes (Alling, 2005).

Prior to retirement, Rugg's travels were extensive and had furnished some of the materials and insights for his textbooks. Before 1924 he had never left the United States. That year he spent a significant amount of time in Puerto Rico as a consultant. He was to develop a long-term consulting relationship in Puerto Rico and returned a number of times. He later served as a consultant in the Philipines, China, Japan, and Hawaii. His travels also included South Africa, New Zealand, Australia, and most of Western Europe, either on travel grants or attending meetings of the New Education Fellowship.

The Ohio State Controversy. With Rugg, it seemed controversy was never far away. Shortly after his retirement, he gave lectures at Ohio State University, Columbus, Ohio, on July 10 and 11, 1951, at the annual Boyd H. Bode Educational Conference. The speeches were given before an audience of 500 graduate students, most of whom were school teachers from throughout the nation. In his address to the audience on July 10th, Rugg described his approach to teaching as the "good life" and the "new concept." He stated that the enemies of the "good life" are ever present, and cited the "cheap Americanism" of patriotic groups such as the Daughters

Rugg, Kilpatrick and colleagues at Rugg retirement, May 4, 1951 (Courtesy of Katharine Alling).

Wedding of Betsy Page at Rugg home in Woodstock, June, 1952 (Dartmouth College Library).

Rugg and Katharine on her wedding day, August, 1957, at the Rugg home in Woodstock (Courtesy of Katharine Alling).

Ernest F. Johnson, Elizabeth and Harold Rugg (Courtesy of Katharine Alling).

Rugg, a friend, and Ernest F. Johnson at Alling wedding (Courtesy of Katharine Alling).

Katharine and Norman Alling, leaving wedding party (Courtesy of Katharine Alling).

Wedding reception line and view of hills from Rugg home (Courtesy of Katharine Alling).

Earle U. Rugg, 1892-1969 (Special Collections, University of Northern Colorado).

Harold Rugg, 1886-1960 (Photograph by artist Konrad Cramer of Woodstock; Courtesy of Aileen Cramer).

of the American Revolution and Sons of the American Revolution. He also reportedly said:

> I see no hope for the "good life" if business is carried on by private enterprise. It will be the will of the minority ...
>   We've let the Un-American Activities Committee frighten us. (They argue) We should abandon democracy, awake from the dark ages and be prepared to lose our little area of freedom. (Federal Bureau of Investigation, 1951, p. 4)

Rugg also reportedly said that a serious depression might actually help reawaken the American people to their responsibilities and benefits ("Ohio State Trustees," 1951).

In his July 11 speech, Rugg reportedly expressed hope for eventual "world control of power production." He stated that he did not believe his predicted depression would materialize in the near future, but that through a future nationwide period of unemployment people would be made to think. He also reportedly spoke of the growing systems of limitless atomic power production (Federal Bureau of Investigation, 1951, p. 4).

Finally, referring to the controversy surrounding himself and his writings, Rugg was quoted as saying:

> The names of the patrioteers and organizations change, but their devilish motives never change. Most of them are crooked and subversive of the American way. The appalling fact is that parents and teachers of middle age stand and do nothing after the bigoted attacks of the late 30's and early 40's. The Un-American committees have got us backed right out of the ring. They're in every town in America, led by professional rabble-rousers and backed by large sums of money. They are merchants of conflict—yellow newspapers with disgruntled editors, the commentator with a yen for the microphone, lap-dog women, business men's clubs, Rotary, the American Legion, chronic letter writers and the prestige hunters. These are the real enemies—and the active ones—of education. (Federal Bureau of Investigation, 1951, pp. 4-5)

Though Dean Donald P. Cottrell of the College of Education came to Rugg's defense, supporting his appearance on the grounds of academic freedom and the need for diversity of viewpoints, the university president, Dr. Howard L. Bevis, issued a statement stating that Rugg's lectures on the campus implied no sponsorship of Rugg's views by the university. President Bevis also stated that he disagreed with much of what Rugg reportedly said, but that "freedom of speech allows wide latitude of expression" (Federal Bureau of Investigation, 1951). The speech touched off yet another controversy over Rugg, though this time the most heated controversy was largely confined to the Columbus, Ohio, area and its vicinity. The speech also spurred a renewed investigation of Rugg by the Federal Bureau of Investigation (FBI).

Stirred by media reports and a local campaign launched by Rugg opponents, readers of the local papers wrote to express their concerns over Rugg's appearance. Some attacked Rugg and his ideas, while others decried the use of tax dollars to support such a radical guest speaker. Several letters attacked the leadership and faculty of the graduate school of the College of Education who were responsible for, and funded Rugg's appearance. Among the letters were the following:

> We vehemently protest the appearance of Dr. Rugg, author of the controversial Rugg textbooks which have been eliminated from numbers of schools and which have been the target of numerous patriotic organizations.... The Ohio State University is supported by the people of Ohio. Let the people speak! Do we want Harold G. Rugg at our University? (Federal Bureau of Investigation, 1951, p. 1).

> (Rugg) is a notorious left-wing writer of Socialistic textbooks and one of the original group of collectivist teachers who have warped the minds of American school children for two decades.... Harold Rugg is a socialist. He has been the leading part of the undermining apparatus of our education philosophy. He should not have been invited to speak at the OSU conference. (p. 2).

> Will teachers attending this conference bring this so-called "new concept" to our children next fall? Ohio State University needs a thorough investigation by the people of Ohio for bringing speakers of this type to the campus. (p. 4)

> If our nation is to be destroyed by teachers indoctrinated by a bunch of fuzzy-minded, hair-brained, so-called educators, I for one protest having my hard-earned tax dollars pay for that destruction. ("Readers Indignant," 1951)

Following what appeared to be a genuine public outcry over Rugg's appearance, on July 17, 1951, Ohio Governor Frank J. Lausche asked the trustees of Ohio State University to check into the matter. The previous day, two members of the state's newly formed Un-American Activities Committee of the Ohio Legislature and an OSU trustee stated that Rugg's conference appearance would be investigated.

An editorial in the *Columbus Dispatch* on July 23 supported an investigation of Rugg's appearance, "its sponsorship, financing and the political philosophies being fostered in the College of Education." The editors stated, "These moves are in order.... The question is whether or not (teachers) are being indoctrinated with the subversive political ideas advocated by a notorious and discredited propagandist" ("Campus Probe," 1951). A much longer editorial expressing similar sentiments appeared in the *Columbus State Journal* on August 31, identifying Rugg as "the nation's most notorious Marxist educator," and reading:

> The Rugg episode cannot be laughed off. Somebody or a group brought him here for a purpose, if none other than to provide an audience of potential missionaries and to give them the opportunity to hear and see the fountain head, the master, the messiah of the movement to build through the school system a new body of American citizenry, receptive and reconciled and blindly eager to accept an American counterpart of Soviet totalitarianism. ("Rugg Episode," 1951)

The editorial went on to state that it suspected the College of Education at OSU had been "substantially infiltrated," and that many boards of education had avoided employing graduates from the school, especially in social studies.

On August 12, it was reported in the *Cincinnati Enquirer* that the Ohio American Legion had called for the removal of the Rugg textbooks from Ohio schools, repeating their usual charges that the books were "biased in their presesntation by advocating socialistic government for the United States" (Federal Bureau of Investigation, 1951, p. 13).

Most of the letters on the controversy called for an investigation of university policies, but a few defended Rugg's appearance under the idea that one of the functions of a university is to provide a forum for all ideas, even those which are unpopular, so that each may be judged on its merits. Therefore, unpopular persons and ideas should be given a hearing. A number of faculty members apparently expressed this defense of the Rugg appearance, maintaining that a university faculty, within a democracy, has the right to select the program to be presented to its students.

Also coming to Rugg's defense was the Communist Party of Ohio which circulated 250 copies of a mimeographed circular entitled, "The Luxury of Silence," to certain members of the OSU faculty and others. The circular, which blasted the acquiescence of campus liberals to the will of the "DISPATCH gang" in the witchhunt, and "the reality of TRUMAN's bipartisan police state" (Federal Bureau of Investigation, 1951, p. 11).

Then, on September 4, the *New York Times* reported, in its back pages, that the Ohio State University Board of Trustees had attacked Rugg's speech as "un-American" and condemned the invitation given Rugg to speak at the university. In its statement, the board of trustees said, "the function of the university is teaching, not indoctrination. The university must not be used as an agency of un-American propaganda. Every effort will be made to carry out these purposes." The article also noted, "Dr.

Rugg has not been listed by any Government agency as un-American" ("Ohio State Trustees", 1951, p. 29). A similar article, appearing in the *Cincinnati Times-Star*, reported that the invitation was "not in accordance with the traditions and objectives of Ohio State University," and noted that in order to avoid a recurrence of such an incident, all future speakers would have to be cleared through the office of the University president (Federal Bureau of Investigation, 1951, p. 12).

The FBI Investigates. FBI surveillance of Rugg, which covered the Ohio State controversy in great detail, actually began many years earlier, when the bureau began receiving unsolicited materials on Rugg in 1942. The bureau did not begin its Rugg file on its own, but started the file when the Washington Field Office was given materials "gratuitously" by Mr. Walter Steele, publisher of the *National Republic* magazine. One of the earliest items in the file was a manuscript on Rugg by Augustin G. Rudd, titled, "What is the Rugg Social System." This manuscript had appeared in the *National Republic* magazine and was subsequently reprinted in *Rugg Philosophy Analyzed* and circulated by the American Legion. In addition, the file contained an article published in the April, 1938, issue of *The Beacon Light*, a periodical printed by a right wing California group, titled, "Atheistic Communism in Our Schools" (Federal Bureau of Investigation, 2003). The files also reportedly contained reprints of articles by many of Rugg's most determined critics. Despite opening a file, the bureau apparently did little else to investigate Rugg during the war years (Nelson & Singleton, 1977).

However, by the early 1950s, the climate had changed, the cold war was intensifying, the McCarthy era was in full bloom (Shrecker, 1998), and the bureau was apparently moved to launch a security investigation of Rugg following the controversy over his speaking engagement at Ohio State University. A lengthy report was filed by the bureau's office in Cincinnati on October 1, 1951, detailing the controversy and summarizing several other "pamphlets, books, and leaflets" furnished by a local informant, materials "which she had accumulated over a number of years," including *Rugg Philosphy Analyzed, Vol. III* (National Americanism Commission, 1941), and the pamphlet, *Undermining Our Republic: Do You Know What the Children Are Being Taught in Our Public Schools? You'll Be Surprised ...*, published by the Guardians of American Education (Rudd, Hicks, & Falk, 1941).

Apparently no further action was taken by the bureau at that time, but on April 30, 1953, the head of the New York bureau requested authority "to conduct the necessary investigation of this person (Harold O. Rugg) to determine whether he should or should not be included in the Security Index. The request referenced the letter of October 1, 1951 from the Cincinnati office. The director of the New York office was given authorization on May 15, 1953, by the bureau's director, J. Edgar Hoover (Federal Bureau of Investigation, 2003).

The subsequent investigation led to reports by the Boston and New York bureaus of the FBI. Agents in Boston prepared a detailed report based on their contact with Dartmouth College where they viewed his records, including his alumni file which contained a good deal of biographical information on Rugg's life and career. The alumni file included a number of articles critical of Rugg as well as his defense published in the *Dartmouth Alumni Magazine* of January, 1941, titled, "That Men May Understand." In the article, as in his book of the same title, Rugg categorically denied ever being a Communist or Socialist (H. O. Rugg, 1941). The FBI report also contained a report on Rugg's address to the Progressive Education Association meeting in Cleveland, Ohio, on March 2, 1934, in which he reportedly stated that efforts would be made "to organize 14,000,000 persons into a 'pressure group' to force more radical changes in the economic system."

Agents in New York City prepared a detailed, 14-page report which advised the director on Rugg's residences, his professional affiliations, his voting registration ... and included reports from a variety of informants, many "of unknown reliability" and a few who were deemed "reliable informants." The synopsis of facts of the report read, in part:

> Reliable informant advised Rugg not a Communist but "one of CP's favorites..." Reliable informants advised subj. associated with persons known to be members of Communist front organizations, 1949 to 1950.

The report contained a good deal of information and misinformation about Rugg gathered from miscellaneous informants. At one point he is cited by an informant for being openly sympathetic with Communist theories and for his lack of morals. Throughout the report, Ruggs professional and political affiliations and activities were subjected to close scrutiny, including involvement with The Progressive Citizens of America, and the International Judicial Association, both deemed communist front organizations. One dossier cited in the report, Red-ucators at Columbia University, published by Allen Zolls National Council for American Education, listed Rugg as un-American. However, the FBI report stated, It is not to be assumed that because a professor or teacher is included in this list, it is conclusive evidence that he is a Communist. He may be simply naïve (Federal Bureau of Investigation, 1953, p. 4).

The report also included references to selected speeches and writings, reported on charges from the usual critics, and included new allegations from a few loose cannons. In June, 1954, a recommendation was made that a Security Index Card be prepared because Rugg was a Communist.

However, in July, Director J. Edgar Hoover rejected the nomination of Rugg to the Security Index because there was insufficient information to warrant the recommendation. Hoover advised the New York office to "remain alert to report any additional information indicating subject's affiliation with the Communist Party or Communist front organizations" (Nelson & Singleton, 1977, p. 20). From the time of the authorization in 1953 and until his death in 1960, whether he knew it or not, Rugg was under continuing, but apparently sporadic, surveillance by the FBI. Three reports were filed on Rugg in 1959, but they apparently led to no further action (Nelson & Singleton, 1977).

Though the controversy surrounding Rugg's appearance at Ohio State in 1951 was the last major conflagration in which Rugg was actively involved, during the McCarthy era, and even later, there was a continuing series of attacks and critical commentary on the Rugg textbook series and Rugg's educational, political and social ideas. During the deluge of attacks on progressive education that occurred during the 1950s, Rugg and other frontier thinkers, especially Counts and Dewey, were subjected to a revival of those attacks. The American Legion used the Rugg controversy as a continuing warning to progressives and published articles during the 1950s recalling their victory over Rugg. And, one of Rugg's chief critics, Augustin G. Rudd, published a memoir recalling his role in the Rugg controversy and renewing his allegations (1957).

AN UNFINISHED LIFE

During the remainder of his retirement years, Rugg continued to write, travel, and maintain his many professional contacts. He became known as a local icon in Woodstock, and made many friends in his adopted community. He and Elizabeth hosted frequent dinner parties at their home, which one friend described as a "treasure of a house" and often hosted colleagues and local friends as guests (Evers, 2003). During his later years, he was fondly referred to by at least some of the townsfolk as, "old Doc Rugg." By this time he looked the part, with white hair, tweed jacket and a small goatee.

In Manhattan, the family purchased a brownstone on East 58th Street in Manhattan west of Sutton Place, a rather toney area, in 1951 or 1952. They rented out most of the apartments, but sometimes occupied the top floor, with Harold's study at the front. One morning during the winter of 1952 as Harold was working, he was disturbed by the din from a parade of floozies entering the lower level of the house sometime between 9 and 10 A.M. He asked Elizabeth to check on the revelers and ask for studious quiet, only to learn that one of the men was Richard Roger's musical coach, and that the noise of revelry was actually a rehearsal of the many wives of the court of Siam for "The King and I." Rugg's outrage at what he thought was occurring was a good indicator of Harold's strict work ethic. He worked at his writing, either lectures or books, every working day of his life, which was practically every day (Alling, 2005).

During Rugg's retirement years, the family spent most of its time in Woodstock where they would frequently entertain friends and colleagues as houseguests. Among those who visited the Rugg home on Ohayo Mountain in Bearsville were Bunny Smith, Carlton Washburne, Fred Redefer, and Lauren Zilliacus. Zilliacus, from Finland, whom the Rugg's called "Zilly," would usually spend several days. House parties for colleagues often lasted overnight, and would frequently conclude with a long breakfast at the Rugg home, from 9 A.M. to 3 P.M., marked by lively and wide ranging discussion.

The Ruggs also had a number of friends among the arts community in Woodstock and often entertained various artists at dinner parties held at their home. Among the friends who were apt to visit the Rugg home were local painters, writers, sculptors and musicians including painters Emmet and Eleanor Edwards, Ethel Magafan, Bruce Currie, Edward Chavez, Robert Angelock, Georgina Klitgaard, and Konrad Cramer, sculptors Alfeo Faggi, Raoul Hague, and Alexander Achipenko, composer Henry Cowell, poet Rafael Rudnickand, writer Alf Evers, and many others (Alling, 2005).

Harold Rugg was an avid champion of new modes of expression, and came to know many of the men and women of the Woodstock art scene very well during his years in the town. The Rugg family invariably attended openings at the Woodstock Art Gallery, concerts at The Maverick Concert Hall and experimental theater productions. Moreover, there were many other intellectuals living in and near Woodstock with whom Harold was friends, including John Kingsbury, Hughes Mearns, and James Shotwell. Among descendants of the area's previous settlers were many fine craftsmen whom Rugg knew well, such as Ishmael Rose, who with his three sons, built and rebuilt Rugg's home. Rugg was also a patron of the arts and owned numerous works produced by local artisans, including three by the sculptor, Alfeo Faggi. One of the Faggi works was a bas relief plaster nude in profile installed in the living room wall. Another was a reclining, full body sculpture of Walt Whitman which was installed on the grounds of the Rugg home (Alling, 2005).

Rugg's neighbors, Georgina and Kaj Klitgaard, remarked on how much the Rugg's presence meant to them in their "hilly community," and noted, "Your generous-mindedness, your energy, your cheer, and your fight has been stimulating to the environment … (and in retirement) …

you'll be carrying on the fight, cheerfully and energetically as ever (Klit-gaard, 1951).

During retirement, Rugg worked harder than ever on writing projects which thoroughly absorbed his mind. He had a typist, Dorothy Peters, who worked at a small desk in his study, and a gardener who took care of the grounds. His wife Elizabeth, was a wonderful cook and companion, and also served as his first editor and read everything he wrote. His typical working day meant that after a solitary breakfast of eggs, bacon, toast, orange juice, and coffee, he was usually at his desk by 7 A.M., aided by a constant stream of Pall Mall cigarettes and more coffee. He would remain at work until 5:00 in the evening, with brief sojourns to stretch or enjoy a few minutes in the garden. This was his routine, typically, 6 days a week. After working, when the weather was nice he would enjoy a cocktail on the porch. When it was cold or rainy, he would enjoy his drink in front of the fireplace, or meet friends for drinks at a tavern in Woodstock. He enjoyed drinking Scotch, usually "Teachers" brand, but never drank to excess (Alling, 2005).

He also spent a good deal of time traveling and serving as a consultant. During the early years of his retirement Rugg continued his consultancy in Puerto Rico, and wrote to his brother Earle:

> My most important news is that I am now serving as a kind of roving consultant for the University of Puerto Rico.... Elizabeth and I were there for four months last year and ... we are going ... to spend three months more. We are developing various projects as a part of a general program of educational development in the Island schools. (H. O. Rugg, 1954)

Later, after Rugg and his wife Elizabeth spent the summer of 1956 traveling in Europe, he wrote:

> We had a wonderful time abroad—two weeks at the New Education Fellowship Conference in Utrecht, Holland—another couple of weeks driving up the Rhine to Hindelberg and back to Belgium, Holland, and France to England. We then drove for about a month and a half all over England, Scotland and Wales. Although I have been there many times, I really have never seen the countryside as it can be seen from a car. (H. O. Rugg, 1956b)

Rugg loved to drive. His stepdaughter recalls his driving on a number of trips, both in the United States and abroad, and relates that he loved the devil-may-care boyishness of it, hair flying, knuckles wrapped around the wheel, driving on twisty and dangerous roads at what seemed heart stopping speeds (Alling, 2005).

Despite what may seem a busy life filled with travel and engaging projects, in his later years Rugg continued to feel the shadow of the text-

book controversy, and often felt isolated and alone. As he wrote to his protégé, B. Othanel Smith:

May 14, 1957

Dear Bunny,

Day after day Day after day since getting back to Woodstock, Elizabeth and I
have talked about the wonderful time we had with you and Tommy and your
group at Urbana, meeting at St. Louis, and the rest of the marvelous trip,
etc..... I work alone here so continuously, only rarely seeing colleagues from
New York or other places. Until your seminar at Urbana I have had no discussion at all over the direction in which my studies are going. You and your
group helped to re-orient me. In fact, I personally got a new perspective on
the task, and in the two weeks we have been back in Woodstock I have
rebuilt the overall plan of the book. It is now to be one volume instead of
two, even though that may make a fairly large book. I am determined, however, to write with the utmost economy of words....

I wonder if you can get even a small glimpse of what the St. Louis meeting meant to me. For many years of my life I was on the platform of our various associations constantly, much too frequently for my own good, no
doubt. But since the successful attack on by work by the Legion and the
other patrioteers nearly 20 years ago now, almost no institution or learned
association would allows its platform and its members to be subverted.
Hence, I have been almost completely alone, except for you, Ted (Brameld),
Kenneth (Benne), and a few others. The invitation to present a major paper
at St. Louis gave me a tremendous lift, the reception of the paper even a
more powerful one. I am glad that you told me at St. Louis that the invitation sprang from a suggestion of the program committee. I am writing Bill
(William O. Stanley) today to thank him also for his part in it all. Such
friends for a man to have.

Harold (Rugg, 1957b).

On the same trip, in 1957, Harold and Elizabeth stopped in to visit his
daughter, Betty, and her family whom he hadn't seen for many years,
spending a day at Black Mountain, North Carolina. It appears that Rugg
was fond of all his children, though contacts were infrequent. Prior to
their trip, he contacted Betty to let her know that he would be in the area.
Betty responded:

Dear Dad, I was most surprised to hear from you after all these years, and
pleasantly so, believe me. We rarely leave home so you would be sure to
catch us here if you come by. Be quite nice to see you again and I would like
very much for you to meet my family. Just drop me a card when you are
more sure of when you will be here.... Looking forward to seeing you again,
Betty (Betty, 1957).

After visiting Betty, Rugg wrote: "She has grown exactly as I had anticipated, from the lovely child that she was, into a beautiful and confident
young woman of 40 with two remarkable children, the younger about
ready to go to college." During the same trip, the Rugg's also stopped in
Washington, DC, to see Harold's nephew, Dean Rugg, son of Earle, who
was attending graduate school in the vicinity (H. O. Rugg, 1957b).

Though his contacts with children from previous marriages were few, it
seems that he longed for relationship with family and was trying to re-
connect when possible. For many years, he had prioritized his work over
his private and family life, and his family life was tumultuous (J. E. Rugg,
2003). During his later years, and with his marriage to Elizabeth, it
seemed that his appreciation for family connections had deepened and
he tried to make contacts when he could.

During the period of his retirement Rugg's scholarship focused on the
social and philosophical foundations of education, and his interest in aes-
thetics. He published a new textbook in educational foundations, *Social
Foundations of Education*, coauthored by William Withers of Queens College (Rugg & Withers, 1955). The book was largely a repetition of previous Rugg volumes, especially *Foundations for American Education*. From that
time forward Rugg focused his scholarly interest and research almost
entirely on the creative process, writing a draft of a book that would be
published posthumously.

In 1959, Rugg spent most of his time writing, working on his latest
book project focused on the creative process, and, with Elizabeth, traveling around the world. In Finland, they spent an evening with their dear
friend, Lauren Zilliacus, who died later that night. In India, Harold spoke
at the NEF World Conference in Delhi, and spent time with Zilly's great
friend Nehru, who was eager to talk with Harold about India's educational system. They also visited Hawaii, Japan, the Philippines, and Indo-
nesia. In Japan, Harold bought a collection of lovely pearls, to be strung
into a necklace upon their return home.

Since at least 1954, Rugg had been working on what he termed his
"magnum opus on the creative process." Rugg's final publication, *Imagination* (1963), was primarily the result of his labors during the last 8 years
of his life, and partially the work of Kenneth Benne who, at the request of
Elizabeth Rugg, prepared the final manuscript for publication after
Rugg's death. In doing research for *Imagination* Rugg crisscrossed the
country interviewing creative people including artists, writers, dancers,
and thinkers and read hundreds of works by "great" artists in an effort to
answer "a single baffling question:"

What is the nature of the act of thought when, in one brilliant moment,
there is a sudden veering of attention, a consequent grasp of new dimen-

sions, and a new ideas is born? Some autonomous forming process sweeps like a magnet across the chaotic elements of the threshold state, picking up the significant segments and, in a welding flash, precipitates the meaningful response. What is this magical force that forms the bits and pieces of the stuff of mind? (H. O. Rugg, 1963, p. xi).

It was, for Rugg, a new area of focus that grew logically out of his broad interests in education and the arts. The resulting work, though unfinished and somewhat rambling in spots, offered an insightful and comprehensive look at the process of creative thought, examining both the intuitive and the scientific, exploring the conscious and unconscious mind, and both eastern and western ways of knowing and understanding. In hindsight, though flawed by its somewhat unfinished feel, it was a seminal work. At one point in his research for the volume Rugg confessed both his excitement and frustration in his search for understanding "the creative flash." It seemed that many of his interview subjects, among the most creative people in the world, were not able to express in words the flash of insight that lay at the heart of creativity (Hanna, 1974). Nonetheless, the volume was a significant contribution to our understanding of creativity and received a favorable review as "a readable synthesis of many of the best studies on creativity" offering "a grand Toynbee-like tour ... he searched for truth with the eye of an artist, the mind of a scientist, the heart of a humanist, the zeal of a reformer, and the longing of Everyman" (Parker, 1963).

Rugg's final speaking engagement may have been a paper he presented from his forthcoming book, then titled, *Imagination of Man,* at the annual meeting of the Philosophy of Education Society in 1960. Rugg attended the meetings of the society for the last 5 years of his life, partly because his interests dovetailed nicely with the work of the society, and partly because he had many old friends, colleagues, and supporters who were active members. Among them were Theodore Brameld, Wilbur Murra, Kenneth Benne, B. O. Smith, R. Freeman Butts, Gordon Hullfish, Bruce Raup, John Childs, William H. Kilpatrick, and others. Rugg's paper, titled, "The Creative Imagination: Imperatives for Educational Theory," was a long discourse on the nature of creativity taken from the book manuscript, and was presented to the Society the month prior to his death (H. O. Rugg, 1960).

On May 17, 1960, Rugg spent the entire morning at his home in Woodstock, sitting at the great semicircular desk in his study overlooking the foothills, revising the manuscript for his book, while Elizabeth drove to Poughkeepsie to have the pearls Harold purchased for her strung into a necklace. It was a fitting final passage for Harold, spent doing what he loved most. That afternoon Rugg died suddenly while walking in the garden of his home. Upon her return, Elizabeth found him lying in the rose garden with a cigarette in his hand. She called an ambulance, and accompanied him to the hospital, but didn't know he had died until a hospital attendant came out and asked, "How old was Dr. Rugg." He was 74 years old. The immediate cause of death was a coronary occlusion. On her return to the Rugg home in Woodstock, Elizabeth busied herself emptying ashtrays and coffee cups, right away that same day, and did it in a state of numbness, seemingly unconscious. She knew she wouldn't be up to it the next day, when it all sank in. According to her daughter, who arrived the next day, she was "in a state of profound shock" (Alling, 2005). As Elizabeth herself later recalled the event of Harold's death, "he was in the garden, taking a look at things. It was sudden and seemingly without warning, as he would have wanted it" (E. Rugg, 1960). Rugg was subsequently cremated at the Gardner Earl Crematory in Troy, New York.

Rugg's death marked the end of an era. By 1960, the progressive movement in education had come under such severe criticism that its crusade to transform the school was moribund, if not dead. In the mid-fifties, the PEA, once a major voice for progressive change in education and society, had folded up its tent and gone out of business. As in the case of the Rugg controversies, the attacks on progressive education were made on both political and educational grounds. In both cases, the media played a strong role in furthering what amounted to a propaganda campaign against progressivism writ large, comprising a classic case study in support of media as a form of propaganda for the current social order (Herman & Chomsky, 1988), and in the case of schooling, for its more traditional forms.

REFERENCES

Alling, K. (2005). Interview with Katharine Alling, January 20, 2005; letter to the author, January 26, 2005.

Betty. (1957). Betty, Harold Rugg's adopted daughter from his first marriage, to H. O, Rugg, undated, as recorded on tape by George Kay in Rugg's study, October 9, 1965. Rugg papers, tape 5, side 2, letters. Tape in the possession of the author.

Bowers, C. A. (1970). Social reconstructionism: Views from the left and the right, 1932-1942. *History of Education Quarterly, 10*(1), 22-52.

Butts, R. F. (1974). Murry R. Nelson interview with R. Freeman Butts, November 20, 1974 (as cited in Nelson, 1975, p. 184).

Campus probe in order. (1951, July 31). *Columbus Dispatch*, "Rugg" folder, box 69, faculty files, Public Relations Office, Archives, MilbankMemorial Library, Teachers College, Columbia University.

Childs, J. L. (1950). *Education and morals*. New York: Appleton-Century-Crofts.

Confidental. (n.d.). There once was a professor named Rugg ... (poem), "Harold Rugg" folder, box 58, William F. Russell papers, Teachers College Archives, Milbank Memorial Library, Teachers College, Columbia University.

Counts, G. S. (1945). *Education and the promise of America*. New York: Macmillan.

Cramer, F. B. (1941). Personal journal of Florence Ballin Cramer, wife of painter Konrad Cramer and Woodstock resident, June 7, 1941. Photocopy obtained from Aileen Cramer, Woodstock, New York.

Cremin, L. E. (1951). Lawrence E. Cremin to Harold O. Rugg. *Harold Rugg: Letters in appreciation of his frontier work*. Unpublished manuscript. New York: Teachers College.

Cremin, L. E. (1960). *Transformation of the school: Progressivism in American education, 1876-1957*. New York: Vintage.

Davis, O. L. (2006). O. L. Davis memories of seminar discussion with Harold Rugg at Vanderbilt University, Nashville, Tennessee, in 1959. Personal communication.

DeBoer, J. J. (1951) John J. De Boer to Harold Rugg, April 12, 1951, in Teachers College. *Harold Rugg: Letters in appreciation of his frontier work*. Unpublished manuscript. New York: Teachers College.

Evers, A. (2003). Interview with Alf Evers, Woodstock, New York, June 14, 2003, conducted by the author.

Federal Bureau of Investigation. (1951). Office Memorandum, SAC, Cincinnati, to Director, FBI (J. Edgar Hoover), October 1,1951, Rugg FBI file. Washington, DC: Federal Bureau of Investigation.

Federal Bureau of Investigation. (1953). Office Memorandum, SAC, New York to Director, FBI (J. Edgar Hoover), November 25, 1953, Rugg FBI file. Washington, DC: Federal Bureau of Investigation.

Federal Bureau of Investigation. (2003). *Rugg FBI File*. Unpublished papers. Washington, DC: Federal Bureau of Investigation. Material unclassified, November 6, 2003. Obtained under Freedom of Information Act.

Fisher, W. H. (1961). Harold Rugg, 1886-1960. *School and Society, 89*, pp. 304-305.

Fox, L. K. (1951). Lorene K. Fox, Queens College, to Harold O. Rugg, April 16, 1951. In Teachers College. *Harold Rugg: Letters in appreciation of his frontier work*. Unpublished manuscript. New York: Teachers College.

Hanna, P. R. (1974). Murry R. Nelson's interview with Paul R. Hanna (as cited in Nelson, 1975, p. 202).

Hart, M. K. (1942). "Who seeks to commit us to world revolution?" *Vital Speeches of 1942*, pp. 588-590.

Herman, E. S., & Chomsky, N. (1988). *Manufacturing consent: The political economy of the mass media*. New York: Pantheon.

Klitgaard, K. (1951). Kaj Klitgaard to Harold Rugg, April 10, 1951, in Teachers College. (1951). Harold Rugg: Letters in appreciation of his frontier work.

National Americanism Commission. (1941). *Rugg philosophy analyzed: Vol. 3. Textbook abstracts*. Indianapolis, IN: The American Legion.

Nelson, M. R. (1975). *Building a science of society: The social studies and Harold O. Rugg*. Doctoral dissertation, Stanford University.

Nelson, M. R., & Singleton, H. W. (1977). *FBI surveillance of three progressive educators: Curricular aspects.* Paper presented at the Society for the Study of Curriculum History, Annual Conference.

News Release. (1951). News Release on Rugg retirement dinner and symposium, May 3, 1951, "Harold Rugg" folder, faculty files, Public Relations Office Papers, box 39, Milbank Memorial Library, Teachers College, Columbia University.

Ohio State trustees assail Rugg speech. (1951, September 5). *New York Times,* p. 29.

Page, K. (1956). Katharine Page to Harold Rugg, January 1956 on the occasion of Harold Rugg's 70th birthday. Personal papers of Katharine Alling.

Parker, F. (1963, August 17). A study of creativity. *Saturday Review, 46,* p. 49.

Readers indignant about Dr. Rugg's OSU appearance. (1951, July 11). *Columbus Dispatch* (as cited in FBI, October 1, 1951, pp. 1-5)

Redefer, F. L. (1974). Murry R. Nelson's Interview with Frederick L. Redefer, November 20, 1974 (as cited in Nelson, 1975, p. 184).

Retirement Dinner. (1951). Rugg retirement dinner tapes, Lincoln School, Teachers College, May 4, 1951. Tapes in possession of the author.

Rudd, A. G., Hicks, H., & Falk, A. T. (Ed.). (1941). *Undermining our republic: Do you know what the children are being taught in our public schools? You'll be surprised.* New York: Guardians of American Education.

Rudd, A. G. (1957). *Bending the twig: The revolution in education and its effect on our children.* New York: New York Chapter of the Sons of the American Revolution.

Rugg, E. (1960). Quote from Elizabeth Rugg on Harold Rugg's death. In Ernest F. Bayles (Ed.), *Proceedings of the Philosophy of Education Society,* p. 109.

Rugg, E. U. (1966). The Earle Rugg tape. Prepared by Earle U. Rugg in response to questions posed by George A. Kay and Elmer A. Winters. Tape and transcript in the possession of the author.

Rugg episode calls for thorough stock taking. (1951). *Columbus State Journal,* editorial page, August 31, 1951, "Rugg" folder, faculty files, box 39, Public Relations Office Papers, Gottesman Libaries, Teachers College, Columbia University.

Rugg, H. O. (1931). *Culture and education in America.* New York: Harcourt, Brace.

Rugg, H. O. (1936). *American life and the school curriculum: Next steps toward schools of living.* Boston: Ginn.

Rugg, H. O. (1941, January). That men may understand. *Dartmouth Alumni Magazine,* pp. 10-13.

Rugg, H. O. (1943a). *Now is the moment.* New York: Duell, Sloan and Pearce.

Rugg, H. O. (1943b). We accept in principle but reject in practice: Is this leadership? *Frontiers of Democracy 10*(81), pp. 70-72.

Rugg, H. O. (1947). *Foundations for American education.* Yonkers-on-Hudson, NY: World Book.

Rugg, H. O. (1952a). Harold O. Rugg to R. Freeman Butts, January 15, 1952 (as cited in Nelson, 1975, p. 199).

Rugg, H. O. (1952b). *The teacher of teachers: Frontiers of theory and practice in teachers education.* New York: Harper & Brothers.

Rugg, H. O. (1954). Harold O. Rugg to Earle U. Rugg, November 30, 1954 (as cited in Nelson, 1975, p. 199).

Rugg, H. O. (1956a). Cold Spring Tape, Tape 3, track 1, June 16, 1956. Rugg speaking at New York Geriatric Society, Cold Spring New York, transcript, p. 10.

Rugg, H. O. (1956b). Harold O. Rugg to Earle U. Rugg, October 3, 1956 (as cited in Nelson, 1975, p. 199).

Rugg, H. O. (1957a). Cold Spring Tape, Tape 5, Side 2, June 22, 1957, Rugg speaking at New York Geriatric Society, Cold Spring New York, transcript, p. 11.

Rugg, H. O. (1957b). H. O. Rugg to B. Othanel Smith, May 14, 1957, as recorded on tape by George Kay in Rugg's study, October 9, 1965. Rugg papers, tape 5, side 2, letters. Tape in the possession of the author.

Rugg, H. O. (1958). Harold O. Rugg to Earle U. Rugg, Christmas, 1958. Rugg noted he, "stayed younger than ever by having this absorbing search for new ideas through my books. No textbooks!" (as cited in Nelson, 1975, p. 181).

Rugg, H. O. (1960). The creative imagination: Imperatives for educational theory. In E. F. Bayles (Ed.), *Proceedings of the philosophy of education society*. Lawrence, KS: Philosophy of Education Society.

Rugg, H. O. (1963). *Imagination*. New York: Harper & Row.

Rugg, H. O., & Brooks, M. (1950). *The teacher in school and society*. New York: New World.

Rugg, H. O., & Withers, W. (1955). *Social foundations of education*. New York: Prentice-Hall.

Rugg, J. E. (2003). Interview with John E. Rugg, Denver, Colorado, nephew of Harold O. Rugg and son of Earle U. Rugg, conducted by the author.

Rugg, J. E. (2005). Interview with John E. Rugg, Denver, Colorado, nephew of Harold O. Rugg and son of Earle U. Rugg, conducted by the author, Spring 2003.

Rugg, whose texts drew wide criticism, to retire form Teachers College faculty. (1951, May 5). *New York Times*, p. 15.

Shrecker, E. (1998). *Many are the crimes: McCarthyism in America*. Boston: Little, Brown.

Teachers College. (1951). *Harold Rugg: Letters in appreciation of his frontier work*. Memory book presented to Harold Rugg by the Department of Social and Philosophical Foundations of Education, May 4, 1951, on the occasion of his retirement.

Whitman, H. (1954, May 14). Progressive education—Which way forward. *Colliers*, *133*, pp. 32-36.

Winters, E. A. (1968). *Harold Rugg and education for social reconstruction*. Unpublished doctoral dissertation, University of Wisconsin, Madison.

CONCLUSION

What can we learn from the Rugg story? It is certainly a story full of drama, with a cast of heroes and villains, and key turning points which capture, in microcosm, some of the basic ideological conflicts in American political life, as well as the competing interest groups in American curriculum history, especially in social studies. As one observer noted in a letter commemorating Rugg's retirement, "The Rugg books story has made for itself a powerful place in the annals of American education. It is a story of the perpetual struggle of the schools for intelligent democratic action. The intensity of your fight through all theses years has been in direct proportion to the good it has served countrywide" (Fox, 1951).

Since the Rugg textbook controversy, there have been many similar episodes. One of these occurred on the heels of the Rugg controversy. Allan Nevins' article in the *New York Times Magazine* which charged that United States history was no longer sufficiently taught in the nation's schools inspired a spirited and protracted episode of controversy during the Second World War. Another prolonged episode of attacks on social studies developed in the 1950s as part of an assault on progressivism writ large. Intellectual critics such as Arthur Bestor called social studies an anti-intellectual "social stew," while red-baiting critics characterized it as a forum of propaganda for Communism. Yet another round of criticism came in the aftermath of the new social studies and took the form of a series of academic freedom cases involving individual teachers, followed by the larger controversy over MACOS (Man A Course of Study), an inno-

This Happened in Ameica: Harold Rugg and the Censure of Social Studies
pp. 293–301

vative project of the era. Most recently, attacks on social studies were a core ingredient of the revival of history during the 1980s and 1990s, which led to dramatic growth in history offerings in schools and a narrowing of the social studies curriculum, with less attention to issues (Evans, 2004). During all of this, critiques of Rugg have continued, usually in the background, with Rugg portrayed as the poster boy for everything that is wrong with social studies education in schools. Contrary to the critics of Rugg, of recent or more distant vintage, I believe that Rugg's achievement was the pinnacle of progressive reform in social studies. Moreover, I think there are several things we can learn from an examination of Rugg's life and work, and the controversies he inspired.

In a very real sense, the Rugg textbook controversy served as a watershed in the history of social studies. The controversy and subsequent events marked the censure of progressive social studies in schools, and led inexorably to changes in the curriculum. The Rugg controversy, and the general failure of issues-oriented social studies to find greater success in social studies classrooms, has inspired more than one scholar from the issues-centered camp to reflect seriously on future prospects for reform (Evans, Avery & Pedersen, 1999; Gross, 1989; Oliver, 1978; Shaver, 1989). One of the main reasons that issues-centered education, broadly defined as attention to social issues of past and present in the curriculum, has had relatively limited success in the nation's classrooms is that we seem to have something of a cultural taboo against raising certain questions in the public schools, especially when they touch on some of the basic, and sacred, pillars of American economic and cultural success (i.e., capitalism, the Constitution, the founding fathers, etc.). A significant and vocal segment of the American populace does not want such questions aired in schools, and instead prefers imposition of an "our country right or wrong" mentality. In addition, there seems to be general support for history as the core of social studies among historians, and among many citizens, thus eclipsing visions of an integrated synthesis, as represented by Rugg and many other progressive reformers. Moreover, historians are a strong and prestigious interest group when compared with teachers and teacher educators. Finally, advocates of any alternative to traditional, discipline-based approaches face an up-hill battle in part because so little knowledge and understanding of the alternatives exists among the general populace. The focus in schools on the disciplines of history and the social sciences, and the de-emphasis or omission of social issues and controversies, might be seen as part of what Tyack and Cuban have termed the "grammar of schooling," aspects of schooling in America that seem so commonplace that they are taken for granted as the way schools are and the way they are supposed to be (1995).

The Rugg textbook controversy was an especially dramatic and important episode—the turning point at which criticism of social studies became a sort of national pastime. Prior to the Rugg dust up, critical and issues-centered approaches to social studies appeared to be headed for greater prominence in the nation's classrooms. Afterwards, social studies itself appeared to be on the run, in a defensive posture and losing ground to advocates of more traditional approaches to learning and to more conservative visions of the American way. One of the key implications of the controversy is that criticisms often stick, despite defense and counter-arguments. The sensationalistic charges of subversion and un-Americanism that conservative, "patriotic," and Fascist critics attached to Rugg frequently appeared in prominent spaces, while Rugg's defense was too often relegated to the back pages. Over the years, similar criticisms of educators, and especially of social studies, have take their toll on the vitality and public impression of the field and have contributed to the decline of progressive social studies, the revival of traditional history, and a narrowing of the social studies curriculum and the range of ideas and questions considered in the nation's classrooms. The sum total of criticisms over the years has left the general impression that social studies is an unsound educational idea, developed by second rate scholars in schools of education, and dominated by radicals with an inclination to use the schools to subvert the social order.

Rugg's example illustrates the importance, and the potential impact, of dreaming big and bold visions of reform, not only as a well-spring of inspiration, but as a source of ideas for practical action, praxis, with the aim of social improvement. Rugg had a worthy social and pedagogical vision combined with a bold personality and the courage to persist in upholding his convictions. His educational vision was pedagogically advanced, and forward-looking. He seriously questioned capitalism, its apparatus and influences. Moreover, Rugg's basic critique is largely still relevant. We need a renewed questioning of capitalism and of the mainstream institutions in American life. I believe it is healthy to ask such questions, and to ask school children, beginning at a fairly early age, to wrestle with these questions. In short, today's education can benefit from the contributions of both past and present advocates of education for social justice.

At its heart, the progressive approach to schooling championed by Rugg and others held that students must be challenged to confront social realities, to understand how the problems and dilemmas of the contemporary world came to be what they are, and to think about what might be done about it. In his later years, Rugg captured the essence of the matter in one of his many talks about his work on the creative process:

One of the very essential factors in the creative process, it seems to me, is the concept of integrity. It's involved in that very homely phrase, "I say what I think my way" ... An authoritarian world will not permit that question to be asked, "What do you think?" ... Why it's revolutionary!... So you could generalize that, ... and you could put it into schools. And (it) consists of teachers honestly asking, "What do you think?"

I think we've seen almost a vicious expression of the very opposite of this. Not what they really think, but what ought to be said to fit in with the controlling interest, with the boss, with the owner, the employer, with the party.... And you see it worse in all these fascist organizations, and you see it in complete form in any authoritarian society, whether it be the Russian one, or Hitler, or Mussolini, or the Japanese war party, or whether it be the same kind of thing in a democratic society where the powers that be control.

Educationally, I would go back to what seems to be the heart of it, getting teachers to understand, that no matter what the board of education has prescribed, no matter what the superintendent and the principal, and the supervisor have said must be done, that basically, this group of children and I have got to explore life ... together, honestly, and confront the problems ... in spite of the possible authoritarian (reaction).... The teacher would have to bring them right down to this village, this town, this neighborhood, this school, this class. Our problems. (Rugg, 1956)

Thus, Rugg's work was revolutionary in character. It was a call to action, a call to confront the persistent issues at the heart of our social and economic structures that are typically left out of school. He called for students to find their own individual voices, "to say what I think, my way," as they confront the most persistent social dilemmas of our times.

The Rugg story touches on several important areas of concern in social studies education mentioned in the introduction. Each of these deserves further comment:

Definition of Social Studies. Rugg's approach to social studies serves as a seminal foundation for progressives in the ongoing debates over what form social studies should take in our schools. His work is a touchstone, a source of inspiration and ideas for advocates of a meliorist, Deweyan, issues-centered social studies as well as for advocates of a social justice oriented curriculum (Ayers, Hunt & Quinn, 1998; Engle & Ochoa, 1988; Evans & Saxe, 1996; Hunt & Metcalf, 1955, 1968; Oliver & Shaver, 1966). Moreover, his pamphlets and textbook series serve as a useful prototype, demonstrating how innovative and reflective teaching techniques might be built into course materials. The Rugg materials provide examples of the kinds of difficult issues and questions that must be a focal point if students are to meaningfully examine the most persistent issues of our society and the world.

Curriculum Scope and Sequence. Rugg's critique of the existing curriculum and of common practices of the 1920s is eerily reminiscent of what goes on in schools in the twenty-first century. Moreover, most of his comments are still valid. We need to shift the mood of classroom discourse from the declarative to the hypothetical, focusing on consideration of issues and alternatives, consequences, evidence, and consideration of our most cherished values. In Rugg's words, "To keep issues out of the school, therefore, is to keep thought out of it; it is to keep life out of it" (Rugg, 1941, pp. xv-xvi). Despite current trends which have considerably narrowed the curriculum and placed greater emphasis on history, geography and civics, we would do well to re-create a strong movement for a new synthesis. Not just history, but a broad synthesis something like Rugg proposed, with issues as the hinge for opening consideration of alternatives and evidence. This is justified partly as a means for creating interest, motivating, and making connections, and partly on the grounds of educating our population for thoughtful citizenship. In the 1920s, Rugg wrote, we have a "troubled world." We still have a troubled world facing many similar, increasingly complex dilemmas. Thus, Rugg's rationale for an issues-centered focus is as relevant as ever.

Pedagogy. Issues-centered, problem-posing forms of pedagogy are both appealing and elusive. It will take a supreme commitment to create this form of pedagogy in classrooms because of the commonplace emphasis on teacher talk, and the persistence of banking approaches to schooling which have proven stubbornly resistant to reform. Making a difference in the pedagogy of the typical social studies classroom will mean creating and distributing new materials which are as innovative, exciting and as well written as the pamphlets and textbooks created by Harold Rugg. But, as the Rugg brothers learned, it will take more than new materials to make a lasting difference.

Structural changes in the grammar of schooling will also be required, giving teachers time and material support to develop thoughtful, interactive approaches to teaching. Time and the requisite support will be expensive, but worth the effort. The persistence of recitation and low-level approaches to teaching conditioned by institutional constraints seems an almost insurmountable obstacle to the wide implementation of innovative, issues-oriented approaches. As Tyack and Cuban illustrate, teachers tend to teach as they were taught (1995). Overcoming the weight of classroom constancy and persistently didactic methods will require time and positive incentives for teachers to learn, grow and adapt.

Texts and Materials. In interpreting the meaning of the Rugg textbook controversy for today's social education, it is important to recognize that we now have a textbook machine by which certain books are approved, but only after they are altered, sanitized to reflect "a vision of America sculpted and sanded down," in which many important voices, episodes, and perspectives are de-emphasized or omitted (Fitzgerald, 1979; Loewen, 1995; Tyson-Bernstein & Woodward, 1986). This is, in part, a direct legacy of the Rugg the textbook controversy, and of other similar controversies over the years. The pattern of culture wars focused on school materials has had the impact of limiting or narrowing freedom to teach and freedom to learn (Zimmerman, 2002). We have reached what amounts to a state of perpetual censorship of school materials, partly as a result of the Rugg censure. This situation requires serious and sustained attention. It is one of the few areas of agreement among liberal social studies theorists and neoconservative critics (Apple, 1993; Leming, Ellington, & Porter, 2003; Ravitch, 2005). This dilemma deserves the sustained attention of educational professionals and a high level of public interest and discourse.

To make a difference, we will need new and innovative materials which focus on persistent issues of the past and present. The Rugg pamphlets and textbooks provide a seminal model of what may be possible, as do other reflective and issues-centered materials created over the years. A twenty-first–century version of the Rugg pamphlets might stand a chance of being used if adapted to teaching common offerings in the existing curriculum (i.e., history, geography, and civics).

Indoctrination and Social Criticism. We can also learn a great deal about the fine line between engaging in social criticism and incurring the wrath of critics by examining the Rugg textbook controversy in some depth. Curricula cannot be neutral. But it can strive to present multiple alternatives and to be fair to a full range of perspectives. Given current trends reflecting the conservative restoration in schools and society, we need a greater emphasis on social criticism in social studies. Questions of social justice seem especially pertinent today, given the economic stratification and hegemonic power of elites in our nation and the world. In the United States, wealth is highly concentrated: the top 1% control 40% of the financial wealth, and the top 20% control 84% of the wealth, leaving only 16% of the wealth to be shared among 80% of the population. Moreover, numerous studies show that the distribution of wealth has been extremely concentrated throughout U.S. history. Wealth translates into power and influence. The United States is a "power pyramid," making it difficult for the majority to exercise much influence (Domhoff, 2006).

Given these realities, progressive educators cannot allow social studies in schools to further retreat from the prospect of a bold and forward looking curriculum. The current focus on standards and high stakes testing diverts the mainstream from progressive change. Progressive educators must resist current trends and reassert a progressive agenda, promoting a new critical and democratic education driven by questions, issues, and concern for social justice. The study of issues can incorporate strands of disciplinary materials focused on issues and problems of both past and present examined against a backdrop of utopian visions and values.

Yet, as we continue to advocate a progressive vision, we must acknowledge that Rugg did make a few mistakes. Education for social justice can take many forms. In the Rugg materials, it seems, there was some justification for the charge that he presented more evidence on the side of the questions which he supported. After all, the materials were a reflection of the frontier thinkers, those on the cutting edge of knowledge. So, it seems, we must learn to include a balance of materials, sources, and interpretations, and challenge students to make up their own minds about the meaning of the past, present institutions and societal dilemmas. Though this may not silence all critics, it is more easily defensible as part of the "American way," and as a clear example of John Dewey's method of intelligence applied to the social studies arena. The Rugg episode tells us that the forces of reaction are always with us, and that the price of freedom is, as Rugg himself once wrote, "eternal vigilance." At the same time students must confront the truth, the hard reality of social relations conditioned by a capitalist patriarchy. Doing so effectively will mean bringing in content that is often omitted, focusing on the struggles of the oppressed for freedom and a good life, emphasizing critical perspectives on the dominant structures of society and the voices of those who have challenged the way things are.

Censorship. Though his textbooks and ideas were sure to inspire some criticism, Harold Rugg did not deserve his fate. On the contrary, I believe that he fully deserved to receive the recognition and financial fortune that sometimes accompany a brilliant idea combined with hard work. The controversy that engulfed Rugg, and the defense offered by Rugg and those who rose to support him, suggests that some dreams are worth fighting for, even though the struggle may take its toll.

In the present era, we have entered a time during which respect for the professional intelligence and knowledge of teachers, and the freedom to choose alternative paths, has reached low ebb. Curriculum reform is increasingly mandated by centralized authorities and driven by a conservative corporate agenda for which the kinds of questions raised by Rugg and other similar social studies reformers are no longer welcome. During this era, it is especially important to keep alternative visions alive, to nurture deep dreams of justice and fair play, and to make sure that critics of a progressive or issues-centered social studies are met with a stout defense. The attacks on Rugg, and especially the sustained campaign carried on by the American Legion, the National Association of Manufacturers and other business groups, present early examples of the power of interest group financing and organization. In more recent years, foundation supported financing has proven, once again, to have a significant influence on the direction of education, and social studies in schools (Selden, 2004; Singer, 2005). Moreover, business leaders and a business mentality permeate current efforts at reform (Cuban, 2004). Behind the growth of interest group financing and business influence on schools and social studies is a power structure in which the few have great influence over the many, driven by private interests rather than the public good.

Given the high level of interest among social studies professionals in critical and social justice approaches to education, and the present climate of national and international crisis, it behooves us to be aware of, or be defeated by, the successes, the failures, and the mistakes—the "lessons" of the Rugg controversy. Threats to academic freedom must be taken seriously. Moreover, I believe that the current trend toward the restoration of traditional history in schools, and the standards and high stakes testing that support it, must be challenged, openly confronted by those supporting alternative visions of social studies education and of democratic life. These trends run counter to the notion of social studies focused on questions, and are leading to what Paulo Freire has called "the castration of curiosity" (Freire & Macedo, 1998, p. 222). One way to challenge the conservative restoration might be to offer teachers, administrators, and the concerned public a clear, uncluttered view of some of the main choices for educating children in a democratic society. My hope is that this account of the life and work of Harold Rugg, the story of one person's attempt to improve social studies education and the general quality of American democracy, may prove helpful in that quest.

REFERENCES

Apple, M. W. (1993). *Official knowledge: Democratic education in a conservative age.* New York: Routledge.

Ayers, W., Hunt, J. A., & Quinn, T. (1998). *Teaching for social justice: A democracy and education reader.* New York: The New Press, Teachers College Press.

Cuban, L. (2004). *The blackboard and the bottom line: Why schools can't be businesses.* Cambridge: Harvard University Press.

Domhoff, G. W. (2006). Wealth, income, and power. Retrieved September 14, 2006, from http://sociology.ucsc.edu/whorulesamerica/power/wealth.html

Engle, S. H., & Ochoa, A. S. (1988). *Education for democratic citizenship: Decision making in the social studies.* New York: Teachers College.

Evans, R. W. (2004). *The social studies wars: What should we teach the children?* New York: Teachers College.

Evans, R. W., Avery, P. G., & Pedersen, P. (1999). Taboo topics: Cultural restraint on teaching social issues. *The Social Studies, 90,* 218-224.

Evans, R. W., & Saxe, D. W. (Eds.). (1996). *Handbook on teaching social issues* (Bulletin No. 93). Washington, DC: National Council for the Social Studies.

Fox, L. K. (1951). Lorene K. Fox, Queens College, to Harold O. Rugg, April 16, 1951. In Teachers College. *Harold Rugg: Letters in appreciation of his frontier work.* Unpublished manuscript. New York: Teachers College.

Fitzgerald, F. (1979). *America revised: History schoolbooks in the twentieth century.* Boston: Little, Brown.

Freire, M. A., & Macedo, D. (Eds.). (1998). *The Paulo Freire reader.* New York: Continuum.

Gross, R. E. (1989, September-October). Reasons for the limited acceptance of the problems approach. *Social Studies, 80*(5), 185-186.

Hunt, M. P., & Metcalf, L. E. (1955, 1968). *Teaching high school social studies: Problems in reflective thinking and social understanding.* New York: Harper and Brothers.

Leming, J., Ellington, L., & Porter, K. (Eds.). (2003). *Where did social studies go wrong?* Washington, DC: Fordham Foundation.

Loewen, J. W. (1995). *Lies my teacher told me: Everything your American history textbook got wrong.* New York: The New Press.

Oliver, D. W. (1978, November/December). Reflections on Peter Carbone's "The social and educational thought of Harold Rugg." *Social Education, 42*(7), 593-597.

Oliver, D. W., & Shaver, J. P. (1966). *Teaching public issues in the high school.* Boston: Houghton Mifflin.

Ravitch, D. (2005). *The language police: How pressure groups restrict what children learn.* New York: Knopf.

Rugg, H. O. (1941). *That men may understand: An American in the long armistice.* New York: Doubleday/Doran.

Rugg, H. O. (1956). Rugg speaking engagement at Cold Spring Geriatric Society, Cold Spring, New York, June 15, 1956. Transcript and tape in the possession of the author.

Selden, S. (2004, April). *The neo-conservative assault on the undergraduate curriculum.* Paper presented at the annual meeting of the American Educational Research Association, San Diego.

Singer, A. (2005). Strange bedfellows: The contradictory goals of the coalition making war on social studies. *The Social Studies, 96*(5), 199-205.

Shaver, J. P. (1989, September/October). Lessons from the past: The future of an issues-centered curriculum. *Social Studies, 80*(5), 192-196.

Tyack, D., & Cuban, L. (1995). *Tinkering toward utopia: A century of public school reform.* Cambridge, MA: Harvard University Press.

Tyson-Bernstein, H., & Woodward, A. (1986). The great textbook machine and prospects for reform. *Social Education, 50*(1), 41-45.

Zimmerman, J. (2002). *Whose America?: Culture wars in the public schools.* Cambridge: Harvard University Press.

EPILOGUE

Earle U. Rugg lived in Greeley, Colorado, and served as professor and director of Teacher Education at Colorado State Teachers College, then as director of the University Library for many years. He died on November 19, 1969, at the age of 77.

Louise Krueger was headmistress of the Walt Whitman School in New York City during the 1940s. Following her divorce from Harold Rugg, she remarried. In 1949 she became headmistress of the Arizona Desert School in Tucson. After 4 years she returned to serve as headmistress of the Walt Whitman School in New York from 1953 until her retirement.

Harald "Hal" Rugg became a steel guitar player and joined the Grand Old Opry in the 1960s. He had a long and legendary career as perhaps the leading steel guitar player of his generation. He spent most of his adult life in Nashville as a session musician and recorded with stars such as Loretta Lynn, Roy Price, George Jones, Joan Baez, and Buffy Saint Marie. He lived during most of his later years in Tucson, Arizona. He died in 2005. Hal really did not know his father and had only infrequent contact with him following the divorce in 1943. Describing his steel guitar playing, Joan Van Dyke, his friend and longtime companion said, "It cries ... Hal's music cries."

Elizabeth Rugg remarried in the 1960s and lived in Florida with her husband until her death on March 24, 1999.

This Happened in Ameica: Harold Rugg and the Censure of Social Studies
pp. 303–306
Copyright © 2007 by Information Age Publishing
All rights of reproduction in any form reserved.

Katharine (Page) Alling, Elizabeth Rugg's daughter and Harold Rugg's stepdaughter lives in Rochester, New York, with her husband, Norman Alling, a mathematician of some renown.

Donald Alan Rugg, Harold and Berta's adopted son, apparently had a difficult time in life. He showed up at his uncle Earle Rugg's home in the 1960s and asked for money. Because the family believed he would spend it on wine, they denied his request.

The Rugg home in Woodstock was purchased by Bruce Bodner of New York City in the late 1990s who renovated and updated the home and grounds. At the time of the author's visit in 2003 it was in beautiful condition.

William H. Kilpatrick continued as professor emeritus at Teachers College, and as perhaps John Dewey's chief disciple, until he died in New York in 1965 at the age of 93.

George S. Counts retired from Teachers College in 1955, then served as visiting distinguished professor from 1962-1974 at Southern Illinois University in Carbondale. He died in 1974 in Belleville, Illinois, at the age of 84.

John Dewey had a long career as perhaps America's greatest public intellectual. He is recognized as one of the founders of the philosophical school of pragmatism, and is often referred to as the "Father of Progressive Education." He died in 1952 in Tucson, Arizona, at the age of 92.

Franz Boas was a pioneer in modern anthropology and is often called the "Father of American Anthropology." He was thoroughly devoted to "absolute academic and spiritual freedom" and believed that anthropologists have an obligation to speak out on social issues. He was a tireless advocate against racism and for intellectual freedom. He died in December 1942, at the age of 84.

Elizabeth K. Dilling, author of *The Red Network,* continued to speak and publish anticommunist and anti-Semitic literature, and was a known Nazi sympathizer. She and her former husband, Joseph Dilling, were among the defendants in the 1944 Sedition Trial. She was shown to have heiled Hiter at the Nuremburg party congress and to have associated with members of the Luftwaffe. In her later years Dilling published the anti-Semitic, *The Plot Against Christianity* (1964). She died in 1966.

General Amos A. Fries and his wife Elizabeth continued to edit the *Friends of the Public Schools Bulletin* and to warn against subversive influences in education. In 1948 he accused the National Education Association of distributing pamphlets and books containing un-American propaganda and criticized the schools for not teaching patriotism. He died in 1963 at the age of 90.

Merwin K. Hart continued his affiliation with the New York State Economic Council. In 1943 the name was changed to the National Economic Council. He was among the defendants in the 1944 Sedition Trial. Hart was also a member of Robert Welch's John Birch Society and continued to support Fascist, anticommunist, and anti-Semitic groups until his death in 1962.

Major Augustin G. Rudd, the Legionnaire who instigated the American Legion campaign against the Rugg textbooks, continued his campaign against Harold Rugg and progressive education. In the late 1950s he authored a book, *Bending the Twig: The Revolution in Education and Its Effect on our Children* (1957), published by the Sons of the American Revolution. The book tells Rudd's story and elaborates on his critique of Rugg and the social frontier group.

H. W. Prentis, Jr., president of the National Association of Manufacturers in 1940, continued to serve as president of Armstrong Cork, Lancaster, Pennsylvania, until 1950 when was elected chairman of the board of directors. He was appointed "Honorary Vice President for Life" by the National Association of Manufacturers in 1946, and received the NAM "Man of the Year" Medal in 1953. He also received the Lancaster Citizenship Award for 1948 from American Legion Post 34. In his later years he served as a director of Mellon Bank, the Borden Company, Atlantic Refining, and Alco Products. During his tenure as president of the NAM in 1940 he visited 32 states and held meetings with about 22,000 businessmen. He died in 1959.

Walter D. Fuller, president of the NAM in 1941, continued to serve as president of Curtis Publishing Company until 1957, when he became chairman of the board of directors. He served as president of the National Publishers Association in 1947, and served as chair or member of several prominent NAM Committees including the governing board of the National Industrial Information Committee, which funded its propaganda campaigns. He died in 1964.

Ralph W. Robey, author of the NAM textbook abstracts, continued to serve as a writer and editor for *Newsweek,* and later served as economic advisor to the NAM. He died in 1972.

Walter S. Steele continued to publish *National Republic* magazine for the remainder of his life. Known as a "professional red-baiter," Steele served as an official with the American Coalition of Patriotic Societies and was active in the Christian American Crusade. His 1947 testimony before the House Un-American Activities Committee regarding Communist activities in the United States was 176 pages in length. Upon his death in 1960 the magazine ceased publication.

Printed in the United States
212226BV00002B/10/A

9 781593 117658